"This book can't fail to prompt managers to streamline their company's revenue building and cost reduction operations. There are many illustrations of just how companies can exploit the new tools of the electronic age to jump-start their productivity and profitability, and set on a sure path to profitable growth.

Read this book to learn how you can use the new technology tools to create more profitable buying, producing, and distributing of your products. Michael de Kare-Silver convinced me that tomorrow's winners will be those companies that learn how to streamline and enable, automate and innovate their business processes."
Professor Philip Kotler, *Distinguished Professor of International Marketing, Kellogg School of Management.*

"This book looks past the hype of the Internet bubble. Instead it clearly identifies the commercial benefits that can be derived from the application of new technologies. *Streamlining* is a must read for any executive looking to reshape their company at a time when growth is generally harder to come by."
David Grigson, *Chief Financial Officer, Reuters.*

"In 2002, no company has realized more than 10% of the productivity gains made possible by information technologies. Incremental productivity improvements are boring, and as Michael de Kare-Silver tells us, don't ensure long-term advantage. Companies that engage in streamlining can grab big chunks of the next 90%, experiencing the thrill of transformation and seizing leadership in existing and new markets."
Professor Fred Phillips, *Oregon School of Science and Engineering.*

"As detailed in this book, the new technologies are clearly providing an absolute opportunity to each and every business to make itself sleeker, faster, simpler and more efficient. Vast benefits will accrue most to those businesses that respond best to this challenge."
David Grainger, *Chairman, Grainger Inc.*

"Those businesses that wish to turn the stagnation of today into the growth of tomorrow must read Michael de Kare-Silver's outstanding new book. We are all aware of the bursting of the IT bubble. *Streamlining* makes us aware that the technology that has become available can be applied in all parts of the business. The book is full of practical examples."
The Rt. Hon. Lord Walker, *Deputy Chairman, Dresdner Kleinwort Wasserstein.*

"*Streamlining* pinpoints the key managerial challenge in the faster technology-driven economy. This book will take you on a voyage of discovery that will re-energize your business."
Kevin Lomax, *Chairman, Misys Plc.*

"Through a number of relevant corporate insights, this book is a warning to all of us not to ignore the long-term implications of e-enablement."
Patrick O'Sullivan, *Chief Executive, Zurich Financial Services.*

"E-technology is transforming the presentation, delivery and impact of our online products. The same technology has the potential to make a huge impact on our operating procedures and costs. *Streamlining* articulates very effectively the change process taking place in our business and gives many examples of the impact which the technology is having on business worldwide."
John Saunders, *Chief Executive, Experian International.*

"*Streamlining* makes a strong case for re-examining the opportunities afforded by Internet technologies now that the hype has died down."
Jon Symonds, *Chief Financial Officer, AstraZeneca plc.*

"*Streamlining* addresses many of the issues companies face today as they seek to transform themselves to meet the challenges of the Internet-enabled world. Michael de Kare-Silver examines how this transformation will be driven by the dynamic inter-relationship of three broad market forces: intelligent, connected devices and environments; an always-on Internet infrastructure; and a new generation of business and personal solutions and applications. These market drivers, de Kare-Silver argues, will be the fulcrum around which enterprises will discover new revenue streams and efficiencies. Embrace them and evolve; ignore them and die."
Borel Setten, *Chief Marketing Officer, Hewlett-Packard Europe.*

"With the collapse of the dot.com bubble, some people seem to think that the importance of the internet has been overstated and that the impact of e-business is not nearly as significant as expected. As *Streamlining* shows, nothing could be further from the truth. We have yet to appreciate, let alone exploit, the full potential of the e-world."
George Cox, *former Chairman of Unisys.*

Streamlining

Using new technologies and the Internet to transform performance

Michael de Kare-Silver

palgrave

Published by
PALGRAVE
Houndmills, Basingstoke, Hampshire RG21 6XS and
175 Fifth Avenue, New York, N. Y. 10010
Companies and representatives throughout the world

PALGRAVE is the new global academic imprint of
St. Martin's Press LLC Scholarly and Reference Division and
Palgrave Publishers Ltd (formerly Macmillan Press Ltd).

ISBN 0–333–99456–6

This book is printed on paper suitable for recycling and
made from fully managed and sustained forest souces.

A catalogue record for this book is available
from the British Library.

A catalog record for this book is available
from the Library of Congress.

10 9 8 7 6 5 4 3 2 1
11 10 09 08 07 06 05 04 03 02

Editing and origination by
Curran Publishing Services, Norwich, Norfolk

Printed in Great Britain by
Creative Print & Design (Wales), Ebbw Vale

Contents

Preface   *vi*

1 Streamlining: an introduction   1
2 Overview of book   7
3 Meet seven pioneers   11
4 The Internet revolution in context   33
5 Getting started on *e·a·i*   50
6 Streamlining in procurement   67
7 Streamlining in supply chain   84
8 Streamlining through knowledge management   104
9 Streamlining in CRM   125
10 Wireless interactivity: Internet on the move   148
11 iTV   170
12 e-learning   184
13 Making it happen   194

List of figures   *216*
List of tables   *218*
List of abbreviations   *219*
Index   *222*

Preface

The trigger for writing this book was the series of full page ads taken out by Oracle proclaiming they'd saved $1bn "by e-enabling the business." That's a big impact. It's making a significant difference to their reported earnings. It's holding up profits, despite the early decade slowdown. And it hasn't stopped there. For 2002 Oracle are targeting $2bn. Others like Cisco, GE, BP, big companies and smaller companies that we'll meet in this book are all vigorously following suit.

So what's going on? What are these organisations doing? How come they're getting value – and such significant payback and returns – out of their 'e'-initiatives? It's especially challenging since after the dot.com bomb many have become skeptical, given up, or relegated this whole area down the agenda. And while some others have persisted they haven't seen anything like the same returns.

What then are the lessons learned? What are the tricks of the trade, how get started and perhaps most importantly where to start, how establish the priorities, how mobilise the workforce to hard drive some selected opportunities? Indeed, is it really about e-business or is it more broadly about new technologies and new tools? The Internet seems so pervasive, it seems to affect everything we might do or touch. Should we suddenly shift our entire technology platform onto the Net, should we abandon our expensive high tariff ERP environment? And everyday there's a new software solution, an apparently better package, an alternative way of doing things. Buy or rent via ASPs, off-the-shelf or bespoke? And where does wireless fit into all this? Is 3G going to happen, will the benefits materialise and if so when? Should we equip everyone with a new laptop and instal XP or should we wait for the next generation pocket PC with wireless internet connection?

Streamlining provides a solution path. It identifies ways to cut through this raft of issues and opportunities. It builds on the learnings and techniques developed at Oracle and other pioneers. It pinpoints three key tools for transforming business performance. It shows just how *enabling*, *automating* and *innovation* can impact the business. It identifies the means for improving productivity, speeding up interactions, strengthening customer relations, reducing costs and refocussing the energies of the organisation on tasks and activities of leverage. It shows just how the new technology tools can be employed effectively, can in some circumstances force a complete reappraisal of the way things get done and drive to new levels of competitive advantage.

As usual writing this book would not have been possible without the support of my darling wife Deborah. It's also been inspired, unwittingly, by our new baby boy Alexander. Deborah has provided the practical critique and commercial reality-testing. Alexander has pushed and shouted and cried and encouraged his Dad to both moments of high emotion and a determination to get on and finish!

Thanks also go as ever to my editor at Palgrave, Stephen Rutt, whose own commitment and enthusiasm has been so important. Colleagues at PA Consulting provided input and examples. Bernadette Heenan and Lorraine Oliver were superb workmates in typesetting and proofing, and had many good suggestions. Finally three business friends deserve special mention: Lord Peter Walker, a true professional and business leader, Walter Goldsmith so full of business acumen, and Robert Heller a fellow author and soulmate.

Thanks and I hope you enjoy the book!

1 Streamlining: an introduction

We've had the go-go years of the 1990s, now we've got a period of slower growth. A time for readjustment. Profits are harder to come by and management teams are under new pressures. Investments must be reexamined, some projects just stopped, jobs are being cut, there are redundancies and uncertainties still about future prospects. It's a difficult period.

Once the initial storm of September 11 and recession has passed, managers are left to pick over the pieces; they must manage the downside but they have to move on. There's no indulgence, no forgiveness, no time to mourn for what might have been. Shareholders, analysts, the media, customers, suppliers, and employees themselves want to see the plan for recovery. How is the organisation going to rebuild, what are its expectations, is this the best it can do, does the revised business plan inspire confidence, is every stone being turned, are the assets being sweated, is the cost base being realigned?

Is this in fact an opportunity? Is there now, in the wake of a crisis, a chance to do things differently, to operate smarter, leaner, quicker and more effectively, to be in a stronger position to weather the next downturn or continuing weak demand? Can the company build a more competitive platform, create new sources of advantage over rivals so its products come quicker to market, its supply chain carries less inventory, its manufacturing processes are more productive, its customer service more responsive, its sales teams more effective? Is it possible to review the company, make it even more vital and build in change that has a lasting and durable effect?

At this juncture, companies have choices. On the one hand they can slash and burn, jobs can go, sweeping cutbacks can be made. That gives short term gains and benefits, but there's not much about "corporate renewal" or rebuilding a lasting future.

There is an alternative. And we can call it *streamlining*. It's about a program of change. But the difference, the key enabler, the thing that distinguishes it, is new technology. And yes, let's use the words deliberately but in context, it's about e-business, it's specifically about the new e-technologies, tools and applications. It's about new approaches to business. But importantly, approaches which have already proved themselves. Proven to deliver cost savings and performance improvement, proven to enable an organisation to do things better and reach out to those targets and goals that ambitious teams aspire to.

'e' need no longer be associated with hype and disappointment, with confusion and uncertainty, with false expectations and desires. 'e' can and is being reborn and rediscovered. Its revival comes in the context of performance improvement in the processes, tasks and activities *inside* the corporation. Its scope includes how they interface with the external network of suppliers, partners and customers. 'e' is now a catalyst. It's a catalyst that *enables* things to be done differently. It is new technology. It has spawned a growing list of applications. It has encouraged software providers to produce solutions that can be quick and easy to implement. Via the already ubiquitous web browser, companies can talk to other companies, individuals can communicate, even though they have different underlying operating systems and platforms.

'e' has enabled global data transfer, real time, 24/7 at low cost and with ease. Now everyone who wants to be can be connected. There is no limit. It means data transfer that involved manual intervention can now be reorganised. It can be *automated*. Information can be transferred, if appropriate at "zero touch." As an employee I could get my training online, take courses electronically, store education materials on my hard disk. I could submit travel requests automatically to an airline and get a ticket reference number, instead of a ticket. I can work on a project with all the materials kept in a single virtual data room. The blueprints, the designs, the project "papers," the critical path, the actions and responsibilities can all be recorded in one place. If one part of the project team has to change something, everyone can be automatically, and immediately, notified. No need for phone calls or faxes, no excuse for error or delay. If I want to review progress with a customer, I can access on one database who last contacted the customer, the nature of it all, the response, the last order, all the key people in my organisation who have contacts with the customer, whether I've got the right team in place, whether the customer's technical queries have been addressed. And I can do all this and much more through the Internet. And I can do it either at my office or if I'm out and about using my wireless connections.

There's no limit to what can be *streamlined, e-enabled* and *automated* using the new technology. Each process of the company can be examined, challenged and if appropriate redefined. There's fresh scope for challenge and innovation. No need to stick to old processes that are slow, cumbersome and frustrating. No need to be constrained by old approaches or clunky ERP systems. Now's the time to reappraise, *innovate* and discover new forms of competitive advantage.

Here's one example, and more of them later. Take Progressive Insurance. Three or four years ago they were a sleepy US auto insurer, no. 10 in their markets. A new management team comes in and wants to improve, wants to change, wants to revitalise. They had a choice. They could embark on a process of incremental improvement and change. A bit here, a bit there. Making some progress, but slowly. Or, they could look for a quicker win, a bigger success, but one that would require more radical action, one that would involve using new technology to "streamline."

What did they do? They looked at their value chain and business processes. The key area of underperformance was "claims settlement." If policy holders had an auto accident, they had to get a claims form, fill it in, send it through, chase it. It took weeks of hassle, the form was often completed incorrectly, customers got very p***** off.

They could have tried to improve the claim form process. But the Progressive management team determined to cut through all that. They've changed the whole thing. They've *innovated*. They've come up with the simple idea of "roadside settlement."

So now, if there's an accident, a 1–800 call through to the company call center and the "mobile claims assessor" nearest to the scene of the accident is automatically contacted. The goal is to get to the customer asap, and if possible "within 20 minutes." And once there the claims assessor uses a pocket PC with a wireless Net connection. Dials up to the data warehouse, checks the policy details and claims record, assesses the accident and if appropriate clicks "submit." A check in settlement for the policy holder is automatically dispatched. The claim is "settled" right then.

On the back of that, Progressive's revenues have doubled in three years. It's shot from a "sleepy no. 10" to "fast-tracking no. 4" player in its industry. Its streamlining has simplified and automated a previously high cost, poor service process. Costs have been reduced, delays completely cut out, and now the call center can focus on customer sales and service, rather than handling complaints.

Streamlining is a simple idea. It's not some rocket science. It's not complicated. It's what many businesses have been doing for many years as they try to improve competitiveness. So what's new? What is new and different is the new technology. What's creating a dramatic new opportunity are the new e-business tools. It's streamlining with *e·a·i* – through enabling, automating and innovating. It is enabling things to be done that just could not be done before. It is facilitating new levels of efficiency and effectiveness. It is establishing an environment where streamlining becomes a reality.

Here are some examples and recent news headlines of streamlining in action:

- "Procter & Gamble, Philips and Coca-Cola are backing a new web-based approach that will streamline the development of global marketing campaigns: 'automation of laborious processes will give more scope for innovation, save cost and speed up campaign development.'"
- "UK Government has pledged to streamline business for offshore oil and gas operators in the North Sea by developing an e-commerce portal for the industry. The aim is to speed up application for consents, approvals and reporting: 'it's vital that business and government make the most of cutting-edge technology to make daily business easier and faster.'"
- "Dutch distributor Van Gerd and Loos is investing in a new scanning and wireless computing solution to streamline and fully automate its distribution process to provide parcel tracking via WAP phones over the Net."
- "Michael Dell attributes his company's success to ruthless streamlining of its manufacturing processes and linking its suppliers on the Net to deliver build to order and eliminate inventory."
- "Covisint aims to streamline an entire industry by moving business to business processes online for major automakers and establishing an industry-wide e-marketplace with the broadest possible OEM participation: 'this streamlines the industry supply chain by simplifying procurement, reducing costs and speeding up the order to delivering process.'"

A colleague of mine has described streamlining like this:

> Imagine two boats on a river. They're both rowing boats. One is one of those big, clumsy and cumbersome wooden boats. It's got a crew in it but as they row their timing is poor, there's a lack of coordination, the boat is wallowing. It's not quite going round in circles but progress is painful.
>
> Now see the other boat. It's the Harvard 'A' crew. The boat is made of lightweight carbon fiber. It's sleek. It's streamlined. The crew are coordinated, in time. They've had all the best training facilities, all the latest technology to improve their performance. The boat cuts through the water like a knife.

Enable, automate and innovate – it can become a simple mantra to guide corporate agendas over the next few years. It can be the rallying cry that captures the imagination of the entire workforce. It can be the catalyst that encourages the stretching of horizons, the uplifting of ambition, the setting of a new strategy and action plan to carry the company forward. It could be the vehicle for a new round of performance improvement, it could actually leverage what the Net is most obviously geared for – enabling business to communicate internally and externally, at last in an open universal easy access fast network, and operate together more efficiently.

enabling is about taking existing products or services and using new technology tools to reach out to new customers and new markets; enabling is about taking an existing process e.g. in sharing knowledge or managing customers and reconnecting it and networking it on the Net so it extends the enterprise and provides communication and captures and transmits data recognising no barriers to time or distance; enabling is about networking different teams and different businesses who have different proprietary systems which were incompatible – except now for the Net which provides a communication pipeline that cuts through all that using a mix of Html and Xml or Java.

automating is about cutting out time and cost. It's streamlining at its most basic and fundamental. It's about taking out layers of intervention and approval, cutting "like a knife" through a process or a structure and determining the most leveraged, effective and enduring way to deliver the necessary benefits. It's about simplifying and standardising and taking advantage of open standards and universal communication to make sure the enablement is done in the most productive way.

Figure 1.1 Streamlining: the new agenda

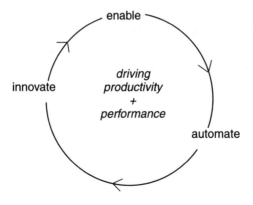

innovation is about challenging the very process or product or service itself. How can it be improved? How can new technology be applied to change the game, to reinvent the rules, like Progressive or like other "pioneers" we shall look at, from Cisco and Oracle to less familiar examples from Herman Miller or Grainger or Weyerhaeuser or Fisher Scientific? Innovation gets a new lease of life with the Internet. It's the driver and force for change and has that performance-transforming capability that every organisation is ultimately investing and searching for.

Figure 1.2 Internet as catalyst

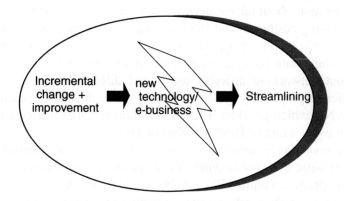

It's principally the Internet, but also the developing wireless applications. This is the catalyst, the enabler for "the revolution" in how things can get done. This is the force that's encouraging reappraisal and challenge. This is the spark that's ignited passion and enthusiasm for people and organisations who want, desperately, to do better and prove themselves the most successful in what they do. This is what encouraged Jack Welch when at GE to get 'e', Larry Ellison of Oracle to restructure his entire organisation, the President of Siemens to announce demanding new cost savings targets, and Tony Blair, Britain's prime minister, to get the vision that his country "become the best nation in the world for e-business." And it's what will excite a host of others to do the same and more.

2 Overview of book

There are four main chunks of streamlining opportunity set out in this book. They form the heart of the content here. They range across the value chain of every company and represent the key areas of performance improvement and business gain.

Figure 2.1 Streamlining: key points of leverage

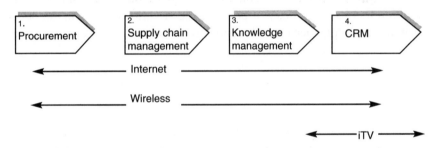

In addition to the Internet as an all-pervasive new technology power-house, wireless connectivity and networking is rapidly emerging as a major force for change and reworking traditional business models. That wire-free way of doing business has so much as yet untapped potential that it deserves and requires specific attention.

Interactive TV is the forgotten-for-now medium and business communication tool. Because its main application is B2C, it's been tarnished by the dot.com fall out. But it remains a unique platform not only for reaching into every home in the land but also potentially for business and government to interact with target groups.

Setting the scene for streamlining, the immediate next three chapters look at "pioneers" and lessons learned, establish the context, and explore how best to get started and get an organisation mobilised behind these opportunities. In "Pioneers" we consider "Seven of the best." They are using streamlining tools and approaches deliberately and successfully, and demonstrate a challenging array of applications and case examples. The "Internet revolution in context" chapter encourages a longer term view of the impact and potential of this technology "discontinuity" or revolution. It reminds how history is full of examples of technology change – railroads, electricity, radio, motor cars – where initial boom was followed by pause, reappraisal, even some busts, before consolidating and re-emerging but in a more robust and business-realistic form.

Chapters 6 through 11 then introduce, describe and illustrate the "four main chunks" and related applications and technologies in wireless and in iTV. Through a mix of case study, research and interview, the options in each area are examined, pitfalls identified and ways forward defined.

Finally we consider ways in which organisations can best capitalise on the ideas and insights here. One opportunity is to build an "e-learning" environment where 'e' and new technology awareness and skill get built into the very fabric and soul of the company and its workforce so that, as Dell employees put it, "the Internet is part of our core value set." In addition there's a summary of points made at various stages in the book, bringing it all together into a blueprint for "making it happen"!

Oracle saved
$1 billion in 1 year
using our own E-Business Suite.

The Oracle E-Business Suite

is engineered as a complete

and integrated system.

We finish our software

so you don't have to.

You save time and money.

You get better information.

Simple.

ORACLE®
SOFTWARE POWERS THE INTERNET

Get the facts at www.oracle.com

THE BEAR MARKET: HOW IT AFFECTS THE U.S. ECONOMY

BusinessWeek

EUROPEAN EDITION / MARCH 26, 2001   A PUBLICATION OF THE McGRAW-HILL COMPANIES

SPECIAL REPORT

RETHINKING THE INTERNET

ABU DHABI......DH 15   BELGIUM....B FR 166   FINLAND...F MK 24.00   GREECE......DRS 1000   ITALY.....LIT 7,500   NETHERLANDS...FL 8.75   PORTUGAL (CONT) ESC 750   SPAIN.........PTS 695   UNITED KINGDOM...£2.50
AUSTRIA.......SCH 56   DUBAI........DH 18   FRANCE...F FR 27.00   HUNGARY.....FT 900   ISRAEL.....NIS 18   NORWAY...N KR 35.00   SAUDI ARABIA...SR20.00   SWEDEN...S KR 37.00   UNITED STATES..US$3.95
BAHRAIN......BD 1.900   DENMARK....D KR 34   GERMANY.....DM 7.90   IRELAND......IR £2.95   KUWAIT.....KD 1.600   POLAND.......Z 13.50   SOUTH AFRICA...R 16.00   SWITZERLAND...S.FR 5.9   NUMBER...3709-1039

3 Meet seven pioneers

Despite the recent economic slowdown, the synergies of new key technologies has
significantly increased the potential for productivity growth.

(Alan Greenspan, Chairman of US Federal Reserve)

Who's leading the charge on streamlining and e-business transformation
and how are they doing it? It's all very well to talk the theory but what
about the practice?

There is a small but growing band of organisations who *have* taken the
bull by the horns. They've realised just how big is the profit gain and
potential. And through a gradual program of change and restructuring
they've gone after the benefits with increasing commitment, rigor and
determination. They've made mistakes, for sure, but in doing so have
learnt how to do it better. It's not all worked right first time but because
of the "size of the prize" and senior management's personal engagement
they've not been put off. They've pressed on to win.

The good news is that these "lessons learned" are now being captured
and written about, so companies coming along in the next wave don't
need to see themselves as risk takers. They're not "betting the farm" if
they push down this route themselves. On the contrary, the approaches are
proven and more importantly the new tools that need to be employed are
reliable. Organisations have also recognised that they don't need to be
slaves to the technology, it's as much about changing behaviors, processes
and organisation structures.

Alongside this, the clincher is the range of benefits companies have
achieved by pushing down these paths. In many cases it's straightforward
cost savings through streamlining business processes. In other examples
it's about productivity gains, output and more effective ways of working.
In still other arenas it might be about better communication between
teams and groups and affiliates and partners to get to market quicker and
more effectively to drive up revenues. In yet other areas it's about using
data more effectively to boost collaboration, share know-how, improve
education and bolster morale. The gains are potentially available in every
part of the organisation.

Table 3.1 Pioneers across most sectors

• Financial services	Fidelity	• Banking via mobile phone/PDA
	WellsFargo Bank	• No. 1 banking/investment community online
	Progressive Insurance	• "20 minute claims settlement"
• Retail	Tesco	• World's largest online grocer and profitable
	Amazon	• A $4bn company in 5 years
• Manufacturing	Honeywell	• myplant.com
	Solectron	• Leading web-connected outsourcing
• Energy/utilities	BP	• $100m + of e-purchasing savings
	Dynegy	• Online energy
	TXU	• Knowledge sharing/employee collaboration
• Construction	Webcor	• Virtual project management
• Computer services	Dell	• Automated customer supplier ordering
	Cisco	• Majority of orders online

Oracle $1bn, Cisco $800m growing to $1.4bn through 2002, Dell's S, G&A (sales, general and admin costs) down below 10% (industry norms are 20%), BP £200m, GE $200m announced in just one division and expecting $1.6bn to be announced, Siemens hitting on €1bn, Progressive Insurance doubling revenues ... the profit impacts are so significant and the "softer benefits" in organisation and culture are so far-reaching that this whole opportunity must be examined with some care and rigor. For many companies fighting in today's tough markets the prize could add up to a near doubling of profits over time, if the Cisco e-transformation is the benchmark. Let's look at some stunning examples. We have seven industry pioneers:

1 **Nestlé**
2 **Cisco**
3 **Oracle**
4 **Dell**
5 **Nordea Bank**
6 **Moen**
7 **Microsoft.**

1. Nestlé

Nestlé is a $50bn revenue company employing more than 200,000 people in 400 factories in 83 countries and producing more than 8000 different consumer product lines – everything from cat food to Perrier water.

Headquartered in a sleepy town in Switzerland it's as "old economy" as you get, but together with Siemens and ABB Asea Brown Boveri it's leading the charge in continental Europe among the major industrials to take advantage of the Net and new technology.

CEO Peter Brabeck-Letmathe has announced a $2bn investment over three years to become one of the world's "web-smart elite." The company wants to overhaul its buying, producing and distribution processes and establish an "e-revolution." Though this revolution is a three to four year journey! not the kind of overnight trip that might have been advocated when 'e' was at its full hype.

Early results have been encouraging with profits and margins up and with e-initiatives claiming some of that success. In addition investor expectations have been raised that at last this big and somewhat bureaucratic company is on the move, and the share price has started to respond. "For big companies like us the Internet is particularly good because it shakes you up.... It also gives us the chance to get further economies of scale while still remaining locally responsive."

Nestlé has identified a series of internet-driven initiatives. First up is a program to streamline its operations:

- Consolidating IT – Nestlé had, according to a *Business Week* interview, five e-mail systems and 20 different accounting, planning and inventory management software tools. Country operations used different computer codes for the same products and so comparing or aggregating or leveraging any of the data across the company was very time-consuming. Now Nestlé has moved to one package that's web-linked, and has forced the consolidation of product codes to make that single package work.
- Providing employees with "useful information" – most people had no access to data or sales or production from other countries as their systems didn't link up. Now there is a single database available via the web-browser on everyone's desk. In particular the single database is providing insight because the data is at last transparent. A buyer in country X now knows what his counterpart in country Y is paying the same supplier for the same product.
- Streamlining purchasing – while Nestlé is looking at ways to leverage its new internet network to reduce supplier costs, it's also looking to improve its whole purchasing process. The company has plans to tie together its far-flung operations, partner with suppliers and customers, and examine ways to reduce costs and inventory throughout the whole

supply chain. "This is as much about us increasing our own internal productivity as working smarter with others."

On the back of its initial purchasing review Nestlé has consolidated its supply base cutting out more than half and reducing costs both in its own purchasing processes and also on materials by 20%. "For example we had 12 buyers in Europe dealing with 14 suppliers of lactose – a key ingredient in chocolate bars. Now we only use four suppliers and costs have come down. Only because we got the online information did we identify this."

"The web also enables us to communicate more easily and real time with partners, and all at once outsourcing is back on our agenda as we have a chance of being able to manage it more effectively."

- Customer service – Nestlé is putting effort into using the Net to improve and strengthen customer relations. For example it set up EZOrder.com for its US customers. This encourages customers to order online and track order progress. The aim is also to eliminate c. 100,000 phoned or faxed orders the company gets each year, which require significant resource to process them. Nestlé reckon initiatives like this could cut global admin costs of some $3bn by up to 20% once the program is in place.

Not surprisingly, it's Nestlé's US division who are leading this Internet charge. Among other things they are holding weekly e-training sessions with employees with the topic: "how can we use e-business and the Net to help unify the company?" The US team are also spearheading experiments with inventory management – sharing data electronically with retailers on demand forecasts – and also with knowledge management – ensuring key best practices discovered in one operation get posted on the intranet to enable others to improve their own productivity or ROI. "For the first time we are learning to take advantage of Nestlé's size."

As CEO, Brabeck-Letmathe has been given a clear signal by investors and employees: the company has to concentrate on improving efficiency and the company is clearly now responding. Internet-based initiatives are spreading, there's an eagerness to test-pilot new ways of working from procurement to interactive TV shopping, and commitment is growing. "No one here underestimates the challenges ahead; we have to learn to manage through uncertainty and turmoil but the Net is contributing a huge amount to our restructuring."

2. Cisco

Cisco's $1.4bn of cost savings is equivalent to 7% of its sales. 7% of sales or 7 net margin profits – would certainly be equivalent to a doubling of profits for many organisations. Looked at another way, 7% of US manufacturing costs is equivalent to $300bn! That's one big potential cost saving number.

And for Cisco, the catalyst for all this, the driver behind the achievement of these gains, the enabler has been the Internet.

Cisco is often written about despite the downturn in its order book but here are the stark facts:

- 70% of orders, and growing, are placed and fulfilled over the web.
- Indeed one customer did $100m of business without any human contact!
- 70% of service calls are resolved online, relieving the call center to focus on new orders rather than being bogged down with old queries.
- Cost of Finance function halved from 2% to 1% of sales.
- Company accounts automated and can be closed within a few hours of any given day.
- Manufacturing orders reworked down from 33% in 1995 to under 1%.
- Using the Internet for data transfer and project work has saved $40m in paper alone.
- Streamlined inventory and ordering systems connecting suppliers to forecast demand enables real time adjustments to product orders, increases as well as decreases, to meet changing customer needs.
- Web-based procurement boosted gross margins to 60% plus, cutting processing time by 70% and requisition handing costs by 50%.

John Chambers is the CEO and driving force of Cisco and it's no fluke they've got as far as they have. Look back to their annual reports for example as early as 1994–5, and you'll see a stunningly clear statement of strategy and vision around the Internet and the products required to ride that opportunity. "Cisco uses the Web like a weapon," is the way one analyst has put it. And now with Internet traffic doubling every 100 days or so, whatever the skeptics might say, the demand for infrastructure products of the type Cisco provide is not going to go away. Quite the reverse.

Not surprising then that when you meet with people from Cisco you find that many "live and breathe" the Internet and its applications. They've been part of the team that's delivered the benefits that all can see. In fact when Cisco's 35,000 strong workforce are evaluated, they get brownie points and bonuses based partly on their ability to improve operations using the Web.

We'll see this is a characteristic running through all these pioneers and success stories. In each case "living the Internet" is part of the way these companies think – every day. It's something ingrained in each and every employee. They're taught the benefits, training courses are geared to exploring the how and the why, war stories abound around what's been achieved and the contribution of individuals to it, and the bonus rewards they've received for their insight and innovation.

It's a belief that's developed over time so that the organisation's leaders don't have to keep "pushing" the benefits and the opportunities; individual employees are now "pulling" at their colleagues and associates to find new ways to use the Net. And while a lot of the talk is around cost savings, there's just as much about better/smarter/more effective ways of working.

Here's one example from Cisco's early internet developments. The company had a large sales/technology support team. Their job was to chase new customers/new orders but also continue to support existing customers. However they were getting bogged down. Existing customers had so many queries that the sales/technology team just weren't getting around to new customers. New customer growth was falling, existing customers were getting irritated at delays in getting a response, the sales team weren't reaching their bonus targets. The system just wasn't working.

One solution: have more sales people, but that wouldn't fix the underlying problem. So Cisco decided to use the Web to change the process instead. The company set up extranet links for customers and identified the FAQs (the most frequently asked questions and issues). It launched this as a new customer service initiative: get an immediate response to your problem now and do it online.

There was some hesitancy at Cisco: would customers be satisfied with an electronic interface? Would they not still demand human contact? What they found however was that customers naturally responded to the FAQ initiative. There was a "modularised" set of answers but Cisco found it answered most questions, and certainly took the pressure off the need for an immediate response from the sales rep.

Within months the sales technology team were noticing a significant drop off in customer queries. At the same time the FAQ web site was relaunched with extended technical and other information. In addition, as pressure in the call center also started reducing, call center operators were redeployed to act as online intermediaries and experts. So there was an "e-mail the expert" facility, initially at only certain times in the day but eventually extended to 24/7. All this done online and real time.

Of course as this initiative succeeded so the win:wins began to emerge. For the sales technology team, more time available for new customers, more time to get to their targets; for existing customers an easier and more immediate response; and for new customers a faster turnaround time on initial enquiries. And for Cisco, more profits.

Looking forward, Cisco is now wrestling with the questions of what should be the best organisation model to facilitate its next moves in the Internet economy and how to take advantage of the Net to drive out further efficiencies.

The company's current model was established largely in the mid-1990s when it decentralised IT and gave all business unit managers the authority to make whatever investments they felt sensible to increase sales and customer satisfaction. (This contrasts strongly with the centralised model we'll see next at Oracle.) The company acknowledges that this structure was not the reason by itself for its subsequent e-business success but it was strongly reinforced by an incentive system that focussed on "customer satisfaction" and held those same business unit managers accountable. "This combination of structure and aligned and targeted incentives was key for us.... It forced us to deepen customer relationships and made IT especially responsive to customer need." It also led to a strong entrepreneurial/innovation culture as managers were encouraged to take any initiative provided they could sell the payback.

The only qualifications to this decentralised model have been efforts to standardise B2B commerce platforms. The Internet has helped the achievement of this because the largest customers, who may have run across different Cisco businesses, were provided with one common purchasing platform and only one entry point to the order management system. Nevertheless, even with this is in place, there remain questions as to the extent individual business managers might protect their autonomy and continue to operate orders locally.

So the Cisco system is not perfect. But because it's worked so incredibly well, fuelling the growth and success that at one point made the company the biggest in value terms in the world in spring 2001, there is a reluctance to change it too dramatically. However inevitable questions are being asked about how this model should evolve, especially as growth rates slow and the economic slowdown affects orders and highlights issues. Is it leading to too much duplication of effort, are there synergies which are substantial which just aren't being captured, is the global customer being best served if there are many different local approaches?

Streamlining

Centralising a decentralised organisation structure is a substantial task that can take many years, but it is apparently on the agenda as the company looks to continue its market leadership. It's likely however that any initial moves will be more tentative and focus around some central technology research team to try to capture and exploit cross-company initiatives. "We have been extraordinarily innovative to date but we don't want to be complacent, and feel we have to evolve if we are to take advantage of the best e-business practices."

3. Oracle

Oracle has saved $1bn in annual costs and is now talking of raising that to $2bn annually.

What's that in relative terms? $1bn equates to a 10 point improvement in operating margin; let's repeat that – a 10 point improvement in operating margin. One thing we need to stress here as this book unfolds is that you don't have to be big to get the benefits. Indeed go to www.oracle.com and look up its "customer database." There are lots of examples there where Oracle has helped quite small organisations achieve success.

For Oracle, those 10 points pushed their margin up to over 41%. It contributed over 20% to year 2000 net income and contributed significantly to the company's cash. Inevitably it's been an important addition too during the more challenging 2001/2 results period.

What lies behind this substantial cost reduction and profit boost? For Oracle, it's all about e-business. It's about using the Internet to replace "the complex with the simple." It's about "using the new technology to build a cost-cutting and performance improvement engine." It's streamlining. It's about so effectively integrating the Internet into the existing business processes that it replaces or changes them forever. It's about restructuring the way the organisation operates so that not doing things 'e', not using the Internet, becomes unthinkable. The old ways just fall away.

In doing this, Oracle have used these new tools to:

- consolidate servers worldwide
- standardise architecture and peripherals
- streamline databases
  - e.g. 100 customer databases into one
  - 140 product/pricing databases into one
  - 70 HR databases into one
- convert 97 e-mail databases into one unified e-mail system

- centralise processes/tasks where there is clear scale leverage, e.g. supplier procurement
- putting online what was previously offline, e.g. automating sales order processing.

At Oracle, they see the Internet as a global network and opportunity to put in place a global database. Their goal was to establish single unified databases on the Net to integrate all aspects of doing business. They also wanted to do this across every business function – marketing, sales, supply chain, manufacturing, customer service, accounting, human resources – everything. Connecting everybody up with all the information in one place on one unified system.

Oracle began this process back in 1995–6 and developed its own Internet application software to facilitate this changeover and run the business. They don't pretend it was easy. They had to replace old client/server systems which had grown up bespoke. Each country and each function had developed its own operating systems and this was leading to issues of incompatibility, data reworking, data delays, different product codes in different countries for the same products, irreconcilability of accounts, different invoicing terms in different countries for the same customer ... inadequate decision making, duplication of cost, extra effort and resource to manage the incompatibilities ... and so the list of inefficiencies went on. "Data was so fragmented it was difficult for people to quickly find the information they needed to do their jobs. Also separate databases meant it was difficult to share information so people didn't collaborate or cooperate. In the end it was not just a cost issue but a revenue problem as well."

When this transformation process first began, it seems there was quite a lot of internal resistance. Some saw no reason to change systems that already worked well for them; others were prepared "to explore options"; only a handful were sufficiently swayed that they were ready to initiate the changeover program. And of course it only needs a few champions, combined with the total commitment of the business leaders, to get the whole program under way.

Oracle spent a lot of time up front clarifying and defining the benefits. A key to the change argument was understanding those benefits and identifying what the new situation would look like, how it would work and how it would resolve many of the existing process, data and decision-making systems. As Larry Ellison, CEO of Oracle has pointed out "I talk with CEOs almost every day. Virtually none of them have access to all the information they need. If we could do that for ourselves then we'd really learn and be in a much stronger position to do it for others."

To take a specific illustration, Oracle found many of its problems lay in poor customer relationship management. There was a catalog of missed orders, wrong supply, part supply, delays, failing to respond to customer queries, not responding at all to some new order requests! and general dissatisfaction with the sales/marketing process.

Digging into this, Oracle discovered it had six separate customer databases: marketing, web store, telesales, field sales, accounting and services. And that was just in the USA. Around the world there were over 100, scattering customer information. Backing that up, each country had its own data center filled with its own computer hardware configuration with its own IT staff who were experts in maintaining its own separate and unique system. Compounding that problem, since each organisation had its own system, each organisation had constructed its own business processes and had then tailored them to its own local environment. So in each country there was a separate and different process for customer marketing. Everything therefore was non-standard. And it meant a huge amount of duplication. That was not just each country doing the same thing for itself, but also each country reinventing the wheel because it couldn't easily discover that the wheel had already been invented! "We were in effect a feudal operation run by a group of autonomous general managers inventing their own policies and procedures." "We didn't set price once, we set it about 150 times. We didn't develop one marketing program, we had 150."

Sounds familiar?

To facilitate the change, Oracle did three key things.

1. Streamlined IT, bringing it into one global organisation with one head across each company.
2. Changed the compensation plan of the country general managers. Their bonus was based on target profits. If they used the global IT division rather than their own IT, then they had that resource for "free." There was no charge, for two years, for global IT services.
3. Initiated the first major program for change. For this they landed on a global e-mail pilot project. They discovered there were 97 client/server e-mail systems. These were replaced with a single Internet e-mail running on just two servers in a US data center.

The pilot project was key. It was set up as a critical early win and it did deliver. Everyone in the company was migrated onto one unified e-mail platform, and the costs were reduced by 90%. It was more reliable. It was more secure. It was available in local languages. And it was free to country managers.

With this achievement behind them, the Oracle team then did the same to marketing. A global marketing executive was established, services provided free to country managers, marketing people themselves still located in the regions, databases consolidated, sales support services automated. With this in place, marketing costs went down as duplication was eliminated. Instead of many different marketing, pricing and sales programs, there was now one. There was one view of the customer and the customer had one view of the company.

As additional innovations on the back of the unified Internet-based system, Oracle took to hosting global seminars on the Net, inviting attendees from many different countries at much lower cost to them and to Oracle. All product demos were moved onto the Net so that anyone could see a demo by clicking for it. This tool was then taken up by the sales force to support the sales process and boost orders. All visits to the web site are logged and captured, providing hosts of new leads for sales and then tracking step-by-step the sales development process. Like Cisco before them, online support is growing, call center staff are being trained into online experts, FAQ service is expanding and product/technical information on the Net available to would-be or existing customers is substantial and growing. It also leads to 24/7/365 support as problems anywhere in the world can be dealt with immediately.

> "When we globalised our business onto the Net, our operational inefficiencies began to melt away. It was amazing. New ways of working developed. Cooperation and interdependency replaced the silo mentality. The culture changed and the values of the company changed. The more we've learned about working in this way the better our business decisions have become."

4. Dell

Dell has become the world's largest PC maker (although the HP/Compaq deal temporarily at least takes that title). It claims that a key reason is its low cost model. This enables it to price aggressively and beat out competitors. "We've got the business model to tough it out and grab share from weaker rivals." S,G&A (sales, general and admin costs) at c. 10% are roughly half the industry average and continue to decline. Inventory is down to an amazing just four days, working capital is substantially cash

21

positive and there is almost no debt on the balance sheet. How has the company achieved this? What extraordinary steps have been taken to arrive at this ground-breaking business system? What have been the key levers to drive these changes through?

Dell's answer lies in the Internet: "the most important development at Dell is the degree to which we have transitioned our business to the Internet." It's about building revenues as well as streamlining operations.

Dell now does more than $50m per day of business on the Net. By itself that's well over half of Dell's daily sales and makes Dell one of the largest online Internet businesses in the world. "Our customers recognise that we have the knowledge about how the Internet works, how 'e' works and because that's something they're asking about, they cite it as a key reason why they come to us."

Dell.com gets over 40 million individual visitors every quarter. The physical infrastructure required to support that needs to be substantial, but it also needs to facilitate a seamless online order flow into Dell's order entry and manufacturing systems, otherwise things would collapse very quickly. It also means that given Dell's business model it needs to link current order patterns into future demand and requires real time updating to ensure inventory stays at four days and doesn't creep up.

Through 2001 Dell shipped c. 12 million computers to over 150 different countries. "The Internet has become our essential tool for dealing

Figure 3.1 S,G&A costs as percentage of net revenue for Dell from 1997 to 2001

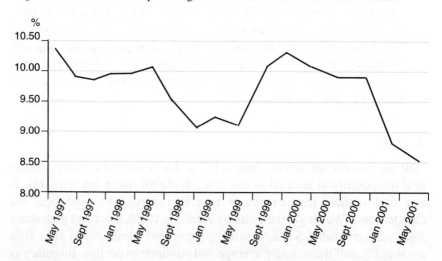

Source: Dell

with volumes and cutting a way through business complexity." Two key goals have been set for continuing to provide an automatic real time interface with customers.

1. "Provide a superior web experience for customers." Part of this is achieved though "support@Dell.com." Here all customers can get personalised access to Dell products, specs, special pricing, order tracking and order customisation. For larger customers, these customer pages are called "Premier Pages" and there are over 50,000. The aim is to "let the customer inside the business." For Ford for example, one of Dell's largest customers, there is an automated procurement process integrating into their purchasing system. It provides access to the Dell account team managing Ford and a range of support tools.

2. Build the online environment so that by 2002 80% of customers go online for product-ordering and technical help. Automating the whole ordering process is seen as a critical step. It's Dell's key to driving S,G&A even lower and keeping that low cost model as competitive as possible: "the way we see it, a call center call into Dell's support operations typically costs between 3 and 10 dollars per call. An online call, once the infrastructure's been built, is 'close to zero.' That's partly because it's accessing information we have already compiled. As the online interface has improved – it started in 1994 – it's reached a point where 70% of queries are resolved first time without the need for any subsequent call center discussion or technical support needing to be sent to the customer site. Alongside this there are less 'quantifiable' benefits in terms of speed and quality of response that play a role in delivering customer satisfaction."

In addition pushing back up the supply chain, Dell uses the Internet to manage its own supplier relationships. Over 80% of suppliers are dealt with directly over the Net. In particular it manages the purchasing of its 25,000 employees who are spending c. $5bn each year on non-production supplies – everything from consulting services to office equipment.

Dell used to have a purchase order process requiring completion of a three part form. With each requisition, employees had to hand-code information about suppliers, part numbers and item costs as well as manually collect up to ten approval signatures. At the same time employees were responsible for entering the handwritten data into two separate systems. This was clearly time-consuming and it was worked out that each requisition was costing over $100; "this was a process ripe for change if we were to improve profitability in an e-business driven economy."

Dell looked for an internet-based solution which would significantly lower costs. It also wanted to take advantage of the change to shorten procurement cycles, streamline the supplier base and eliminate "maverick spending." Dell had five criteria for the e-procurement solution:

- ease of use for employees
- optimisation on Dell servers and Microsoft Windows NT platform
- e-commerce connection to suppliers
- integration with Dell's back-end systems
- cost.

Dell has now established its Internet requisition tool (DiREQT), which is a fully automated process. It's integrated into Dell's legacy systems including purchase order, cost centers, accounting code data, catalogs and HR. The result is a 62% reduction in requisition time and a reduction in average cost per requisition of nearly $70. Combined with better value buying from a rationalised supplier base, this produced savings of well over $100m after the first year of implementation.

The bottom line of this activity and Dell's other Internet-based initiatives is a dramatic increase in its measure of ROIC (return on invested capital). This has gone up from 34% in 1996 to 294% in 2000! While it's been partly affected by the changing economic climate during 2001/2, it's still delivering substantial returns for shareholders.

"Despite all this success we believe we've not yet begun to tap the full potential of the Internet. We're still in the infancy of a revolution in how the world works and communicates. Our only certainty is that the Internet is a powerful tool and it's growing. For businesses, integration of the Internet throughout all relationships and processes is no longer an option; it's a requirement for success."

(Michael Dell in a speech at University of Texas)

5. Nordea Bank

More than any other bank in the world, Nordea is tapping the Internet. Its goal is to "woo customers and streamline operations." Its bottom line is to boost profits by $250m, that's 10% a year each year for the next three years. And it's targeting that achievement to come half through revenues and half through reduced costs.

Nordea is in the process of slowly transforming itself into an Internet-enabled operation. It's a group that's only recently come together, being the result of mergers between several Scandinavian mid-sized retail and wholesale banking institutions. Finland's MetaBank joined with Sweden's Nordbanken and then embraced Denmark's Unidanmark and Norway's Christianbank. Several other mergers have subsequently taken place including Sweden's Postgirot and also the Insurance operation Tryg-Baltica.

The mergers are proving a huge success with annual profits for 2001 scheduled to hit €2.5bn, up 22% from the previous year. But what's drawing the headlines is the Internet activity of this growing and ambitious outfit.

Nordea has c. 2.5 million net customers. Around 7 million transactions are expected to be completed online, such as paying bills, buying/selling shares etc. That level of online activity puts Nordea up there with the other big internet banking operations such as Bank of America and Wells Fargo, and it's more than double the number of transactions per month of the largest Net only bank – UK Prudential's Egg bank. "When it comes to mixing banking bricks and clicks and getting value out of the Net, Nordea are among the best," is the view of analysts at Morgan Stanley.

Moreover, the step-by-step e-banking strategy that's being employed is already contributing significantly to the profit base. Nearly half the branches of the bank in Finland have been closed as business has deliberately been shifted online. It's also meant a reduction of over 5000 staff as these business changes roll out across the new Scandinavian-wide enterprise.

Nordea has been quick to capitalise on its established brands and physical presence on the local retail scene. While an Internet only bank can find itself paying more than $200 in marketing costs per customer captured, Nordea reckons it's only spent $18m over five years building its strong Net franchise. Furthermore it's not been afraid to charge fees online for its services – in fact some of its online fees are higher than its branch fees – but it's all helped ensure the Net operation is positively profitable.

The size of this achievement must be measured against others. Not just Prudential's Egg, but Cahoot from Abbey National and Commerzbank's Comdirect have variously struggled to see profits. Switzerland's Vantobel had to write off $150m after its "YOU" e-bank failed, and Norwich Union are under pressure to get returns from their $250m financial services/insurance/banking web site.

Specifically as a result of Nordea's move, a number of internal processes and procedures have been automated, delivering cost savings or freeing up time to enable staff to focus on more value-added activities. For example 96% of all deposits and withdrawals are now processed electronically "so we have time to call customers, say hello and see what we can do for them." That approach alone in one branch network pushed revenues by 50%; "instead of a lot of manual work it's more interesting to sell loans or other products."

Other initiatives and benefits include:

- Online transactions actually now cost Nordea an average of just 11¢ each. That compares with around $1 for transactions in branches, and is saving the Bank at least $40m each year.
- Customers can apply online for loans up to $15,000 and decisions get e-mailed back within 15 minutes. By approving loans over the Net, the Bank saves around 30% of the normal processing costs per loan.
- Nordea has also set up an online marketplace for SMEs. There, small businesses can also market their services to Nordea's other customers ("everything from sausages to saunas"), paying the Bank $18 per month and a 25¢ transaction fee.

These and other initiatives are all springing up on the back of the pervasiveness of the Net in the way the Bank's staff approach day to day transactions and business processes. If there's a short cut via the Net that can improve customer service while cutting costs, then the business investment is quickly approved.

The next stage is to start taking advantage of wireless technologies to deliver selected product services to customers' mobile access devices. These would include stock buying, and Nordea is also looking at schemes enabling customers to use their mobile phones to purchase all sorts of other products – food, movie tickets, drinks etc. – with purchases debited directly from Nordea accounts.

> "Key to our success is our long-standing commitment to the potential of internet technology. We've had a program of continuous improvement while recognising any commercial limitations. We are evolutionaries not revolutionaries but we have shown just what can be achieved."

Figure 3.2 Netbanking at Nordea

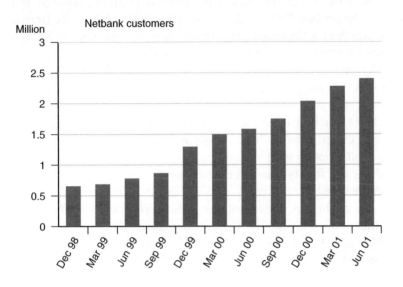

Source: Nordea Bank

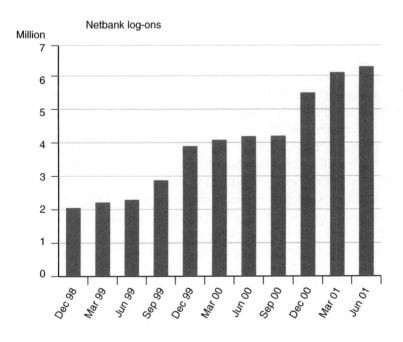

Source: Nordea Bank

6. Moen

Moen is one of the world's largest manufacturers of plumbing products and is the no. 1 faucet brand across the USA. It's part of the Fortune Brands portfolio, which is a US-based $5bn brands company manufacturing and distributing everything from Moen to Jim Bean whisky.

Moen has grown sales by 17% from 1998 to 2001 in highly competitive markets. It's jumped share from no.3 to no.1 ahead of its archrival Delta Faucet with a c. 30% slice of the America's $2.5bn faucet market.

It attributes much of its success to the Internet. It has focussed on its total supply chain process. It has innovated in the way it works with suppliers, collaborates with outside contractors and partners, develops new products and finally brings them to market.

Its approach has been "steady drip." There is a 20-member Internet Program office which is responsible for setting priorities, identifying the "things that can realistically be accomplished with the resources available" and establishing the change program and solution. Moen reckons its web investment has only been around $2m and that's mostly been on hiring software developers for work that's largely been driven in-house. "This is our new model for an effective Net strategy: a clear focus on the bottom line and an understanding on how to deliver a return on the investment."

Moen's vision was driven by their understanding of their markets and their customers. Historic buying patterns saw customers purchasing new faucets an average once every nine years. Moen used to bring out one new range each year. Moen wanted to become the "Donna Karan" of its market producing regular fresh and accessible new designs, enabling customers to mix parts, inject some style into the market and excite more frequent replacement and refurbishment.

Its goal was to "turbocharge product design and manufacturing." This meant going back to the drawing board and reconfiguring its entire supply chain process. By reducing "product to market" time from 24 months, Moen realised it could at the same time unleash its 50 engineers from time-consuming, inefficient project development and focus them on delivering between 5 to 15 new lines a year.

Moen's first challenge was to clear up its own clogged product development pipelines. One of its engineers would typically work six to eight weeks to come up with a new design. That would be "burnt" onto CDs and mailed to suppliers who were making the many parts going into one faucet.

But suppliers would find they couldn't meet the required spec, so they'd make changes and send new CDs back to Moen, who would then review all its suppliers' changes, redo the spec, put it onto CDs, send it out .... this process would take months till finally resolved.

So Moen launched "ProjectNet." This is an online site where the company shares digital designs simultaneously with suppliers all over the world. Each supplier is encouraged to respond immediately, and others can equally see the various changes taking place and can comment on their ability to respond. Moen then consolidates all the design changes into a master web file that all can access real time. Problems are uncovered instantly, adjustments can be made real time and the final design can get approval in just three days!

On another front Moen has launched "SupplyNet." This streamlines the parts ordering process. Suppliers have been "encouraged" to link up if they want to participate in Moen's growing business base. Orders are now sent online and suppliers can check a Moen forecast table at any time to help manage their own inventory and scheduling. Moen will make changes to orders as its own customer needs vary and again suppliers are automatically notified. It's reckoned that this has reduced

Figure 3.3 Fortune brands

the company's product costs in just six months by 9% and also seen significant reductions in inventory in the supply chain.

None of this is especially revolutionary. But it's moving at "light speed" compared to competitors in an historically slow-moving industry sector. Moen is emerging as "a clear step ahead of its peers in embracing Internet technologies," concluded a Forrester Research report on the industry.

> "For us the web is a natural.... Its streamlining has become our means of gaining competitive advantage by speeding up product development, reducing inventory and freeing up both resources and cash to be used more productively.... We want to become a web-smart company."

7. Microsoft

Microsoft has itself been through wrenching change internally, although its struggle to get Net-literate took place a bit earlier than most in the mid-1990s. During 1995 and 1996 for example, with the advent of the Net, the success of Netscape and the emergence of the likes of Sun Microsystems, research group Gartner was publishing papers wondering if Microsoft would be "killed off by the Internet." Its software solutions were so orientated to the traditional desktop environment that commentators wondered if the company "could go through the necessary network reinvention from the ground-up."

This was how the challenge was described in one of Microsoft's own internal newsletters at the time:

> Our competitors were laughing, said our network was a fake
> Saw the Internet economy as simply theirs to take.
> They'll regret the fateful day
> The sleeping giant does awake.
> We embrace and we extend.

At the time, Microsoft had been so obsessed with Windows '95 and beating back government regulators worried about alleged anti-competitive practices that the company had completely missed out on early Net developments. In 1995, others had taken control. But Microsoft then embarked on an intensive program of Net-transformation which still hasn't stopped.

It switched a significant part of its resources. Gates himself went on record acknowledging the company has missed the early developments and the speed of the Net's commercialisation. He publicly announced a U-turn in the company's strategy. "Our goal is turn ourselves into being web-centric, to leave behind what doesn't fit and reshape everything else."

With that new framework established Microsoft announced a series of initiatives: (i) increasing R&D by 50% "mainly to meet the challenges posed by the Internet"; (ii) forming alliances with MCI, Intel, Hughes and others; (iii) making a number of relatively small acquisitions to access/buy in the know-how; and (iv) establishing a wide array of tie-ins with all the major commercial online services and ISPs to make its new web-browser the standard tool to surf the Net.

It showed extraordinary commitment and determination right across the company. Gates realised early enough just how powerful a tool the Net would become and invested considerable effort to get the company back into the forefront:

Oh our eyes have seen the glory of the coming of the Net,
We are ramping up our market share, objectives will be met,
Our browser will be everywhere, you ain't seen nothin' yet.
We embrace and we extend!

Microsoft's desire to win has carried it through to its more recent "Dot.Net strategy." In a *Fortune* magazine article entitled "The Beast is Back," it becomes clear just how determined Microsoft is to extend its influence into everything from hand-held devices to high-end servers, and to turn the Internet into a big operating system that delivers services to PCs, PDAs and other access devices. The technology goal of the Dot.Net strategy is to plow through the competing standards and other roadblocks and create a web where it's far easier for servers to communicate.

Among other things this has led Microsoft into investing heavily in building its web services and its Net platform now competes head-to-head with Sun Microsystems' Sun One architecture. It's also built up an array of developers – some 7 million – who have been trained and certified and provide worldwide back up, installation and maintenance. And as an example of its "Net-spread," the company has now established a signif-icant lead in secure payment systems for consumers and SMEs online with c. 200 million "Passport" accounts opened up, providing a single sign-on identity authentication service.

Microsoft is also a powerful advocate of "distributed computing." This is a way to create an array of software programs linked over the web that can tap into each other directly, as though they were all on one machine. It's computer to computer communication that takes advantage of new standards such as Xml (extensible mark-up language) to allow computers to share software processing tasks and manipulate data autonomously. "We think we can make the Internet experience even better through technology," comments one Microsoft VP. "Services will be accessible from all access devices whether it's the X-box games console, Ultimate/web TV, Pocket PCs, cell phones or the PC on the desk."

All Microsoft's services and software (including its XP release) will now sync up with Net technologies. "Our goal," says Gates, 'is to move beyond today's world of stand-alone Net solutions to an internet of interchangeable components where devices and services can be assembled into a cohesive user-driven experience."

* * * * *

"Join the web-smart elite," "use the web like a weapon," "new ways of working," "internet as part of our core value set," "streamlining for advantage," "mixing clicks 'n' bricks," "embracing and extending" – whatever the mantra these pioneers have adopted, they've developed a vision of how the Internet and new technologies can transform their organisations. They've taken significant steps to change and transform the way things get done, how processes get carried through, how they're organised and how they 'woo' customers. Besides satisfying their shareholders and other stakeholders they also, most importantly, act as models and benchmarks for how the next wave of companies can join in this success story.

4 The Internet revolution in context

The dot.com revolution may have been and gone, but as we are discovering it has given birth to something much more substantial.

As the seven pioneers and others are demonstrating, in fact we just ain't seen nothing yet. (Challenge yourself with some basic Internet "did you knows" at the end of the chapter.) There's a growing recognition that business has only just begun to realize the potential. As Jeff Bezos in his inimitable style has put it: "today is just Day 1 of the Internet and it's just 1.00 am on Day 1." We may have overestimated the short term but "we usually underestimate the long term" (Bill Gates). And as the indomitable Peter Drucker has commented: "investment in building information highways and communication pipes is estimated at c. $1 trillion per year – all that effort, passion and activity cannot have been for nothing!"

What type of perspective on 'e' is now appropriate and how should business be thinking about new technology over the next two to three years? Evidence and research is showing that in general business leaders do remain enthusiastic and committed to the "new economy." But they do also have somewhat more realistic views on what can be achieved.

- "We believe that productivity is the promise of the Internet and we are just beginning to see the payback of Internet applications and networking technology.... Demand for network equipment has fallen sharply during this economic downturn, but we are in the very early stages of a major technological revolution and the long term outlook for this industry has not changed" (John Chambers, CEO of Cisco).
- Microsoft CEO Steve Ballmer kicked off the Industry Standard's third annual Internet summit declaring that the Internet's promise has yet to be achieved but reckoning that another revolution is just around the corner. It was an impassioned talk to a group of hundreds of industry leaders who have seen values plummet. Ballmer declared that companies are just beginning to get to grips with the

new opportunities. "There are a number of major innovations in the pipeline around software, bandwidth and access which will transform Internet applications ... but usage will need to reach critical mass before the real impact" (Industry Standard/Computerworld report).

- "At Unilever we still believe e-business can be a major driver of productivity and growth helping companies improving earnings. Unilever has a strong platform for its moves into B2B and B2C activities.... We think online shopping could eventually account for between 5 and 10 per cent of consumer buying. Prospects in B2B are even more encouraging. We see between 10 and 15 per cent of transactions online by 2004" (Peter Slater, IT head of Unilever).

- "Business chiefs bemoan internet backlash in a recent survey. A majority of FTSE 350 chief executives felt the pendulum has swung too far suggesting all things B2C and B2B are unattractive. 44% expected to increase internet spending despite current slower economic conditions" (*Financial Times*).

- "To think that the new economy is over is like somebody in London in 1830 saying the entire industrial revolution is over because some textile manufacturers in Manchester went broke" (Alvin Toffler, author of *Future Shock*).

- "Since so many dot.coms turned into dot.bombs, we have stopped seeing the big headlines about the e-commerce revolution. But that does not mean e-business has come to a halt. People have learned their lessons and seen how internet technologies can simplify business processes, improve customer communications and save money. The publicity pendulum has swung away from e-business but in some ways the revolution is continuing. It is just quieter this time" (Phil Smith, Director of Business Development, Cisco).

Companies are learning to see through the original hype. They are beginning to reappraise the potential and re-evaluate what is feasible and possible. What they realise for certain is that there are new technologies with new applications which just did not exist commercially ten years ago.

It's extraordinary to reflect on the power of these new communication breakthroughs. Even more startling that all three came through in such a short period of time. During the 1980s and even the first part of the 1990s, business was just waking up to the power of the computer. But it required dedicated leased lines and networks of modems, it was expensive to build, costly to maintain, complex and largely the domain

Figure 4.1 The three core new technologies

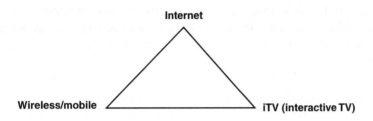

of big business. Yet technology continues to evolve and no one could have predicted even ten years ago that three revolutions would take place almost simultaneously.

The Internet has morphed from a military/academic/research industry communication tool into a public commercial and universal network. It now links millions of servers stuffed with data in a world-wide web accessible anytime anywhere and enabling seamless, low cost data/voice transmission in a common language. The mobile phone is becoming a "mobile command module" for global communication, but also for accessing the Net and reaching into that data/knowledge-sharing environment while on the move however remote the location. You can even use it to buy a can of soda from a vending machine, catch the latest promotion in a supermarket as you walk up the aisle, check on how your bid is doing in the current online auction.... And interactive TV, often

Table 4.1 Technology innovation continuing fast

1970s	⇒	Mainframe computing	IBM, Computer Associates
	⇒	Minicomputers	Digital, Oracle, IBM
	⇒	Personal computers	Microsoft, Intel, Lotus, IBM
	⇒	Desktop publishing	Apple, HP
	⇒	Local area networks	Novell, 3Com
	⇒	Unit server computing	Microsoft (Windows 3.1), Oracle, SAP
	⇒	Home computing	Microsoft (Windows 95), Nintendo, Dell
	⇒	Wide-area networks	Sun, Compaq, Cisco
	⇒	World-wide web	Netscape, Yahoo!
	⇒	Intranet	Netscape, Microsoft (Windows NT)
	⇒	Wireless telephony	Ericsson, Motorola, Nokia
	⇒	Handheld devices	3Com (Palm Pilot), Psion
	⇒	Application service providers	Oracle, IBM
	⇒	Voice/data IP	Cisco, Lucent
	⇒	SMS	DoCoMo
	⇒	Wireless internet	Motorola, Vodaphone

the forgotten member of the triumvirate, brings interactivity into people's homes, enabling social and sociable access to the Net or more simply a return path to program, content, product and service providers to shop, order, bet, bank, book holidays or access video on demand, turning a passive viewing experience into a major commercial and communication tool.

No wonder that companies are agog at the opportunity but also struggling to make sense of it all. It's happened too fast and many are unclear about its value and potential, what it means for their companies and, most critically, how best to take advantage of it.

And in case we wonder whether the pioneers here are something special, some unique corporate environment which is not applicable to another company, a technology company like an Oracle or a Cisco and therefore not replicable by "mere mortals," let us read what *Fortune* business magazine is also saying about the size of the e-business/e-enabling/new technology opportunity.

In an article entitled "Will your e-business leave you quick or dead?", *Fortune* editor Geoffrey Colvin goes on to point out how a few winning companies like General Electric, Cisco and Southwest Airlines are using the Net to stave off earnings misses in these periods of economic uncertainty. For these and all other corporations, Colvin comments, *"the Internet now is a set of tools that are among the most powerful for building shareholder wealth that business has been given in a century."*

Business executives across the world are waking up to the recognition that 'e' is no longer about building fancy new web sites. It's not just about building new business models to drive out new sources of customer and revenue growth. That opportunity still exists, but more immediate and more tangible and more accessible are the means for improving productivity and for cutting costs, for *streamlining* the organisation.

There are many who will still try to dismiss 'e' completely. Their view is that 'e' has become just another tool in the employ of the IT department; no need for separate staff, separate teams, it's not anything unusual; it's just an alternative software solution, so hey ho it's back to "business as usual." But they miss the point completely! They underestimate the effect of this technology revolution. They need to visit companies like Oracle, Cisco and Dell and a growing list of others to appreciate just how different these companies really are. In those places 'e' is not just about new technology, it's also become a catalyst. It's become a reason for challenging "what we do and how we do it."

Figure 4.2 Key business drivers for adoption of e-business solutions

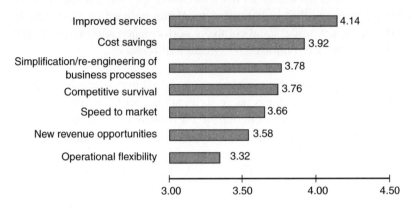

On a scale of 1–5 where 1 = 'not important' and 5 = 'very important'
Source: PMP Research

Just as Y2K became an excuse to replace systems that had for years been out of date and urgently needed to be updated and upgraded, so 'e' is the opportunity to reappraise how an organisation functions, to review the continuing viability of the existing web of different data-bases, different systems spread all across the organisation with all the consequent costs of complexity, maintenance, delays in information flows, insufficient knowledge management and inadequate decision making.

In today's highly competitive environment, an information and communication network that does work collaboratively and efficiently in real time will be a major contributor to a company's success. It can enable fast response to customer requests, it helps capture customer information, it enables marketing to that customer in a much more

Figure 4.3 'e-business' as catalyst

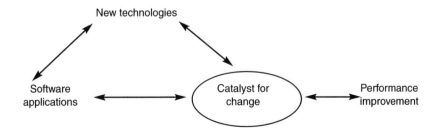

detailed one to one program. It can help manage complex supplier networks to ensure the company has a common approach, it captures the purchasing leverage that it is entitled to. It can help employees tune in to what's going on, understand company performance and their role in it better. It can empower employees to make a difference:

> "Today it's easy to believe e-business is not all that impactful. But the reality is that e-business is a tremendous tool for performance improvement and cost reduction. It's a tremendous tool to help you get closer to your customer. It's a tremendous tool for what used to be called "old economy" companies to apply to our current processes. The winners will be those that view the Internet as a complement to and not a cannibal of their traditional ways of competing."
>
> (Brian Kelley, VP e-business, Ford Motor Company)

Companies must appreciate that like any major technology change, internet development is going through cycles. Growth is through a series of 's' curves. Periods of fast growth will alternate with plateaus during which sales growth falters, confidence is shaken, doubts creep in about the full potential, and then the *next wave* kicks in, driven by innovations in software or hardware, or by breakthroughs in bandwidth, or by novel design for access devices, or competitively driven reductions in costs (we've had free PCs, so how long before free mobiles and free voice calls?).

Figure 4.4 Cycles of Internet development

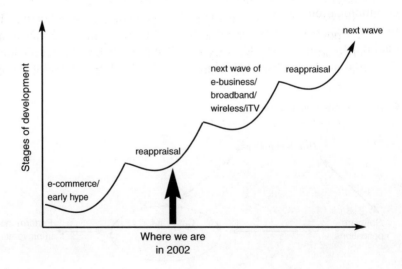

We need to remind ourselves that internet penetration is now up to 45% in households in UK and Germany, nearer 55% in the US, nearer 65% in Sweden and Singapore, with other nations still catching up as distribution, price competitiveness and deregulation develop. We also need to remind ourselves that there's a whole generation growing up totally "Net literate," for whom the Net is as comfortable and familiar a communication tool as the fixed line telephone has been for their parents. Indeed the Henley Research forecasting center in a survey of 16 to 24 year olds found 80%, yes 80%, expected to do all their shopping and banking over the Net in the future.

Many commentators in fact have drawn parallels with twentieth century history, showing how time after time major new technology innovations have been accompanied by tremendous hype but then by periods of consolidation as the technology and its potential get better appreciated.

Three brief case studies illustrate this hype, bust and renewal. Development in the auto industry in the early 1900s saw substantial investment in production and a surge in share prices. General Motors' share price, for example, increased 5,500 per cent from 1914 to 1920. But by the mid-1920s it was becoming clear that the short term potential had been exaggerated and no way were companies like GM going to meet the overblown profit expectations. Share prices plummeted, GM's own price lost two-thirds of its value. It took some time till the reappraisal of potential set in and a more realistic but still promising view took hold.

The next lesson from history comes with the development of radio. Early pioneers worked specifically on point-to-point communication. The idea of "point-to-many" took a long time to gain acceptance and prospective advertisers were wary of paying for airtime. When broadcast radio did develop it quickly mushroomed to nearly 50 different stations on the east coast and north west USA, but within five years half these stations were bankrupt. Share prices fluctuated wildly. RCA, one of the survivors, saw its price rise twenty-fold only to fall back during the 1930s, and it took till the 1950s till the price recovered its earliest highs.

So more recently PC usage went through initial rapid growth among early adopters, slowed in the late 1980s, then re-ignited in the early 1990s with the advent of computer networking and then the rise of the Web. Share prices of the early PC manufacturers like Digital, Amstrad, Acorn, Atari, Commodore and Sinclair all rose to great heights in the early period but had already crashed by 1985–6. At that point the Luddites of those days scoffed that the PC boom was over and we would all realise that individuals would have no use for "toy computers." Wasn't it Ken Olson, CEO of Digital (a one time $10bn computer powerhouse), who at one point said "there will be no market for PCs in the home"!

In these circumstances, it's often the pioneering companies who get caught in the loss of confidence following the early hype. Good businesses go bust because they can't deliver an often exaggerated business plan and so fail to meet investor expectations. But the underlying model is still sound and so a new wave springs up. Companies doing similar things but with more realistic outputs, who've learned from the pioneers, understood the mistakes that have been made and come back to take the more mature market. Stand up the PC successors: Dell, Apple, Compaq/Hewlett Packard and others.

What else does history teach us? Whether we look at the early Californian gold rush of the 1840s, the oil boom of the 1860s, the birth of the railroads in the 1920s, all these new breakthrough innovations and technologies were driven by early hype, initial disappointment, subsequent reappraisal and then more realistic business development.

What's more encouraging is that when the new industry sector comes back, it typically does so stronger than ever. So the 1890s slump in railroad development was followed by a resumption in expansion such that from 1900 to 1915 passenger traffic tripled and investment boomed correspondingly.

If we consider the whole "Infotech" surge during recent years and the consequent boost to productivity, it is hardly surprising that we needed a pause for breath – before the next wave. As Governor Lawrence H. Meyer has pointed out via a paper to the Federal Reserve Board: "productivity growth during 1889 to 1995 averaged 2%. In the slow growth years it fell to around 1% and in the higher growth times it has reached up to 3% each year. Each surge in growth has coincided

Figure 4.5 Stages in technology development

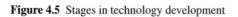
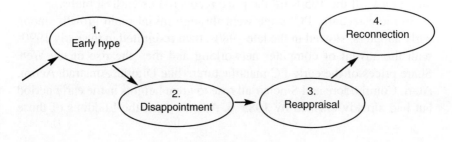

Figure 4.6 US productivity: IT investment

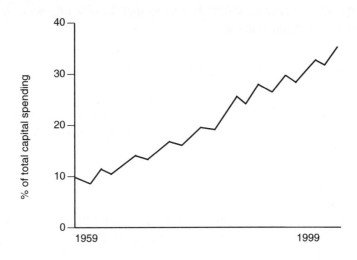

Source: US Federal Reserve

US productivity growth

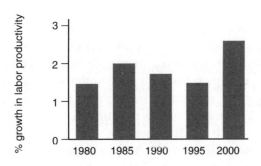

Source: US Federal Reserve

with periods of technology innovation and the trend is to look at waves of rapid development followed by periods of consolidation."

The current early decade plateau and consolidation in infotech investment should thus come as no surprise after the 1995–2000 productivity uplift. But already among e-business technologies we are beginning to see some signs of the "stage 3 reappraisal" of what can be achieved. In other

41

words, a recognition of what has taken place and a gradual reawakening to the next round of opportunity. In fact it's worth reappraising just what has been achieved in just the few short years that the new internet technologies have been commercialised.

Internet-based models are beginning to deliver profits

As a *Business Week* article has highlighted, many fund managers had gotten so stuck on falling internet stock values that they'd missed the more robust business models which *were* now starting to deliver and whose stock had gone up, not down. Examples include:

- Monstor.com: TMP Worldwide job hunting site, profitable from inception.
- Priceline: restructured business to focus only on selling plane tickets and "that is very profitable."
- Expedia: online travel site became profitable Q2 2001.
- Travelocity: rival to Expedia and also moved into profit Q2 2001.
- eBay: "continues to beat earnings estimates every quarter."
- 1-800 Flowers: "business is on a sound footing."
- NetBank: "an online Bank that pays its way."
- Lastminute.com: "on track to operating profit/growth continuing."

For the more savvy investor, identifying these more profitable ventures would for example have delivered a very satisfactory capital gain through the first half of 2001, before terrorist activity gave markets a further shock.

Other companies emerging from the pack in this way include Ameritrade on line brokerage, real estate listings site Homestore.com, and TicketMaster which does both online ticketing as well as city guides. Other smaller sites such as Register.com and Findwhat.com have muscled their way into profitability. Even more encouraging are sites that are breaking the "everything's for free" model of early Net plays to show it *is* possible to charge successfully for services. Companies like Goto.com, the pay for performance search engine; Alloy Online, the teen-oriented web site and Moviephone.com, the AOL/TimeWarner-backed operation have all moved their business models effectively from a free to a pay basis.

People are beginning to sit up and take notice that there's a quiet e-revolution taking place here. A number of companies are just getting on with it. Taking simple robust business models, applying sound common

Figure 4.7 Dot.coms digout: total operating income of the 35 companies in the Dow Jones Internet Index

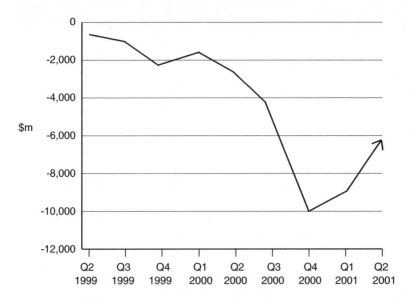

Source: Dow Jones

sense business principles to the operation, building slowly but efficiently and laying the foundation stones – as any would-be business leader would want to – for *future* success.

Indeed, it's not just the headline-grabbing quoted companies who are operating in this way. There's a host of small "mom and pop" online businesses being established, many doing c. $1 to $5m of turnover now but operating across a vast range of different industry sectors.

Small Business administration chief Robert E Beney and William Dunkelberg of the National Association of Independent Businesses point out that currently "small businesses produce more than 40% of US GDP." Beney forecasts that by 2005 there could be more than 2 million small businesses (up to 10 employees) online. "This could account for billions in online revenues and start making a significant contribution in the round to US growth."

Of course it's easy to dismiss these forecasts based on the disappointment around e-business during 2000/1 and subsequently, but we're talking sound businesses here, with sensible business plans that are profitable, that are simply providing their customers with a better proposition.

Infrastructure has been built

Look at the network-build chart from Britain's Thus plc, a "Tier 1 alt-net" or new telecomms carrier (Figure 4.8). In the past two years, Thus has built a powerful national network with global links to carry voice but also, more critically, internet data traffic. What they have achieved in an extraordinary short period of time has been mirrored in many other countries where local operators have completed networks to provide the information highways of the future.

Figure 4.8 Thus plc: telecomms infrastructure

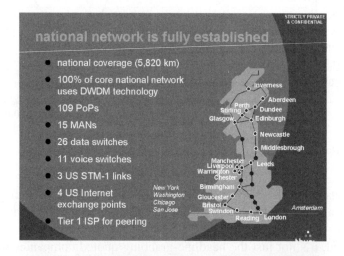

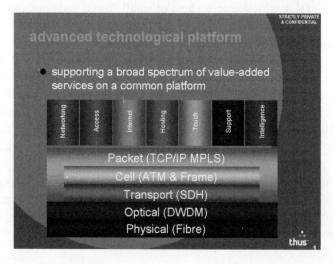

The capacity is in place and it's better than anything previous. At Thus, the 5820 km of fiber contain all the latest technology, using innovations like DWDM (dense wave division multiplexing) to more effectively compress data and speed up transmission. With growing demand from business for bandwidth-intensive applications, innovations like DWDM use optical networking technology that enable Telcos significantly to increase capacity over existing fiber. At the same time it reduces the cost of transmitting information through better fiber utilisation and so creates a truly enhanced service environment.

If Drucker's $1 trillion infrastructure investment estimate is right then there's no doubt that the e-economy is being enabled fast and getting better too. No one is claiming it's all perfect or that the end of the journey has already been reached. It's just that it is now possible to communicate and transfer voice and data cheaply, quickly, conveniently and efficiently all over the world, linking customers and employees in one network.

What's more, key infrastructure concerns like "security" are being constantly addressed, with organisations like Internet Security Systems (ISS) developing systems to protect companies from online break-ins, damaged systems and lost information. And, Verisign is not only the dominant "dot.com" domain register but provides leading edge software for verifying online identities and reducing fraud.

Equally, "greasing the wheels of the virtual world," companies like Actrade are now established as providers of online credit, payment and settlement systems for big ticket B2B transactions. And EMC data storage and others have built substantial capacity to store all the huge volume of electronic data being generated, from documents through to digital video movies.

Some sectors have already been changed forever by the Net

We could take many examples but let's consider one case study in the area of foreign exchange.

Historically, it's been the preserve of the investment banks' forex trading floors who've acted as middlemen to buy and sell foreign currencies on behalf of corporate clients. Daily trade amounts to a staggering $1.5 trillion. Corporate treasurers typically phone the bank dealers. The dealers themselves buy and sell electronically, taking an additional profit on the spread between the price communicated on the phone and the price actually booked electronically. It's easy business and it's nice business, with relatively decent margins and an estimated $10 billion annual profit for the banks. No wonder there's no impetus from them to change. In fact more than 25% of Deutsche Bank and Citigroup profits came from foreign exchange in 2000–1.

But all this is changing and changing fast. In 2001 only around 10% of foreign exchange trades were done direct online by companies themselves, cutting out their bank trader intermediary. But by 2003 a *Business Week* review expected that to go up to 75%. If that happens it will create far-reaching changes in the role of bank forex trading departments. Perhaps in future only the biggest trades, e.g. over $50m, or the more complex, will be placed via the banks for discretion or particular expertise.

Enabling corporates to act directly in this way has been driven by the development of a number of online currency exchanges or portals. The most established is FX Connect, started in 1996 by State Street. But others have set up, most notably Currenex, a venture backed by Royal/Dutch Shell, FXALL which is backed by Bank of America, UBS and 12 other banks, and also ATRIAX supported by Citibank, JP Morgan Chase, Deutsche Bank and Reuters.

Capterpillar Inc was an example of a corporation using traditional phone calls to bank trading desks to get forex quotes and place orders for billions of dollars worth of currencies each year. Often the phone call deal took several minutes before it was completed and in the fast changing FX market that was just too slow. The best price was gone by the time the trade went through. Now Caterpillar does these deals online using FXtrades, a unit of Currenex. Caterpillar can now compare prices online and when it places an order the trade is done right then – immediately.

Currenex has probably been the catalyst kick-starting this online revolution. This is partly driven by its impressive global spread of 40 Banking members including Barclays, ABN Amro and Hypo Vereinsbank. Besides speeding up transactions, it has streamlined the whole operation. It has reduced costs of a trade significantly, increased transparency within the corporation and cut out errors. More particularly Currenex has attracted top-name customers like Mastercard and Ericsson, showing just what can be accomplished.

Of course the banks are fighting back with their own rival online exchanges, but it's clear that the future for foreign exchange trading lies online and the days of the big bank forex trading desks are numbered. Internet and Treasury Director Ted Orban at Motorola sums up the situation, "I only need two or three currency portals at most and will probably settle eventually on one regular place to do business. The Internet is the best deal here."

Other sectors are also changing ... for ever

Two further examples: in the UK alone it's reckoned that 25% of all families or single households that booked holidays went online to do their research before booking. And of course a number went on to book directly. Indeed one UK airline, Easyjet, claim nearly 90% of all their tickets are sold online. Not surprising then that bricks 'n' mortar travel shops like the AA (the Automobile Association) have closed all 130 of their stores because in their research they found people preferred the Internet or telephone access.

In banking, most have internet banking facilities for clients and many with UK operations have taken advantage of the local infrastructure to also pioneer interactive banking via the TV. While it's early days, especially on the TV front, no one in research by Datamonitor doubted that internet banking is set to grow, increasingly undermining the economics of keeping open the physical branch network.

And consumer behavior is going through a sea-change

It's not just the Internet that's challenging the way commerce is done. With the mobile phone, many people believe mobile shopping will be the "next big thing." That's not so much accessing the Internet over the phone, but more likely and more immediately using the mobile to pay for goods or services.

For example Swisscom (the Swiss phone giant) has teamed up with Coca-Cola to produce a drinks vending machine that you dial into. The cost of the can is charged to the mobile phone bill. In Tokyo leading mobile operator DoCoMo has done a similar deal with Coke, and in Helsinki Coke have done another deal with local mobile shopping service Scan. In Stockholm you can pay for the parking meter via the mobile, and in Germany Paybox have a mobile payment system which has already signed up 5000 shops. Paybox lets you use your mobile as a debit card. Pay for taxis, CDs, movie tickets, restaurant meals or a pair of jeans, or simply transfer money by way of payment or a loan to a business or a friend. Simply call the Paybox number, enter the amount and the mobile number of the person getting the money and within seconds the transfer has taken place!

* * * * *

What's all this adding up to? At one level, as Professor Gary Hamel has pointed out, the Net has moved on from the "sandal-wearing, ponytailed Webheads fond of aphorisms like 'follow the free'." It's become more serious, it's become more business-oriented. It's about profits and it's about success. Business models and ventures abound and some, as has always been the case, are not well thought-through or have the wrong management team and will never work. But the well-built, sound businesses are emerging just as the more insightful users of the technology are developing.

It's in this latter area that the "bean counters" (as Hamel calls them) are getting excited. They can see the opportunity for increased efficiency, improvements in performance, productivity gains, automation of existing processes, more transparent data to streamline inventory and procurement, real time sharing of information to increase project collaboration and reduce time to market, improved information availability to aid decision making and speed up communication, virtual knowledge sharing for global teams to improve team working and morale ... and all this leading to lower costs across the board, in administration, in the supply chain, in delivery and in service.

While in the rest of this book we examine the case study evidence to show what can be achieved to please the bean counters! we will also continue to stretch the imagination. We want to understand how e-business can be the "mother of all efficiency programs" but also how it can be the catalyst for "amazing new services" that will excite and change the name of the game.

Enjoy the case studies and success stories in the next few chapters and it will become clear just what can be achieved, just what "quiet" revolutions can take place, and just how much the new technology is increasingly going to dominate business thinking and planning and execution over the rest of this first decade of the twenty-first century.

INTERNET "DID YOU KNOW's"

Do you have the answer to these "top ten" internet/new tech stats?

1. How much is Internet traffic growing each year?
2. How many SMS text messages are being sent around the globe each month?
3. How much quicker can you download a report using 3G wireless technology than with today's (2G) GSM?
4. How many people are online around the world?
5. Which country has the highest percentage of its population online and what is that percentage?
6. How many people have shopped at Amazon?
7. What level of sales is Dell doing over the Net?
8. What's the percentage of government services available online in UK and in Singapore?
9. How much revenue was generated in B2B and B2C through the Internet in 2001?
10. What's the forecast, assuming normal economic conditions, for 2004?

Answers

1. It's approximately doubling each year (source: AT+T).
2. 20bn (source: IDC).
3. 300 times quicker (source: Psion, Vodaphone).
4. 459 million in 2001 (source: Cyberatlas).
5. Sweden, with 65% of its population using the Net (source: Cyber-atlas).
6. 29 million (source: Amazon).
7. $18bn in 2001; that would rank the online business as no. 122 in the *Fortune* 500 list (source: Dell).
8. 42% UK and 55% Singapore (source: Office of the UK e-Envoy).
9. $400bn (sources: Gartner, PwC).
10. $3 trillion (sources: Gartner, PwC).

5   Getting started on *e·a·i*

Pioneers seem to have worked out how to establish an *enabling, automating, innovation* momentum. They've got project teams engaged and committed. They've got a series of initiatives in place. It's happening right across their company. And it's delivering results. They have become case studies in their own right about how to get 'e' and how to get streamlined. But just how did they get started? What triggered this new phase of company evolution? How did they get going?

From interview and discussion with people involved there appear to be three particular keys to unlocking this opportunity:

- pilot and test
- sort out the existing 'e' legacy
- find the hot spots in the value chain.

1. Pilot and test

Especially in these uncertain economic times no organisation is going to commit huge resource and funds to something if it's still unfamiliar, is untried and untested in the company itself and is therefore reckoned to be risky. Many organisations will have invested in 'e', urged on by the hype, but quickly become disenchanted. Investments have not yet delivered, targets have been missed and often there is still a degree of skepticism about anything to do with new technology and the Net. And even less reason to invest when there's no immediate and pressing need. After all, it *may* be a good idea but if it waits six months will that matter? Getting internet-enabled *may* drive cost and performance benefits, but unless there's a business case for a clear and early payback is it the sort of thing that could just be shelved for another discussion?

In this climate companies that do get going are often investing smaller amounts, typically in pilot or test mode, but with intent to generate a fast and clear ROI. The view from the champions pushing this forward is: let's start somewhere and provided we can show it

50

works, it gives us the ticket to the next stage. Here are examples of companies doing just that:

- Hill & Knowlton, the PR firm, invested $300k in a new knowledge management system. Within 12 months it had generated a return of $2m by helping execs get the right information together for new client prospects.
- GE invested only $15k to pilot its first e-procurement project. That paid back within weeks and gave the team permission to advance its much more ambitious business case.
- Fisher Scientific, the lab supplies distributor, invested $50k to pilot a new Web-invoicing system that promised to reduce payment processing costs by 80%. The initial test was positive and got support from suppliers, and costs started reducing within a few months. Payback is predicted within six months and the operations team, now converted and enthusiastic, is already looking for new opportunities to extend the web initiative.
- It's all relative, but for DuPont their bet of $5m a year for three years was seen as a measured investment to attack a $4bn annual purchasing spend. The plan is to move procurement onto the Web completely, but to do it step by step. Prove one bit works before embarking on the next. The payback promise – within one year – was seen as aggressive but the target's been met with an estimated first year saving of c. $200m! And that's expected to double in year 2.
- Herman Miller (of whom more later), the furniture maker, has continued its commitment to internet-enabling its business. Its most recent project has been a relatively modest $1m to link its 400 dealers and distributors to the Web to give them access to product info, order status and other customer details. "For us the $1m was an attractive project because it was affordable, could be finished quickly and makes a practical difference to our business today."
- Otis has been on a web journey for several years now. It's on a program of continuously testing and trialing new technology ideas with a view to learning what will work and what will payback when rolled out. For example Otis put web screens in some of its elevators with the idea of running ads to its "captive" audience and getting a new revenue stream from web advertisers. Maybe a good idea, but with the dot.com collapse revenue prospects dwindled and the scheme's been stopped. But the company continues to experiment. Its new initiative is a streamlining exercise to link suppliers and customers via the Web to ensure spare parts

reach customers as quickly as possible. It's also hoped to make ordering more accurate, i.e. the right part only gets ordered when it's going to be used and doesn't sit in inventory. Savings are expected in the inventory area especially and if this test works payback is quick and high.

2. Sort out the existing e-legacy

The key is putting the money in the right place. Research shows there's often a lot of e-activity already happening in organisations but progress is typically uncoordinated. It means there are often numerous "e-projects" (at companies such as BMW, Reuters, Siemens and CGNU the latest count exceeded 300 different e-initiatives), but there's often no alignment, no leverage, no real synergy capture, no sharing of know-how. It's haphazard and, not surprisingly, it's often failing to deliver anything like the potential benefits.

So Step 2, before attacking the "hot spots" and setting the ambitious vision and target, is to sort out these existing e-business related activities. "Get the value out" of existing investments. Restructure and refocus the portfolio so that people elsewhere in the company can begin to see just

Figure 5.1 e-business progress

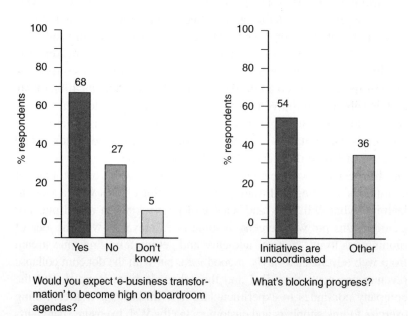

Would you expect 'e-business transformation' to become high on boardroom agendas?

What's blocking progress?

Source: PA Consulting Survey

52

Figure 5.2 Three steps to *e·a·i*

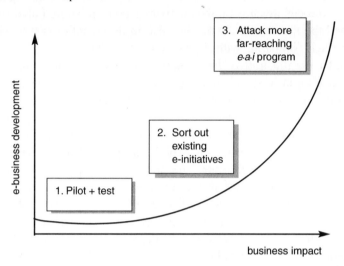

what can be delivered and achieved. Only by doing this is it possible to build a platform for change, a consensus around the opportunity and establish the position for moving forward and capturing the big prize.

With the greatest respect to Stern Stewart and their economic value added EVA program, it would seem that what the business world needs right now is an e-business VA instead. That's an e-business value audit. There needs to be a rigorous assessment of what's adding value and what's destroying value in this arena. There needs to be a program of accelerating some activities but stopping others. There also needs to be a resetting of targets and expectations. The following steps are being taken by pioneers and current champions.

e-VA review

- benchmark progress vs. best practices
- evaluate technology fit with "processes + people"
- restructure the portfolio of e-initiatives
- e-training.

Benchmark progress

Understanding how others have achieved certain targets and success ought to be a standard management discipline. It can only add insight to learn how rivals in the same industry or admired companies in other industries are doing things. But the data is not always easy to obtain and there is a natural tendency to focus inwards on the company's own situation, rather than be concerned too much with the outside. But in these still relatively early e-business days, comparing with "best practices" is vital.

Consider the illustrative "benchmarks" set out here and compare with your own e-initiatives. For example a key reason why Amazon.com is successful is its site user-friendliness. Search and navigation is straight-forward, there's a very attractive and simple "one click ordering" process, the pages are "personalised" and there's plenty of opportunity to interact, write reviews and comments, etc. The home page clearly organises and prioritises the product offerings. The product pages provide just enough information and the 5-star user rating provides a satisfying level of assurance. Checkout is secure and reliable, requiring only just enough information, and can be completed quickly. After-sales service is fast and responsive. It works and delivers excellent customer services. None of these better practices are hidden. So what stops other B2C propositions doing the same thing regularly, consistently, for all *their* customers?

Take a similar look at e-procurement. How come BP saved $100m in ten months, getting a many-fold return on their investment? What did they do that others can easily learn from? There's more on this in the e-procurement section later, but their key insight was to work with *existing* systems, product codes and procurement processes, rather than replace them. So existing legacy systems were left untouched but relevant databases

Table 5.1 The benchmarking challenge: examples

Potential areas	Targets (e.g.)	Processes (e.g.)
1. e-commerce revenues	• 78% of companies doing 5% in 2001 • 53% doing 10% in 2003 (CBI surveys)	• One view of customer • 1-click ordering • 'Interest *before* registration' • Personalisation • Affliate partnerships
2. e-procurement	• BP saves £100m in 10 months • Deutsche Telecom save 67% of budget cost	• Cross-organisation participation • 'Data visibility before systems'
3. Intranets	• Cisco claim 5% increase in target customer revenues through knowledge sharing • BP cut costs through employee portal	• *Unified* intranet • Personalised knowledge base • Automation to replace processes

were extracted, middleware was used to link individual desktop web browsers to the data, and existing codes were translated to a common standard that the disparate business units could easily accept. It meant changes for the user were kept to the minimum, the technology was all "hidden" behind the easy web browser, the buying process looked familiar even though it was now online and people could start using it fairly quickly and easily.

There's also insight to be had by learning lessons from successful Intranet development and knowledge sharing. It doesn't work in many companies and one reason is they have separate Intranets for each function and for each business unit. It's been developed in an uncoordinated way. But best practice shows that companies do need first to migrate to a single unified Intranet. Only in that environment does knowledge sharing seem to really start and only in that way can it be cost effective. (More on this also in the knowledge management section later.)

This is not trying to suggest that learn the best practices and the problem is solved. But there are keys to how to make further progress, and there are relevant case studies which show how that can be achieved.

Evaluate technology fit with processes + people

Along with the e-hype came the related software companies that sprang up claiming all we needed to do was buy their software solution and e-procurement savings, inventory reductions and customer service improvements would all come tumbling out of the system.

In fact there's nothing at all wrong with the software provided by the likes of Ariba, Commerce One, i2, Broadvision, Siebel and others. But capturing the benefits does of course require more than just sticking in a new software package. And given the price some of these companies were charging during the hype period, there were even greater expectations of quick returns and other big benefits.

As a result of a fairly blind-sided rush by many companies into buying and implementing the software too quickly, reports show that most such implementations have failed. In fact there's research around suggesting that two-thirds of all CRM implementations have failed. That's a tragedy! A huge waste of investment, a lot of time and effort for nothing. But more critically a big setback for further e-related investments. And so even more reason to sort out existing projects and get the value out of existing investments. Those basic steps have to be done before there's any chance of moving to the next stage. Confidence has to be rebuilt.

Digging into these early software investments and implementations, we find there was a key ingredient missing. Perhaps obvious in hindsight, but many did not look at matching up the technology to the underlying processes in the company, or training or educating the workforce on how to use that technology, or changing the structures and responsibilities to ensure there was accountability and ownership for the new ways of operating.

We'll return to this point as well in the later chapter "Making it happen," but nothing *will* happen unless this total view of the operation is taken. Many are the stories of technology being introduced but the people around it not being adequately trained. As a result, the old system that they do understand is still being used and the old processes (more costly, time-consuming, less effective) are still prevailing. This creates the double whammy where costs actually increase (two systems working side by side) and efficiency further decreases (half the work is in one system and half now in the other!).

There are cultural, attitudinal and educational aspects as well. One reason why many CRM solutions fail is because they require the sales force to adopt a PC-based system to record all customer contacts, orders, complaints and other relevant information. But many sales people are reluctant to use these new systems. It's a mix of technophobia, comfort with established paper-based systems and job protection – somehow if I put on

Figure 5.3 The technology fit

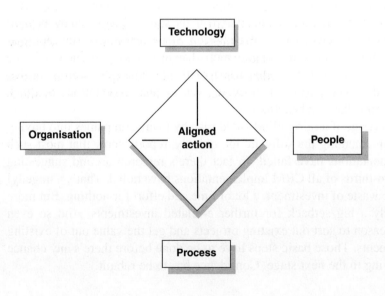

record everything I know about the customer then I've given up my specialist knowledge, am less valuable, could be made redundant. These fears, however ill-founded they may be, nevertheless are legitimate and need to be carefully and thoughtfully addressed. To do that requires a considered program introducing changes over a period of time, establishing each new procedure, "switching off" old systems and demonstrating how the new approaches will be win:wins for the individual, the company and the customer alike.

Like much of what we're talking about here, it ain't rocket science but straightforward implementation disciplines that have become familiar over the years. But the next time a colleague claims these new technologies won't work or won't deliver the benefits, an evaluation of just what's going on in the implementation program may well quickly reveal the lack of "TOPP" (Technology, Organisation, People and Process) alignment.

Portfolio management

Benchmark and TOPP reviews will demonstrate which e-projects have potential. Equally they will show which have no real potential at all. For example the "lessons learned" from others may quickly highlight those initiatives with a high likelihood of failure, and the TOPP review may demonstrate that everything that could be done to ensure an effective implementation has been done; it's the very idea that was misguided in the first place.

The whole range of e-initiatives needs to be proactively managed in this way (see Figure 5.4). Some things may just need to be stopped! Doing that gives clear messages to the rest of the company that "the champions" are getting to grips with the existing e-program, they are controlling investment and they have thought through what will work and what will not. In

Figure 5.4 e-projects portfolio management

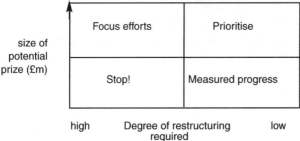

57

the same context, the projects that are to continue may need to be restructured and the targets reset. There may be a sound underlying business model behind some activities but the return may be in three/four years rather than six months, and the ambition may be better localised rather than some global "let's change the world overnight."

In this way others in the company start getting messages of reassurance. e-projects *are* going to be controlled, in the same way all other spend and investment is already subjected to scrutiny and demanding rates of return. Moreover they also start getting the idea that not all 'e' is a waste of time, that some stuff is worthwhile and that there are profit returns that are satisfactory and will add to shareholder, and employee, worth over time.

Training

At this point it's worth referring in a little more detail to training and education around new technologies and things 'e'-related. If the e-VA process can help an organisation collectively get over its cynicism and skepticism and is starting to look forward, then training may be the next step. It can facilitate and enable individuals to latch onto new sets of ideas and opportunities.

This training will likely need to be quite basic in its early stages. How many really understand the difference between the open, universal standard system of the Internet and historical proprietary systems that constitute most companies' legacy networks? The implications are very substantial but it's only when this basic point is fully understood that people's minds can turn to its exploitation. As another example, there are many developments taking place in wireless from GSM to GPRS to UMTS/3G where bandwidth and transmission times will leap and new access devices will establish a much better environment for communication. Is this technology evolution understood, have individuals seen prototypes and demonstrations of what will be achievable? And all these acronyms from ADSL to XML can be confusing and incomprehensible. Which are important, what do they mean and why do I need to know or bother with them?

e-training can be put on line. It can be established in a series of courses and programs. These can be "self-help," do them when you can, and they can increase in sophistication and complexity. In some companies these courses are purely voluntary. In a few companies they are mandatory. Employees are required to get the "self-accreditation" and certification, and are given time-frames within which to pass the tests. There may be additional off-line workshops and tutorials. But the view emerging where these

Figure 5.5 Understanding the new e-business tools

- Speed up time for response and communication, e.g. real time
- Lower costs, e.g. automated contacts, 'zero touch'
- New forms of convenience for customers
- More information/more insight, e.g. 1 on 1 marketing
- New routes to market/new sources of growth
- New ways to communicate, e.g. mobile, virtual learning
- New software tools, e.g. Xml, middleware
- New software applications, e.g. Broadvision, Commerce One
- Competition, e.g. boundaries blur, alliances
- New forms of outsourcing, e.g. ASPs

- Profit growth
- Performance improvement

training courses are "required" is that employees need to know this stuff. They need to get qualified because only if they are can they hope to add value to the future Internet-enabling of their organisation.

3. Find the *e·a·i* hot spots

With a better platform in place, the organisation is now ready to move on. Now is the opportunity to understand just what streamlining can mean for the company, where it can make a difference, what impact it can truly have on the bottom line if we get it right.

In the context of how best to get started, there are four key steps to take. The overall approach is detailed in Figure 5.6 but the specifics are set out below:

- map out the company value chain
- determine the priorities
- challenge + innovate
- establish a disciplined program.

Map out the value chain

Rather than plunge in and pick an area for internet-enabling and automating, the much preferred route is to stand back and appraise the opportunities. If we look at companies like Progressive Insurance, Oracle,

Figure 5.6 Looking for *e·a·i* priorities across the value chain

Basic business processes:

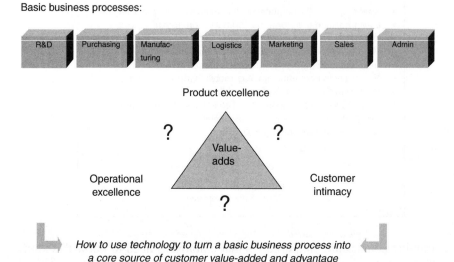

How to use technology to turn a basic business process into
a core source of customer value-added and advantage

Nestlé and others, each embarked on an initial review of the business. They mapped out their value chain. They considered which areas were performing poorly, e.g. were high cost, providing poor service or were weak versus competition, and which areas would have the most leverage in terms of payback, "size of prize" and how quickly the win could be achieved.

This value chain approach forces people to think about the under-lying value-added and define more clearly what are the key levers in the business. It also means that instead of defining a project prosaically as "e-procurement" involving the purchasing function, it could be viewed more broadly as part of a total supply chain project. It could encompass not just cost of goods but how suppliers generally could be linked into the rest of the company's business system and how they could contribute to its further efficiency and responsiveness to customers.

Defining the opportunity most appropriately can be an important step in ensuring the success of the project. Involving key stakeholders across the organisation means that all the players who would be impacted will get involved from the start, and the more collective/coordinated approach provides greater ownership and commitment. That provides a better framework for challenging what goes on today and how the new technology tools could improve things.

Figure 5.7 Fixing on the priorities

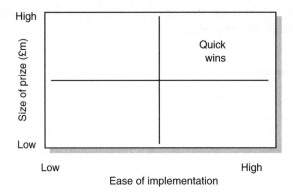

Determining the priorities

Value chain mapping will set the context for deciding which projects to kick off. An additional tool for determining the priorities is to plot the various opportunities on the grid shown in Figure 5.7.

Where to start will in part be driven by where the organisation is coming from. If there's an urgent need for some quick wins to build confidence and get some momentum going, then "ease of implementation" will be the most crucial driver of decision making. If on the other hand the company has already been through an e-VA type process, then it will be better prepared to pick on areas of highest return to some extent regardless of the implementation challenge. Once people have got the

Figure 5.8 New technology tools/approaches across the value chain

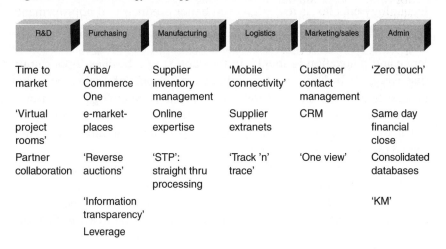

R&D	Purchasing	Manufacturing	Logistics	Marketing/sales	Admin
Time to market	Ariba/ Commerce One	Supplier inventory management	'Mobile connectivity'	Customer contact management	'Zero touch'
'Virtual project rooms'	e-market-places	Online expertise	Supplier extranets	CRM	Same day financial close
Partner collaboration	'Reverse auctions'	'STP': straight thru processing	'Track 'n' trace'	'One view'	Consolidated databases
	'Information transparency'				'KM'
	Leverage				

61

message about what they can actually achieve by streamlining using the new tools, then it is possible that enthusiasm will know no bounds! (We can but hope!) While it's not a complete list, Figure 5.8 sets out a more complete range of the possible opportunities.

Challenge + innovate

"Our performance is the result of constant change, constant forward progress in translating innovations into results. For example, we're unveiling today our "e-efficiency" venture. This is a proven Internet-based service that delivers information about performance of process plant equipment directly to a web browser for easy and secure access by our process manufacturing customers. This innovation makes Emerson the first company to apply the latest Internet technologies to equipment performance monitoring in the process industries."

(Emerson inc press release)

Emerson is a Fortune 500 corporation that is emerging as a leader in surveys identifying the "fast-tracking e-business innovators," outranking even such progressive companies as GE and IBM. As a c. $15bn turnover global manufacturing company, Emerson has enjoyed an unrivalled 43-year earnings growth record (though the 2001/2 downturn ended that winning streak). The corporation has achieved that success on the back of a strategy of "continuous challenge and innovation." "Our strength lies in our commitment to top quality products that meet and exceed our customer expectations. Leadership in innovation in technology enables us to design even better products and improvements in our manufacturing processes."

Here is a company that would claim to truly understand what "challenge and innovation is about." In the context of e-business opportunity discovery, their key was to challenge each one of the value chain processes and ask the question: how can new technology tools transform what we do? There's always the path of incremental improvement, but is there another way which enables us to leap forward and change the whole cost–value equation?

Zara, the Spanish-headquartered women's clothing retailer, is another good example of process challenge and innovation. This company has expanded across Europe and has captured a niche with its smart value clothing, which appears to be always the latest in fashionability. Zara opened its first store in 1975 and has since expanded to more than 400 stores in 25 countries. Sales in 2001/2 run at c. $2bn and that's a 26% increase on the previous year, while profits at c. $150m are up 34%.

How are they achieving that? As they developed they realised that the teams in head office were becoming increasingly remote from the stores and from customers. Standard customer research programs were put in place, but it was felt these were insufficient to really capture and exploit in rapid time that local market knowledge. As the Zara management team looked across its value chain, they realised it was very fragmented. It was functionally based and there was no sense of the underlying processes or their importance. They began to realise that for their business a core process was "new products to market" and, crucially, the time to get them there. But this involved more than just the transportation and marketing departments. It necessarily involved other key groups and especially the stores, who had to feature the new product lines and work closely with the design and manufacturing team to ensure new merchandise ideas got developed quickly.

So important did they decide this value process was for them that they decided to put together an integrated approach and to use the Net. Their aim was to establish a real time 24/7 network that linked what was selling in stores back to design and manufacturing. So committed were they to achieving this that they made the difficult decision of ending their manufacturing outsourcing contracts and bringing it back in-house. The "glue" to hold all this together would be a knowledge-based Intranet. Store managers would signal what was selling in the stores and add their own new ideas. Design, buying and manufacturing would now respond daily to this data, changing manufacturing volumes, managing inventory and, more critically, changing what was being designed and bought. Now stores, merchandising and manufacturing teams are electronically networked and emphasis is placed especially on the role of the store to "trend spot, capture and transmit ideas to other departments at any time on price, color, style and size."

To give the whole initiative a target the team decided upon "two-week product turnaround": from store manager idea to new product back into the store, the company would aim to complete that process within just two working weeks.

The bottom line is that Zara remains highly fashion conscious and responsive to its market place and turnover has continued to increase, both like-for-like in store and through new store openings.

Figure 5.9 Innovation and immersion

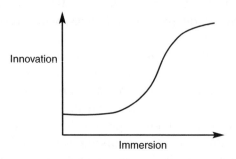

Innovation does not come easily. It's not possible just to "organise workshops" and expect a stream of innovative ideas and challenges to emerge. It comes about by harnessing and exploiting a deep-rooted understanding of the business and its customers, what works and what doesn't and why, what are the key levers, what's already been tried and failed – and why – and what's been a success. There's in fact an observed correlation between the amount an individual, a team, a work-force are immersed in their business and its markets and the amount of effective innovation that comes through.

Companies like Emerson, Sony and Yamaha, who all have an enviable track record of innovation, demonstrate the time and commitment required to get to that point where there is a regular stream of effective new initiatives. Indeed an FT survey of successful entrepreneurs highlighted one of the key factors behind their success: "a thorough knowledge and appreciation of their business and the markets they operated in, often involving a life-time's commitment."

There's further evidence for the value of innovation from the UK Government's annual R&D scoreboard. Their conclusion after evaluating over 1000 companies across the world is that "innovation *does* lead to better company performance." For example, they found the market cap of "innovation intensive" companies had risen by more than twice that of their rivals over the previous four years.

> "Businesses that live innovation have developed a repertoire of attitudes, skills and techniques that enable them to challenge change and be more responsive and they are able to do this in a corporate environment that is distinct and supportive. These companies inspire their people to pursue innovation with a real passion."

Internet innovation is being seen from more and more organisations as each comes to terms with life after the dot.coms. What those who are successful are exhibiting is an increasing readiness to challenge the status quo and explore how new technologies can help them build the next operating platform for their business at new levels of cost and effectiveness.

Establish a disciplined program

None of this will get done unless it's brought together into a disciplined change program. There's more on this in the later chapters but this point is fundamental. We can talk all we want to about new ideas, new technologies, new tools and new profit opportunities but there has to be "effective project management." Without that the entire set of initiatives will result in nothing. At one level project management is a straightforward skill-set, yet many company 'e' and other initiatives will fail because they lack some key ingredients: dedicated resources, change experts and project management disciplines.

- **"Dedicated resources"** means people whose sole task is this particular job. It is *not* an add-on to an already busy, full time, day job.
- **"Change experts"** means people who have a facility for brokering consensus across different teams of people in the company. This will likely involve key individuals within the organisation who have the experience and respect of others, who know their way round and know how to get things done inside the company. Such individuals can be usefully complemented by an external team of consultants who, new to the company, can take a fresh perspective, bring in lessons from other companies and act as an additional catalyst.
- **"Project management disciplines."** It's simple. Some people are incredibly well organised, go through tasks rigorously, complete things on time, keep everyone informed of progress and generally deliver in full. Others contribute in different ways. In some organisations "project management skills" are recognised as a distinct discipline. Such skills are nurtured and every project will be given an experienced project manager whose job is to "deliver the project in the agreed timetable." This sort of input is vital to the team.

These are basic disciplines that we are all tutored on from our earliest management jobs, but somehow in the rush of projects, meetings, committees, tasks, politics and people management things get delayed, deadlines get missed, investment funds – perhaps already committed – get withdrawn, resources get redeployed and project delivery gets put under pressure. What we learn from the e-pioneers is that once these projects get significant in scope and scale then the senior team really gets behind it, makes commitment and delivery public and pushes the whole emphasis right up there as a priority on the agenda.

In every case study success we've described here, these characteristics are common and pervasive. So it's perhaps less surprising that with that degree of conviction paybacks do materialise and so momentum does build for the future. There's so much opportunity across the board that the next few chapters look at each major part of the value chain in turn and look into the detail of how to get started *and how to succeed* in all the key parts of the business.

6 Streamlining in procurement

In a recent National Association of Purchasing Managers survey nearly eight out of ten purchasing professionals expected the Internet to become the primary means of dealing with suppliers. They expected this development especially in areas like shipment tracking, requests for quotes, requests for information and ordering. They acknowledged however that today they are still some way off a streamlined environment. They continue to use mostly phone, fax, and mail for orders under $5000. In addition EDI (electronic data interchange) was typically used in only a few applications in areas of automated billing and payment.

Here's how one purchasing manager of a Fortune 500 company described her operation.

> "Unfortunately there's still a lot of paperwork, checks go astray, purchase orders get lost between incompatible computer systems, procurement officers "guess" how much material to order, information often is inaccurate. As a result there's too much inventory and then we don't have the spare parts we really need!"

In a survey conducted by the Aberdeen Group, they looked at how an automated procurement function that used the Net consistently to link suppliers to their ordering process could save costs in a company. They came up with the figures shown in Table 6.1, after polling some 100 organisations.

Bristol-Myers Squibb reports over $100m saved from initiating its e-

Table 6.1 e-procurement cost savings opportunities

• Print media	8–10%	
• Travel	7–10%	
• Workforce	13–16%	11–15% total
• Facilities	10–18%	savings off cost base
• Direct inputs	13–15%	
• MRO inputs	13–15%	

procurement program with an ROI over 50%. Motorola claims to have saved $54m in the first 18 months of their program. Hewlett Packard claims $70m of savings in the first six months. JD Edwards reckon to have reduced costs of operational goods and services by 11% and to have reached their own ROI hurdle in five months. Fedex saved $12m in just three months and met their three-year ROI target in less than a year.

There are some extraordinary things going on in this e-procurement space. Apparently large and sophisticated organisations with experienced purchasing managers are now discussing new ways to cut costs, streamline their processes and deliver substantial further benefits to their companies. It seems that not only are they buying more cost effectively, but the whole purchasing process is being speeded up, errors reduced and a much slicker operation is being established.

Let's look at a couple of case studies in more detail and examine how for example Eastman Chemical and Owens Corning do it.

Eastman Chemical

Eastman employs around 15,000 employees in over 30 countries. It produces more than 400 types of chemicals, plastics and fibers ranging from animal feed to X-ray film. Whether buying paper clips and white board pens, special lab gloves or raw materials, Eastman has historically struggled to leverage its large company procurement potential. Each plant for example would typically be ordering the same thing from the same supplier but doing it independently and paying different prices. Bringing together the information from the different systems had proved an unending and unhappy challenge.

When the Eastman initiative began, the first step was to get data visibility. What was being bought, from whom and at what price? The initial focus was on MRO. These are the indirect inputs – "maintenance, repair and operational" items – as distinct from raw materials and parts for the core manufacturing processes. Eastman found that with these product categories alone (typically 30% of a company's total cost of goods bill) they were doing c. 30,000 transactions a year at an average value of $45 each. On calculating the cost of processing each transaction, they worked out the average was $115 and was taking 19 person days to fulfil!

Further investigation showed this was just the tip of the iceberg. Including lab supplies, the total "MRO" bill was over $900m in the year. It was spread across 15 facilities around the world and involved 6500 suppliers! Within that, purchases of $1000 or less represented 85% of transactions – but only 3% of total spend. In other words most of the effort was being put against the most commodity-like items, often adding the least value. To cap it all, when Eastman then added in its direct raw material purchasing it discovered total costs reached nearly $3bn and that made it the 128th largest spender on purchased items in the world!

Yet it wasn't as though there were no systems already in place. For example there was an automated system for sending orders through to suppliers. The trouble was it wasn't being used consistently and so the old manual ordering processes still persisted alongside it.

Changing all this was never going to prove an easy task. But once the facts had been made visible and shared with colleagues across the whole company, there was a decision that the area had to be tackled. There was added urgency as margins were eroding generally across the chemicals industry and cost cutting was emerging as top of the agenda.

The first thing Eastman decided to deal with was "front line employee orders of $2000 or less." Employees were buying their own travel and stationery, and using local suppliers as they wanted. Eastman established a Buysite. It was accessible from each person's desktop via their web browser. The Buysite was built by Commerce One, one of the leading software suppliers in this area. Commerce One has established an MRO catalog for office suppliers. In the Buysite there are automatic constraints which can be established for spending levels, which suppliers can be used, and who can buy.

Buysite was first trialled with 50 employees and then expanded to include four of Eastman's US facilities. Investment costs were kept low – Commerce One already had the basic Buysite established for other corporations. The main challenge was getting people to change their buying practices and behavior. That was helped by the ease of use of Buysite but also the quick return. Within months Eastman was getting payback. With all expenditure channeled via one site and an approved (and reduced) number of suppliers, item costs were coming down and requisition processing time was reducing rapidly as this procurement was truly automated.

By the end of the first year of activity, Eastman reckoned it had routed 15% of total expenditures in this way. The total amount being paid to office supplies had reduced by 5% and there were additional savings in inventory and payroll.

While continuing to take things step by step, the roll out across the remaining facilities is now being speeded up, the use of auctions is being planned and there's a section now on the company's intranet highlighting the initiative, the value it's bringing and encouraging people to look out for further opportunities.

"For an old-world company we've moved quickly. We're committed now to adopting Net technologies in procurement. We've started with the unsexy stuff and we're getting more effective in how we roll this out with our suppliers. We expect to handle well over 50% of transactions via the web by the end of 2002."

Owens Corning

Owens Corning is now the world's biggest maker of fiberglass insulation and structural materials. Like Eastman it's a global company, employing 20,000 people around the world with facilities in a number of countries. Again like Eastman, procurement used to be heavily decentralised with consequent inefficiencies, lack of leverage and a large overlapping supplier base.

Owens first came at the e-procurement challenge by looking at how it could use its existing ERP (Enterprise Resource Planning) systems to improve its procurement processes. It was a user of SAP and had wanted to use that software to automate replenishment of supplies through the existing EDI networks.

But SAP at that time was proving difficult to adapt to Owens' needs in this area and also was turning out to be a high cost solution. Owens wanted a purchasing system that was quick and easy to install across all its facilities and also cost effective for the small spot MRO purchases.

So Owens its their own "e-mall." It listed approved vendors by product category and where possible it provided links through to vendor web sites. While relatively unsophisticated in its early days, it helped focus attention on the costs of purchasing and the lack of consistency in choice or use of suppliers. As it dealt with "non controversial" MRO items, it was easier for the different sites to accept and support. Because the cost savings were relatively easy to obtain by combining purchasing through a smaller group of suppliers, the process was quick to build momentum. "We estimate this first step saved the company 10% on the price of goods as well as another 10% due to productivity gains – and it hardly cost us a dime to build!"

The success of the e-mall and SAP's own continued development of its e-purchasing module led to Owens eventually signing up with SAP to establish a single unified catalog dealing with all supplies and services across the company. For Owens the advantage here was clear: "we've replaced the human interface with system knowledge so now it takes one person to do what it used to take three."

Owens has also got involved in auctions. Using software from Freemarkets, Owens now regularly places contracts out for auction, ranging from construction site services through to freight transportation. To make it work best Owens has learnt that a lot of work needs to go into the RFQ (the request for a quote) to specify precisely what will be required. In that way the auction process works better because it simply focusses on price; "market efficiencies take care of the rest." Some $400m worth of contracts were put through the auction process in the first year and that's expected to grow.

> "Our target now is to route 75% of MRO expenditures through our SAP B2B marketplace. We're going to be doing $1.5bn of our $3.7bn total procurement through the Net by end 2001 and we don't see why eventually all our spend won't be done that way."

More generally and across other organisations MRO is getting especial attention for a number of reasons.

- It's seen as being part of overhead, and "overhead" of course is "not a good thing."
- It largely consists of low value items, everything from light bulbs to ladders.
- It's distinct from direct raw material costs, which are the higher value-added items where supplier relationships are more important and the purchasing process is less easily commoditised and automated.
- It's typically fragmented and uncontrolled spending.
- When it's all added up it comes to a large sum of money offering the potential for some "easy wins."

Internet marketplaces, like the Commerce One Buysite, are one straightforward way to start getting costs down in this area. Although the different purchasing items are bought by different people on different sites with different processes, they can all be introduced to a common set of buying rules. The aim is to identify which individuals can buy which products and define their price limits.

It's also easy to get started. At low cost (GE set up their first pilot for $15,000), e-procurement can be trialled say with just one supplier to begin with. All authorised employees can be asked to make purchases only at a specific supply web site and given password access from their own desktop. This can help give a feel for costs and what would need to change to expand the system.

Experience is showing that most employees actually enjoy using the Net to buy! Apart from anything else they find they get so much more

71

useful information. At www.Grainger.com – a company with a catalog of c. 250,000 parts and components for manufacturing businesses – purchasers can get real time order status, total company spend, details of shipments, one consolidated bill, account analysis, details of "top ten items being bought" and so on. The challenge, and we'll come back to it, is getting employees trained and used to using these new tools.

Evaluating how best to start is always going to be an important consideration in getting an e-procurement initiative to succeed. There are in fact a number of options that need to be considered.

1. **Online Marketplaces** – we've already referred to SAP and Commerce One's marketplace sites. Companies like Ariba and Oracle have also established similar web-hosted environments. They are basically catalogs online which introduce purchasers to a potentially vast new range of suppliers from all over the world (Table 6.2). Their functionality has increased over time so that they can facilitate the transaction, protect identities, put payments in escrow till the products have been satisfactorily delivered – some have even offered quality guarantees! They also enable automatic transfer of documentation and can set up invoicing, factoring and insurance services.

Table 6.2 Example of Commerce One marketplace, suppliers included

- Office Depot for office equipment
- Grainger and Graybar for lighting/electrical supplies
- PageNet/Arch Wireless for telecomm services
- Nokia for telecomm equipment
- Wareforce and Converge for computers
- Unisource for cleaning equipment and supplies
- RoweCom for publication
- Standard Register for printing/AV equipment
- Air Products and BOC for industrial chemicals
- Fisher Scientific for lab testing equipment

2. **Trading communities/exchanges** – in most industry sectors now there are groupings of buyers and sellers who have set up web-based marketplaces. Chemdex.com (now hosted by Ventro) is one such example. Here buyers and sellers in the chemicals industry can come together. There is some common information sharing but it's largely intended to enable purchasers to put out RFQs to as wide a range of suppliers as possible.

These trading communities have proved somewhat controversial in some cases. Covisint for example joins Ford and GM in a buying exchange. Is this anti-trust? Does bringing together the two largest automakers in the world put unfair and unreasonable pressure on suppliers? If a supplier is not "allowed" into the exchange, is that excluding that company from reasonable trade and access? So far of course Ford and GM have played down these issues but as the percentage of trade through Covisint increases there's bound to be some "restructuring" required to address these particular concerns.

In response to these sorts of challenges, recent innovation has seen development of **private trading exchanges (PTX)** as an alternative. These are private B2B commerce platforms built and run by individual companies (rather than groups in an industry). The aim is to establish one central platform to unify internal procurement processes and network with key trading partners.

3. **Auctions for SMEs** – auctions are proving especially popular for small businesses. Organisations like Ubid.com provide exciting price-based formats with either no reserve price at all or a notional price of $9. All kinds of office equipment are available and computers and computer peripherals especially can be purchased in job lots at low prices. Bids can be tracked to a predetermined closing time for each auction lot and there's no doubt such format purchasing will grow in popularity. (Ubid.com expect 2002 revenues to hit $1bn.)

4. **Reverse auctions** – here would-be buyers auction their requirements by posting either on their web site or through a marketplace their particular product needs. For example UK retail giant Sainsbury recently experimented with an order for new desktop PCs. The budget for this order had been c. $750k but the company was keen to see what it could save on what it regarded as a commodity item. In the end Compaq bid for and won the contract, but the price paid was c. 55% of the original budget! 50% savings will not be routine but simple examples like this do immediately reveal the power of the auction format over the Net.

5. **ASPs** – application service providers enable companies to rent rather than buy the software, and usually provide hosting and security on their own web servers. They often take on the cost and responsibility of software upgrades as they become available, as well as providing more server capacity if required. So potentially this is a very attractive way for an organisation to minimise investment and risk in the early days of its e-procurement initiative.

Elcom.com is one example of a company providing remotely hosted Internet-based e-procurement solutions for businesses. It will create the e-marketplace or shopping mall, manage the system, load it with appropriate catalogs and help to develop specific rules for purchasing and approvals. It can be integrated into the company's legacy systems or hosted simply on the Net.

What's being described here is an outstanding opportunity to cut into a large chunk of a company's cost base. Purchasing costs in total can be more than 50% of a manufacturing company's revenues. For a service business such as an insurance company they still can run at 10% plus if expenses, IT and facility services are included. Just a 1% change here is a relatively big number and part of the benefit can be captured within days when the next supplier invoice appears.

The benefits range from hard cost savings through to a wider range of process and other improvements:

- improved sourcing by discovering new suppliers
- reduction in cost of goods through more competitive tendering
- more efficient supplier relations by linking, even integrating systems and establishing for example 24/7 real time information updates
- reduction in inventory levels through better monitoring and aggregation of total orders
- reduction in own processing costs
- regulation of buying behavior preventing "maverick buying"
- tracking delivery schedules to match production needs
- freeing up skilled employees as time-consuming procurement tasks get automated
- improving buyer "know-how" as they become more sophisticated in coordinating global supply
- enabling flexible any time/anywhere access
- providing easy access thanks to web-browser technology
- greater security taking advantage of ever developing Net protection systems with firewalls, encryptions and authentication.

While the opportunity here is substantial, there are clearly challenges in fully realising the benefits of e-procurement. Like any Net-enabled change once fully implemented *and* embraced by the employees concerned it can deliver a big prize but there are hurdles:

- understanding the full scope of the opportunity
- getting transparency of data
- getting suppliers onto the system
- migrating from EDI
- authentication
- retaining supplier trust
- training.

Understanding the full scope

It's worth emphasising that e-procurement is *not* just another excuse to beat up on suppliers for lower costs (if it is treated that way then short term possible gains will rarely deliver any lasting benefits). Procurement itself is an extended function which involves a number of different skills and processes spanning analysis through to payment and requiring a tight interface with logistics, production scheduling and sales.

Figure 6.1 Procurement chain

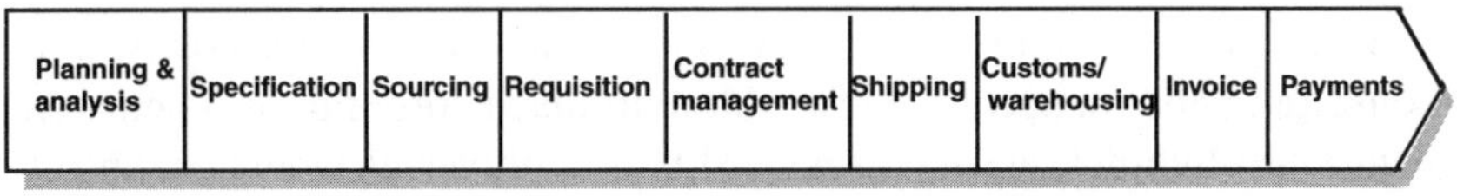

Planning & analysis	Specification	Sourcing	Requisition	Contract management	Shipping	Customs/ warehousing	Invoice	Payments

Experience is showing that it is areas such as transmitting specs, sourcing through global marketplaces, requisition approvals and invoicing that more easily lend themselves to Net-enabled automation routines. But because the range of opportunities can be immense, any move to e-procurement needs to be accompanied by some careful analysis as to which areas to focus on. This is especially true in the early days when the whole organisation is learning about how to take advantage of these new approaches and initial wins are important. This also applies to deciding which product categories to e-procure and it's likely a plan is required to phase in one category after another rather than plan to do all at once.

The message here is that the Net can transform efficiency and effectiveness in this functional area but it should not replace or make redundant the broader function tasks of intelligence gathering about market developments and new products, comparing price of supply with reliability of supply and working with other departments in the company to understand their needs.

Figure 6.2 e-procurement product selection

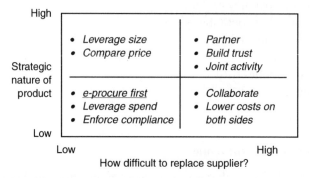

Source: CAPS, Ariba

Getting transparency of data

BP has been developing and improving its systems for worldwide procurement for many years. Yet it still initially struggled to get the leverage it aspired to. This was mostly because so much of the relevant supplier, purchasing and cost data lay in proprietary and different systems in each of the different business units scattered all over the world. Changing to a common proprietary system was seen as most costly, time-consuming and inappropriate for a decentralised corporation. Then along comes the Internet, an open standard with a universal language, and BP started to ask the obvious questions: can we take advantage of the Net to bring together this fragmented purchasing data so we can start getting the leverage that a global company of this size ought to be getting?

BP worked with PA to build a web-based solution. The goal was not to replace the existing systems, nor interfere with them, but to work "alongside them." BP's annual spend was some $15bn and its initial target was to save $100m – a large amount but less than 1% of the total. When the project was initiated BP recognised it was in "pioneering mode" in terms of changing behaviors so it wanted a step-by-step approach. Using the Net meant the software could sit on the Oracle web server and the necessary functionality could be distributed over the Intranet. No need to install any software on the desktop; new users just need to register and away they go.

The key, though, was getting transparency of data. At the start of the project each BP unit used its own distinct product coding, so simply extracting information from the different databases was not going to be enough. Initially there was discussion about changing all the product codes to a standard code (the UN/SPSC supplier standards has some suggested guidelines) but there was inevitable resistance, complaints that it would take months to do that in each business, that there was no resource to do it, that there were other priorities etc.

So PA created a standard commodity/product hierarchy that could link all the code variations together. The software they created was called Oyster and, working with the various parts of the business, they mapped the unit-specific product and supplier codes into the common hierarchy. Once that exercise was completed (and it took weeks, rather than many months), users of the system had the choice of whether to view product/supplier expenditure in terms of their own local codes, or the common code structure.

With this in place, BP purchasing execs were suddenly able to take a global view of their spend. They could see total spend by supplier, identify different prices ("we were buying everything separately, from hard hats to drill bits"), examine the number of different suppliers, average purchase size and quantity and so on. All because they could now aggregate the data previously buried in different systems (Figure 6.3 summarises this diagrammatically).

So successful has this "Oyster" program been that from an initial ten country roll-out it's now global with all the registered users served through a web server, search facilities have been added and it's trans-formed purchasing effectiveness. Savings have grown dramatically. The $100m was achieved within 12 months and the company is now well on target for a 10% plus reduction in total purchasing costs.

Migrating from EDI

EDI (electronic data integration) is a transmission tool which has been around for some years. While the Net environment and applications can replace EDI and establish a lower cost system environment, many organ-isations are showing reluctance to let EDI go. A lot has been invested in installing the technology, most large companies now have it in place and it's become an established way for transmitting purchasing data.

It's probably one of the most mainstream technologies in place today. It contributes little to the sourcing end of the value chain but it is effec-tive at exchanging the relevant documents involved in the process. It's mostly used around the invoicing process for electronic exchange of bills, and links into the payment system. It is not however a streamlined tech-nology like the Net. It is cumbersome, information has to be transmitted from user to user on special lines via a value-added network, application software is required to translate coded EDI messages for processing in a

Figure 6.3 e-procurement through the desktop

Source: PA Consulting

PC, there's no "virtual document area" giving a real time view to every registered user and the basic equipment is c. $100k without adding in the systems integration costs.

Many argue that with the advent of the Net EDI is now obsolete, but recent surveys still show that large corporations like IBM and GM expect to continue to use it at least while that's the critical mass system and till the Net becomes more widely used in this area.

It seems that the interim solution will be adopting some hybrid system that combines EDI messaging sets with transmission over the Net. For example Lufthansa have commented they believe both technologies serve a purpose:

"We've invested a lot now in both EDI and the Net; EDI will provide the logic and structure of the messages we want to exchange but rather than maintain the costs and complexity of dedicated lines we'll start using the Net much more as our communication network."

Authentication

As one of the challenges to establishing a net-based procurement network, security is one of the important hurdles to be addressed. It is a significant concern around all Net applications but there are a number of increasingly reliable mechanisms to address this issue. One function that's going to grow in importance is authentication. That is validating that the person placing the order is really the person authorised to do so and equally checking with the supplier's credentials.

There are a small group of established vendors such as Verisign, Entrust and Xcert/RSA Labs who issue digital certificates confirming identities of individuals or companies. They are known as CAs or certificate authorities. They work around PKI (public key infrastructure) which is ideally suited for e-business. (PKI is a process for exchanging the keys to set encryption and decryption engines. Two keys are used. The public key is used to encrypt and is published freely, but the private decryption key is confidential.) When a company establishes identity with a CA, the CA will generate a unique private signature key together with the public encryption key. It's the private key which passes along the validation and proof of identity.

Companies will increasingly be expected to have recognised digital certificates to authenticate business documents of all kinds, to place orders, to transfer funds and certainly to take many of the actions involved in the procurement process.

Retaining supplier trust

Suppliers are concerned about the Net. They fear automation will replace relationships. They worry that transactions will become commoditised and reduced to lowest price for supply. Of course that risk does exist but it can be managed and dealt with rather than left as an excuse for inaction or delay.

In a recent Harvard study, a Professor Kumar looked at relationships between sellers and buyers and found conclusive evidence that where the parties put significant effort into working together, alongside whatever systems were being put into place, it would result in higher sales and lower costs for both companies.

Complaints about technology displacing value-added are not new and there were similar issues when EDI was first being introduced, but some organisations seem able to stand back from techno-fear and rather seek ways to use it to enhance relationships.

Professor Kumar's research showed that where collaboration did take place and relationships were invested in, then typically sales generated were anything from 11% to 78% higher. "It creates a reservoir of goodwill that helps both parties fulfill their potential ... sharing information, investing in each *other's* business, dedicating people and resources and capturing efficiencies in working together." Kumar refers to Walmart and Procter & Gamble. Even before the commercialisation of the Net, these two organisations had established a single shared sales inventory order system. P&G took responsibility for Walmart's inventory on its products, both on shelf and in the warehouse. In fact P&G now manages the system, sales data is shared, forecasts are developed jointly, delivery volumes are optimised to maximise shipping efficiency and discounts. As the two companies have worked together much of their collaboration is now auto-mated but they still invest considerable effort in projects to continuously improve operating effectiveness.

Training

Both employees and suppliers need to be trained and encouraged to work with the new Net-based systems. The challenge is no greater than for any other change program but because "the size of the prize" here is so substantial there's even greater need to get the right training in place.

Employees can resent what they may see as unreasonable limitations being placed on what they buy and how they buy it. Suppliers, as we've just discussed, will worry that price will become the only buying criteria in an electronic environment.

Implementing the new technologies calls for a program of process and culture change. Companies such as Emerson, Dell, BP and GE have found they needed to establish a pilot to prove the new methods can work, but then define a clear roll-out timetable. That might be as long as 12 months but it gives time for all stakeholders to come to terms with the new environment and accept it. It also provides time to train people in how to use the new tools and become familiar with the benefits and advantages. Moreover it enables suppliers to make their own changes to come on board.

GE set the tone when it first expanded its e-procurement program. Having realised extensive benefits in its pilot phase it gave suppliers a timeframe of c. 12 months. GE made it plain however that unless a supplier was able to deal with GE via its Net-based marketplaces by the end of that period then it would be excluded as a future supplier. Despite the protestations, GE stuck to its guns and it was remarkable just how many suppliers learned what was required, implemented the necessary changes and made the transition by the deadline. In fact GE tended to leave it up to individual suppliers to sort themselves out, but certainly there was also an open door for those suppliers who wanted to explore what the best type of response would be, whether a mix of EDI and the Net would still be appropriate and what other ways suppliers could continue to add value.

Employees too are finding that a mix of online training and workshops plus a recognition that this will be the only system in place after a certain period does sharpen the mind in accepting the new approaches. Indeed because this whole area is typically so productive in terms of its benefits there are few programs, where carefully executed, that have not gone on to deliver significant benefits.

In summary, let's look at two more case studies which appear to capture these lessons learnt on e-procurement implementation success: GE and IBM.

GE

GE effectively started its e-procurement program in earnest at the beginning of 1999, the date Jack Welch got 'e' and announced e-business was "the No. 1, 2, 3 and 4 priority" for the corporation.

Any supplier can apply to supply to GE at www.ge.com. Would-be providers can register free of charge. There's automated software to check whether the company meets a minimum set of criteria and there is a validation/authentication process to check credit-worthiness and identity. Once over that hurdle, each supplier is given its own area on the web site to set out its stall. When a GE buyer is looking for a specific item they'll post their tender to each supplier's area and invite offers. Suppliers then return an electronic form, receive further requests for information and get feedback on how their bid is progressing.

For GE, as a result of this initiative, the costs of processing orders have been reduced by between 50% and 90% depending on the product categories being purchased. Employees now use the Intranet to browse/search the supplier areas and other electronic catalogs, and send their orders directly to purchasing where near real time authorisation (or refusal) is given. Before an order initiated in this way is transmitted to a supplier, it is consolidated with other orders from other departments.

Today all of GE's major businesses run their own Net procurement and web marketplaces, both for internal and external use. Three main initiatives, "e-buy," "e-sell" and "e-make," are digitising all the main functions running the company. GE's declared aims are three-fold: "save money, reach customers faster and through real time data transfer and collaboration extend the focus on quality."

GE say their greatest hurdle has been not the technology but managing their culture. There were still tendencies to use old processes, whether it was the phone or walking round to the local store to order supplies, and these had to be managed. To do that GE experimented with closing the hard copy post room, opening it only one day a week or shutting off the photo-copying facility! "These cultural issues were nevertheless sorted out once everyone got the message that we were committed to using the Internet in everything we do and wanted to take some big bites out of order costs."

IBM

IBM reckons its annual savings through moving procurement onto the Net now run into hundreds of millions. Huge sums but still only a relatively small piece out of a total $10bn plus spend on basic supplies and materials.

IBM decided, like GE, that it would do more than just encourage its suppliers onto the Net, it would require them to operate that way and decided to set deadlines of less than six months. As the company found it had some 18,000 suppliers, it also left it up to each of them to find their own way to respond.

IBM was building on steps it had already been taking through the 1990s to get a better handle on its global procurement budgets and achieve greater leverage in its price negotiations. It had established 24 commodity councils in 1993. These groupings spanned the entire corporation and began to coordinate some product purchasing. That coordination was largely about gathering data to build visibility on supplier/product overlaps and encouraged some migration to a standard common product code.

IBM feels this kind of structural change was a necessary precursor to the introduction of an effective e-procurement system.

> It helped change the culture of the organisation and increased recognition of the value of getting together on this. The Net has introduced centralised procurement and these commodity product councils enable us to have two-way communication between the procurement coordinators and the local buyers.

IBM expects to have 98% of its procurement on the Web by 2003 and plans to move away from EDI to a networked extranet solution.

> While some of our suppliers have been less tech-savvy they've all been able to get online relatively quickly. But it's hard work. The value remains in tight integration of supplier and buyer and we've found there needs to be a customised approach to each relationship if we're to get the value in the long term.

* * * * *

There's no doubt that companies of the size of IBM and GE will use their market clout to drive their suppliers hard. But the overall opportunity is available to any company and it is now possible to test and pilot this at low cost. Some organisations are inevitably going to be faster to take advantage of this area but as Stephen Pownall, group IT director at Pilkington, puts it:

> "We have no crystal ball but we do know that in a few years time we won't be buying at all in the same way we do today ... some initiatives are already in place ... technology and the Web in particular are changing the way we do things."

7 Streamlining in supply chain

Supply Chain Management (SCM) is about the sourcing, making and delivery of materials, and it's rapidly going online. In Europe alone Forrester predict online logistics to grow to €133bn by 2005 equaling 21% of all logistics costs. E-marketplaces, private hubs, more straight-forward bilateral trade and continuing EDI are set to dominate all data transmission and communication links involving inventory management, utilising warehouse and truck capacity, delivery tracking and online transaction management. Recent interviewees have made these comments:

- "Increased transparency through shared online forecasting models will help us identify cost drivers and aggregate shipments."
- "We expect to save 5% in primary logistics costs by opening up the bidding process to more logistics providers in online auctions."
- "The exchange of real time inventory data with our distributors will improve our cycle times and transactional costs will come down."
- "Online logistics enable us to personalise our services to our individual customers.... We expect all our transactions to be online in 2002."
- "Using the Net we've now streamlined the development of our production schedules so that approaching 90% are shared and exchanged automatically with suppliers."

So much of a company's cost and asset base can be tied up directly in the supply chain that this area bears close observation. Companies are continuously reviewing opportunities to reduce inventory, speed up manufacturing processes, ensure on-time deliveries, improve service to customers and manage the cash cycle better. Benefits can appear not only in reduced working capital but also in a slicker operation that can help increase market share. And companies keep on learning about how they can apply new technology tools to network suppliers, partners and their own customers to provide an integrated and more intimate relationship.

Because of the relative simplicity of the Net, expectations of a more efficient and responsive supply chain are now rising, and this is coming especially from customers. The old idea that customers were simply served up what the company could make and deliver – the Henry Ford approach of "any color as long as it's black" – is now gone. Customers now expect to interact at early stages, ordering products they want to the configuration they have specified and still at the lowest possible price. Organisations like Dell have pioneered "build to order" and companies generally now face a situation where they *have* to increase time to market and efficiency way beyond what their internal capability has ever been before.

Researchers have identified a whole list of opportunities for supply chain service improvements and cost reductions that are being enabled through the Internet:

- the ability to track shipments
- 24/7/365 worldwide customer interaction
- real time info on service problems, stock outs, alterations in scheduled shipment dates
- JIT (just in time) scheduling between suppliers, manufacturers and the transportation team
- customers checking status of orders and changing the order (within certain parameters)
- paying electronically (cheaper set up than EDI)
- improved forecasting of demand
- virtual supply management cutting out paper chasing, reducing delays
- automated links through the chain to reduce costs.

Let's consider some examples.

Mitsubishi Auto

Mitsubishi Auto in the US sells coupes, convertibles, sedans and sport utility vehicles. It distributes through 526 dealerships across the country. Getting the right car to the right dealer at the right time when the customer wanted it was proving particularly difficult. It meant that at any one time vehicle inventory on the ground was as much as 100,000 units. But even with those stock levels, delays in moving cars about the country resulted in lost sales and irritated customers.

To address this, Mitsubishi introduced a web-based "order to delivery" network. The aim was to link all the dealers together in a Net-based collaboration system. This enabled Mitsubishi to track sales by type of car by dealer, and develop a profile of each dealership based on factors such as dealer geography, customer buying patterns, product promotions and sales seasonality. The dealers themselves contributed and helped refine these profiles. With the information came insights on customer buying patterns and the ability to better forecast how many vehicles were needed to meet demand. It also brought dealers together in sharing supply chain issues and lessons learned, and encouraged them to collaborate, swap vehicles and speed up the customer lead times to close more sales. The system also allowed 24/7 ordering.

Since going live this "order to delivery" supply chain solution has had a dramatic effect:

- Dealer inventory has reduced by more than half to less than 40,000 units.
- Parts inventory has been eliminated.
- Vehicle lead times have been cut by more than 60%.
- Average age of vehicle on dealer lots has decreased from 166 days to 38 days.
- Sales are up nearly 40%.

Honeywell International

Honeywell determined to take advantage of the Net to build closer links with its customers and set about establishing a virtual supply chain. Honeywell is an "old economy" manufacturer of aerospace systems and factory controls.

During 2000 it launched "myplant.com." That is a business web site that enables companies involved in manufacturing processes all over the world to interconnect. At the site, companies can download software, access training modules, and in particular ask Honeywell manufacturing experts for advice and assistance.

For example, one service on offer helps plants like oil refineries diagnose problems in their processes. A Honeywell customer can send production data over the Net and the aim is to be able to respond "within hours." The training packages have been developed into "scenario simulators" which can teach manufacturing operatives how to respond to a variety of plant problems in their sector. While the training software used to sell for more than $1 million per site, customers can now sign up for as little as $1000 per month. Honeywell is also adding products from some of its competitors in an effort to provide a one-stop shop for plant manufacturers and engineers.

Customers find the benefits are significant in helping them improve their manufacturing supply chain effectiveness. Problems that previously took weeks to solve can now often get sorted in hours or days and that saves time and money. It also reduces risk as this sharing of knowledge enables companies to plan more effectively. For Honeywell the benefits have been wide-ranging. Most particularly it's reinforced their market position with their supply chain partners as the leading innovator. "We're now perceived much more as a leader in our field and it's another factor locking in customers."

Guess? Corporation

The corporation wanted to take a greater leadership position in the apparel industry sector. It decided to "attack the supply chain" because it saw high payback as well as options to cut costs. Its design was to build a specialised vertical portal for the common use of employees, suppliers and retail partners. It realised there would be a number of technology challenges and in a *PC Magazine* interview management talked about how it went out of its way to formally partner with other industry leaders, such as Cisco for some of the hardware, Microsoft for the operating platform, Commerce One for application software and AT&T for the connectivity.

For Guess, this portal was intended not only to give better control over the procurement process but also to integrate that into the rest of its supply chain operations. By forging better communication links with its suppliers generally, Guess wanted to improve quality in raw materials and the downstream manufacturing processes. This should also result in better scheduling and planning and reduce delivery times. Inside Guess, one of the changes that immediately resulted was a change in the role of the procurement team. They changed from chasing paperwork with suppliers to a much more strategic, value-added role looking to optimise sourcing, improve overall supplier relationships and initiate medium term plans for cost and price improvement.

Suppliers now interact with the Guess portal through a browser where they can check inventory levels, agree new orders and prices and input other data to improve demand forecasting. Each supplier has a "customised" set of web pages which immediately updates and reflects latest contacts, orders, changes to specs etc. "There's now an integrated and collaborative approach to the supply chain which we never had before. The web portal has changed many things and we reckon we're way ahead on cost targets and inventory improvements."

These and other more innovative organisations are now seeing the supply chain quite differently. Instead of it being, linear, a chronological sequence of events and activities, the more competitive view is to see it as a collaborative and virtual network (see Figure 7.1). Instead of a back office activity and the concern of a few function managers, the new supply chain network is thrust center stage and can become the driving force for change, improvement and advantage across the entire company. It puts the customer first and puts the whole sequence of purchasing and processing into the context of how to get what's been ordered out to the customer as fast and efficiently as possible.

It's worth emphasising just how vital web technology is to enable this networking and collaboration to happen. It gives companies and their suppliers the capability to access the information they require via the ubiquitous, common, standard web browser interface. And that can be done *without* the need to have all the different supply chain players changing their technology and software architecture just to be able to communicate. Web portals are often seen as part of the solution because they provide the ability to access information held in different databases – again often by different companies – and to consolidate that information on one screen.

While the Net by itself is the catalyst and enabler for these collaboration solutions to work, companies must first agree to share and participate. It also requires intelligence in designing information flows and networks so that they do provide the insights and services that customers and others are demanding. Doing away with sequential processes and implementing "parallel processing" is not a simplistic change, and much has to change around the technology and the organisation structure to make it happen.

In a further survey by Forrester, two-thirds of companies involved in SCM expected to be involved in some form of "virtual and networked collaboration" in 2002. But, to demonstrate the size of the changes required in these companies, only 12% of those in the survey use web tools to collaborate today and as many as 25% still see communication silos – even within their own organisations – as the greatest barrier still be to overcome.

Recognising these challenges, one researcher (Professor Langley at Tennessee University) has identified the "the immutable laws of collaborative logistics" – things that have to be in place for a collaborative supply chain to work. Among his "laws" he identifies the need for "real and recognisable mutual benefits: ... All participants must be able to quantify the benefits they can enjoy and believe those benefits will be equitably shared.... For a collaborative community to be effective companies will incur investment and risk in different measures but they have to see the win:win!"

Figure 7.1 Supply chain evolution

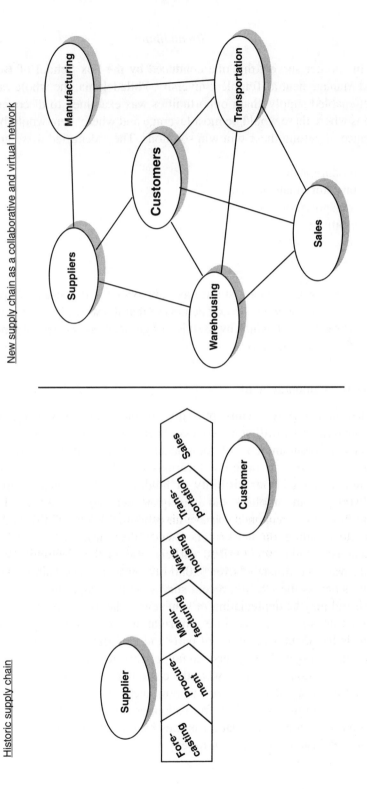

Historic supply chain

New supply chain as a collaborative and virtual network

In another survey, this one conduced by the Fox School of Business and Management at Temple University, Philadelphia, the whole range of Net-enabled supply chain opportunities was examined to discover those areas where there would be most leverage and where there would be most chance of getting these win:win solutions. They identified these areas:

- procurement
- inventory management
- transportation
- e-billing
- order processing
- customisation.

So powerful are the case studies already available in these areas demonstrating what some are already achieving that it's worth looking at each in turn. (Procurement, which by itself is so significant, is considered separately in the previous chapter.)

Inventory management

Traditional supply chains pile up inventory at every stage of the production and fulfillment process. There are safety stocks, cycle time stocks, different amounts of components and raw materials, error stocks, warehouse stock in different locations etc. This is often due to poor communications, poor visibility of holdings and shipments, unreliable deliveries from suppliers and inadequate demand forecasting. The US auto industry is reckoned to have an estimated $50bn of finished goods inventory sitting on dealer lots (hence the particular success of the Mitsubishi initiative described earlier), and in the electronics industry there was an estimate of over $20bn of excess inventory sitting in warehouses across the US in a recent survey. This is unproductive, it ties up cash and may be depreciating in value every day it sits there.

Getting to more accurate information about demand, real time knowledge about availability of parts and materials, and shared planning and scheduling with suppliers can unlock this inventory problem and help the organisation only make what the customers want when they want it.

Automation aided by EDI and now more broadly by the Internet is enabling information to flow from suppliers to manufacturers to shippers and on to customers so that all parties have accurate real time inventory counts and can operate just in time:

- Hewlett Packard discovered that the only way to cut inventory in its distribution center in Singapore was to link its suppliers and share with them
information about HP stocks and demand forecasts that it had previously
regarded as proprietary. By linking them up in a web-based portal,
inventory levels were reduced down to less than two weeks' supply.
- Mazda US introduced a web-based system to increase turn-around
time for cars being repaired and services. They did this by building a
Vehicle locator and Parts availability application, giving each repair
garage access to the Mazda parts inventory to find the part they needed
at the nearest depot.

  "We were able to deploy working technology without spending
months developing applications and retraining everyone. We use
middleware links (MQ series and Universal Database) to our mainframe systems to extract the relevant data and display it on the desktop
via the browser. This enables us to operate without complicated
conversions or extensive programming. We've got a 30% return on our
investment, saved money and improved service."
- Westco-BakeMark (part of Dutch CSM) is a US wholesale manufacturer and distributor of bakery and food service items for hotels,
casinos, restaurants and bakeries. "We recognised early on that
managing our supply chain better could provide us with significant
competitive advantage. Our goal was to delay baking and making till
the very last minute so we responded only to the latest orders and made
only what was required." Westco found its biggest challenge was
convincing customers to use its Internet system. A significant
percentage do now order online but many were hesitant at first, used
to doing things by phone or in person.

  Westco has started passing on some of the cost savings benefits that
the automated process and the migration to the Web has accelerated. The
company not only manages its own "outbound" inventory but also uses
customer order data to manage its back-end purchasing to ensure
suppliers only provide what's needed, when it's needed. "By closing the
loop on the supply chain in this way, our web-based systems have
created valuable synergies. Suddenly, everyone has access to mutual
data they can analyse and use to optimise their own systems and
processes."

While a company has to take responsibility for its own inventory levels,
these case studies demonstrate that it can only really get to grips with this
challenge if it takes a "collaborative and networking" view of its supply

91

chain. Only by linking in suppliers and customers and leveraging information about demand and order patterns, at each stage of the process, can inventory levels really be cut. As the people at Honeywell put it: "we want to replace inventory with information."

Transportation

We all remember the horror stories from Christmas 2000 when so many new e-tailers went online only to find their businesses crash because they couldn't meet deliveries on time. Transportation is a critical function and it too must adhere to sound business disciplines if it's to work, work well and meet rising customer expectations in this new electronic, instant, "now" business age.

The whole transportation industry has in fact been going through significant change. Most companies today have outsourced their warehousing and delivery and while that in principle makes them leaner, more focussed, it has also significantly increased the need for up-to-the minute and effective communication links. As a result technology generally has played a significant part in helping secure and leverage those communication opportunities. Computing networks, satellite, radio, bar codes, wireless links, and now the Internet are being combined to drive the supply network. Companies want to track shipments, manage inventory through the chain, send freight bills, deal with customs and customers – and all on a global basis. Let's look at initiatives in global shipping, from UPS and technologies for the future:

INTTRA

INTTRA is a joint Internet venture put together by leading ocean carriers Maersk Sealand, P&O Nedlloyd, CMA and others. It's the first global transportation portal enabling companies to manage shipping transactions through one common platform. The goal is to become the leading B2B ocean freight service provider. At launch in 2001, the venture covered 35% of the world market and on some routes it covered 100% of all trade.

Before establishing the venture the member companies conducted market research and found strong customer demand for more visibility, greater standardisation and more accurate data along the whole shipping supply chain. INTTRA is a response to provide a "one stop shop" for customers. It provides single point of entry for tracking cargo movements with multiple carriers. It also enables companies to book cargo and schedule routes across several carriers.

INTTRA claims the following general benefits for its services:

- Visibility: web access to all in-transit containerised cargo. Information is shared among all partners including shippers, consignees, suppliers, custom house brokers, forward carriers.
- Simplicity: template-driven booking requests for participating carriers and easy to use tracking tools.
- Efficiency: reduced repetitive phone calls and follow up faxes plus Net access which is fast eliminating long waits for required information.
- Customer service: 24/7 customer service teams in Denmark, Hong Kong and the USA help customers use the web site and support the automated processes.
- Scalability: infrastructure designed to support millions of transactions.
- Standardisation: all participating carriers are standardising their processes to interact efficiently with INTTRA and the aim is to minimise the EDI requirement through the common web platform.
- Security: the IT architecture is open, scalable, distributed and based on common Internet and EDI standards. The comprehensive security includes authentication, authorisation, audit trails, encryption, virus scanning and intrusion prevention.

It's early days still at INTTRA and take-up to date has been slow, but rival online shipping portals have also been launched seeing the substantial potential.

"We expect the shipping industry to take on the new technology at the same rate these initiatives are developing in other sectors," is the comment of rival portal GoCargo.com.

"A carrier pricing manager for example can now be proactive in reducing costs. He can log on and see a shipment from Rotterdam to Sao Paulo which is only 60% full and can now negotiate special rates to get that ship filled.... The web network gives us the visibility to pinpoint these sort of opportunities as well as identify and head-off any problems the moment they arise."

Initiatives such as INTTRA and GoCargo are major steps forward by leading players in that industry. Will all shipping orders eventually

Figure 7.2 INTTRA: customer driven, carrier sponsored

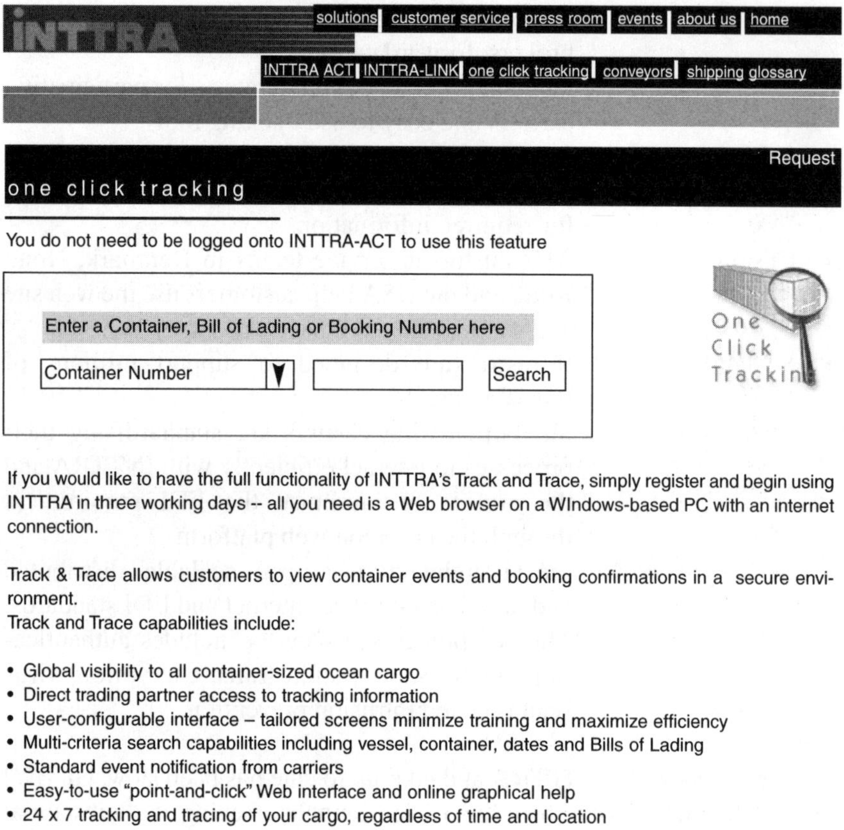

solutions | customer service | press room | events | about us | home

INTTRA ACT | INTTRA-LINK | one click tracking | conveyors | shipping glossary

Request

one click tracking

You do not need to be logged onto INTTRA-ACT to use this feature

Enter a Container, Bill of Lading or Booking Number here

Container Number ▼ | Search

One Click Tracking

If you would like to have the full functionality of INTTRA's Track and Trace, simply register and begin using INTTRA in three working days -- all you need is a Web browser on a WIndows-based PC with an internet connection.

Track & Trace allows customers to view container events and booking confirmations in a secure environment.
Track and Trace capabilities include:

• Global visibility to all container-sized ocean cargo
• Direct trading partner access to tracking information
• User-configurable interface – tailored screens minimize training and maximize efficiency
• Multi-criteria search capabilities including vessel, container, dates and Bills of Lading
• Standard event notification from carriers
• Easy-to-use "point-and-click" Web interface and online graphical help
• 24 x 7 tracking and tracing of your cargo, regardless of time and location

migrate through to the web site, will the services and functionality continue to expand so it genuinely becomes a one-stop shop? Will it be possible eventually to compare prices and services online and choose the carrier whose package is most geared to the company's needs? In these early days for the portal, companies are testing out the opportunity, learning what works and what doesn't, and discovering the key points of benefit and service improvement. But the gains as itemised are high and it's hard to see how competitive pressures won't force the increasing use of this lower cost, faster, more efficient order and tracking service.

Transportation in fact is estimated to account for up to 25% of overall operating costs in a supply chain and so it's not surprising to see significant initiatives in this space. Research at the Fox Business School, referred to earlier, also tells us that tracking shipments is the key concern for both carriers and the manufacturer/supplier. Among other things the research showed that the ability to track 'n' trace helped distribution managers monitor the number of late deliveries and so have the data to make claims and exact penalties for late delivery!

UPS

UPS has stolen a march on rival FedEx in its determination to use the Internet to provide added-value services to its customers, building in track 'n' trace capabilities to provide a whole range of "customer lock-ins." UPS has captured nearly 55% of all e-commerce related shipments compared to FedEx's surprisingly low 10% (according to a Bear Stearns report on "e-gistics").

Instead of the still pervasive phone call and fax links, UPS has gone beyond mere e-mail communication to establish a series of automated processes. It provides ordering, tracking, invoicing and payments all electronically. It provides guarantees to businesses and makes commitments to customers for time, date and quality of delivery so that defects caused by its delivery people can be monitored, and if at fault UPS picks up the tab. It offers these services to individuals and businesses; for example they've worked with Ford to develop better tracking of inventory to deliver cars from factory to showroom faster. They've got it down to five days from nine.

"We can now deliver a message that a package has been received right into the company's accounting system."

More recently UPS have rolled out their "tracking goes mobile" venture. Using wireless technology, it's possible to track packages using a text messaging or web-enabled wireless phone or PDA (personal digital assistant). It will also be possible to confirm transit times, find the nearest drop-off location and calculate shipping costs.

Wireless technology generally is expected to make a big impact on the transportation industry in the years to come. As bandwidth improves, reliability gets better and usage reaches critical mass, there's expected to be a wave of new applications that enables this "industry on the move" to communicate and collaborate. There's talk of "intelligent transportation systems" (ITS) that align satellite, wireless, bar code and other technologies. From package identification through to automated pre-clearance at borders, it's expected that the Internet will help weave together an array of benefits.

Here are two other applications for the future:

- 2D bar codes (two-dimensional in form-stacked, matrix or dot tech-nology) are being developed that allow a far larger amount of information to be integrated so that a product's history can be read at a glance. This is then coupled with intelligent chips that can be implanted on containers and packages for much more detailed tracking and tracing. This is integrated with RF (radio frequency) identification and we essentially have labels with programmable chips that allow for remote, long distance identification. No need for a laser beam to be lined up to read the bar code.

    These "smart" bar codes can be edited to reflect change of destina-tion, new delivery dates and price, and they're "durable." They could for example be embedded in a frozen food container to track temperature and other conditions, ensure supply quality is monitored effectively and improve information flow throughout a supply chain network.

- This next example is already being piloted at PolyOne, a chemicals manufacturer headquartered in Cleveland. They use a mix of wireless and Net technologies to provide just in time service and delivery to customers. PolyOne has installed sensors at its biggest customers' chemical tanks. The aim is to track their inventory in real time. When levels in the tank drop to a certain point, the system automatically sends an order for replacement materials. The order is simultaneously routed to the nearest supplier on PolyOne's "SupplyNet" and replenishment made – all without human involvement!

e-billing

"e-billing" is one of the more recent internet-enabled applications to capture market interest. It can be a complement or alternative to existing EDI networks. Basically if EDI is already in place between a company, its suppliers and its customers, then new Net-based e-billing initiatives can simply act as a catalyst to ensure the existing and available functionality is being exploited and links to legacy systems, for example, are effective in capturing and transmitting data. If EDI is not in place, or doesn't embrace the whole supplier customer network, then a company should consider these new opportunities to further enhance its SCM effectiveness.

"EBP" as it is becoming known, electronic billing and payment, in principle offers a number of advantages:

- enables electronic distribution of invoices
- supports automated invoice approvals

- as a result reduces time for invoice processing
- enables bill details to be uploaded automatically into the accounting system
- reduces paper handling, bill queries (for example the cost of processing a paper bill is estimated at c. $1.10 compared to c. 20¢ for an electronic bill)
- improves accuracy of bill recording and reporting
- allows customers to check/analyse details online.

In the "Getting started" chapter we have already read of Fisher Scientific's own experience of e-billing and how for a relatively modest investment the company has begun to see significant and quick payback in this area. Kingston Communications, the UK-based telco, is another fan of e-billing systems and employs that approach with both suppliers and customers. "We find companies are preferring to deal with bills and invoices electronically because it helps them identify more accurately where costs are going and also to make cost savings." The banks too are beginning to see the potential of the low cost automation of this area provided by the Net and are exploring what role they can play. Citibank for example has developed its e-billing offering to customers and gets its money by charging a fee for each transaction carried out through its systems.

Developing e-billing as the standard transaction method is however going to take time. One not untypical issue in this Internet-emerging space is the range of different standards being employed by the different software providers. That means universal application is impossible till a common language is accepted and adopted. Industry observers in this sector are hoping that XML will emerge as the framework for a common approach and business model, but the time-horizon for that is still unclear.

In the meantime it's providing yet further challenge to traditional supply chain managers. Are the existing internal processes as cost-effective and efficient as possible and, despite some limitations, are there opportunities here to link better with customers and deliver a more responsive range of services?

Order processing

The opportunity here is for "straight-through order processing" (STP). For some, order processing is just another term for e-procurement, but we mean something very different here. We're looking at the opportunity for companies to listen to customers and respond slickly and quickly through the *entire* supply chain to deliver back to customers what they want. It might mean going all the way back to the R&D team and getting them to adapt a product to meet a specific customer need. And this is in stark contrast to the usual procedure where a sales rep. learns of a particular customer preference, possibly captures that via an e-mail back to a regional manager, where it then sinks into a black hole of good and bad ideas that never see the light of day!

Figure 7.3 Order processing

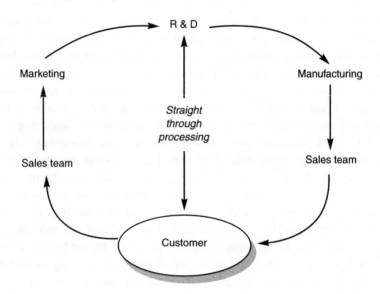

We saw an example of this when we considered Spanish retailer Zara in a different context earlier. Zara has revolutionised retailing by transforming order processing. It can translate the latest customer trends identified by the stores into designs that are manufactured and delivered back to those stores in less than 15 days. It's a form of fast straight-through ordering using the Internet to link all the various parties that no other retailer globally can yet match today. At the same time it sets the next standard. "Other retailers will have to learn to operate in the same way or they won't be in business in a few year's time," comments one retail analyst at Goldman Sachs.

Contrast Marks & Spencer, the once globally aspiring UK fashion retailer (and former owner of Brooks Brothers). For M&S, there's no such thing as STP. It doesn't collect the data, it's got no integrated network, it struggles to turnaround new product ideas, however they're presented or captured, in 15 weeks let alone 15 days. For M&S, trend-spotting revolves around four points in the annual business cycle – spring, summer, autumn, winter – and products are not uncommonly ordered 12 months in advance. That's been the way of all clothing retailers: an old fashioned business model with limited use of technology to facilitate business processes. Not surprisingly in such an environment trying to guess future demand and fashion cycles is troublesome and results in excess inventory and markdowns. But if Spanish "upstart" Zara can do it, there's no doubt others will follow.

Take another example from WW.Grainger inc, the MRO catalog supplier distributing everything from electrical components through uniforms and cleaning products. What might otherwise be a commodity low value aggregation business has been turned on its head by Grainger's e-business team looking to drive out new solutions for customers and streamline their own processes of procurement, inventory management and logistics.

Grainger has worked hard since 1999 to web-enable its products and services and ensure all its suppliers are networked into the supply chain management. To achieve this it has for example seconded its own people to work with key suppliers on their own sites to ensure collaboration takes place and continues to evolve efficiently. It also has Grainger people on key customer sites to ensure the STP actually happens and they can respond fast to new customer demands. The service is 24/7. It provides one integrated order for products from different suppliers (it's Grainger's "problem" to coordinate supplier delivery and rechannel invoice payments rather than the customers').

As the Grainger team say: "Once we get customers we rarely lose them. When they tell us something or request it our processes are geared to responding and delivering – no questions asked!"

To date Internet initiatives around order processing have largely focussed inward on improving the procurement process or looked back up the chain to the supplier. As a result, a lot of gains made by organisations in this space have been around reductions in paperwork, speeding up order cycle time and reductions in the price of raw materials and other suppliers. But STP as described argues for the next stage in order processing applications by driving out and integrating the link from development right through to the customer and their demands.

One further case study here also provides a useful link into the section: on "Customisation" that follows.

Weyerhaeuser

Weyerhaeuser is a Wisconsin-based timber processing and furniture manufacturer that by its own admission was in bad shape. It could often take months to turn around a customer order and it wasn't uncommon for several weeks to elapse before a customer order was even acknowledged let alone scheduled. Costs were high, sales were flat and morale was poor. Commented the CEO recently: "you had to practically beat people with a stick to get them to come back to work every morning!"

Today the company is transformed and as the management team acknowledge: "the Internet was the catalyst." With the help of consultants the company installed a Net-based factory and order management system that can now process orders in just 15 minutes. "Once we received an order it used to take weeks of phone calls and faxes back and forth with the customer to confirm the spec and check it met local and state regulations." Now all this is done automatically online using a rules-based system that immediately detects any non-compliant features in the spec and reconfirms with customers.

"Now customers can place orders and there is constant interaction between us. They can change order details as well and provided that's within certain parameters it's automatically fed back into our production schedules." Customers now feel they're being listened to and their orders are processed efficiently. They also feel they're involved and can contribute to the STP because they can access certain of Weyerhaeuser's own systems to check on orders.

The results of this systematic initiative have been impressive. Deliveries to agreed customer delivery time now hit 97% on time in full (up from a previous low of 40%), revenues are growing at between 10 and 15%, and return on assets is now encouragingly positive after years of losses.

> "It's not been easy but for us it was a question of do or die. The technology has been important but we've had to change the business processes around it too. Initially we held weekly gripe sessions for groups of employees and offered bonuses to those who had positive ideas for improving the situation. Now we've got the platform we can even charge a premium price for our services and still get the job."

Customisation

The next step from STP is customisation or in this context "build to order." Of course, many OEMs have been designing and building large pieces of equipment to customer order specification for many years but until recently no company had cracked this challenge in the arena of mass product manufacturing in areas such as computers, cars or clothing, where there have typically been large batch runs and one-off orders were just too complex and too costly to engineer.

Pioneers in this space have included Levi Strauss. Levi's established an instore fitting program where customers could define size, type, color and style, and a "tailored" pair of Levi's would be available for collection within 14 days. While praised for the innovation, the venture largely depended on old processes and technology to process the orders and costs were too high (in addition other retailers complained Levi's were now dealing direct with consumers, disintermediating them, and resultant protests were another reason the venture sadly got put on hold rather than being improved).

Another pioneer – but this time more successful – has been Dell. Dell now "famously" allows customers to put together their own PC on line from different components and modules that Dell makes available. Orders are then fed through to sub-contract assemblers and it's their task (which Dell oversees but does not manage) to put the customer's tailored order together against fast turnaround deadlines.

Critics of Dell's initiatives initially argued that all Dell had achieved was to push inventory and manufacturing problems back up the supply chain. So far from inventing a new business model, they'd just used their market clout to push the problem on to others. But in fact that's not the case. Dell has worked with its suppliers to streamline the whole supply chain. Inventory levels at its contract manufacturers declined by as much as 44% through 1995 to 1999. As one supplier commented:

> "Inventory has been taken out of the entire system, finished goods only get assembled when an actual customer order arrives, components are industry standard and readily available, variations are tightly managed to minimise complexity and order information is immediately visible through Dell's web gateway to suppliers."

From another perspective within the PC manufacturing and distribution industry, Apple's senior VP Tim Cook puts less of the spotlight on inventory reduction and more on margin maintenance as a key benefit arising through building to order. "In high tech industries where product innovation is key, the ability to control levels of obsolescent stock is vital. This means we make what we can sell at the full price rather than constantly discounting old models."

Some companies are trying to get even further ahead by anticipating customer need using one to one personalisation tools and techniques on the Web. Amazon.com uses NetPerception's software to create personal recommendations. For example it uses customer data and buying patterns to determine which are the most popular products it will hold in its own stock to enable 24-hour delivery, rather than leave in supplier inventory where customer delivery lead times are less reliable.

There's clearly no question as to the value of "build-to-order" and customisation over building to stock. Companies deliver what customers want, avoid inventory, write off and mark downs, and have a more compelling operating model. While the Net has acted as catalyst, as the people at Weyerhaeuser point out, it's not an easy path and there needs to be a strong conviction and commitment that the journey will be worthwhile. The good news is that as more and more companies streamline in this way, so others will both learn what can be done and also be encouraged to follow in similar footsteps.

One last case study here dramatically highlights the value of not just build to order but the whole range of supply chain management opportunities.

Herman Miller

Herman Miller is the no. 2 US furniture manufacturer and, like others in its sector, sat on turnaround times of months for an order to be processed and furniture to be delivered. Frustrated by constant customer complaints, the management team decided to do something about it: "without technology we couldn't lead." With it the company developed its "SQA" ("simple quick affordable") Internet business unit. The goal: "deliver custom-ordered desks, cubicles and chairs in just two weeks against the industry standard of two months."

"We appeal to businesses who value speed over having unlimited choice and options." Miller has made sure its suppliers participate in and contribute to making this initiative work, and set about streamlining its supply chain. Suppliers were rationalised, component orders were held up for delivery into a "just in time" SQA assembly process. "Things happen in parallel" rather than in sequence and each partner in the supply chain is kept informed through SQA's SupplyNet and can track order progress. The sales force are also connected so they can keep the customer informed, and more recent developments allow them to transmit orders direct to the manufacturing team while at customer sites.

Initial results were extraordinary and showed once again the high value of these sorts of innovations. Sales in the first year after launch grew at 25% in an otherwise flat market. All SQA shipments now are over 99% accurate and on time, inventory is down to less than two days and some orders are being processed and delivered within three or four days. Not surprisingly all this has rubbed off on the rest of Herman Miller, which has now gained the ranking of "best manufacturer to do business with in its sector."

* * * * *

The supply chain provides a rich source of opportunity for all those connected with it from supplier to manufacturer, from transportation to warehousing, from procurement manager to inventory controller. Linking it all together provides even more value, whether through simple networking and collaboration or through more far-reaching STP and build-to-order approaches. The case studies make clear just what can be achieved, but the companies going after this are still the exception rather than the rule and examples are found in only some industry sectors. In clothing Zara remains unique, with only Benetton following closely. In automotive all the Big Three are experimenting with various initiatives but Ford seems the most advanced. In chemicals, in contrast, most of the SCM ventures appear tentative with few of the established giants yet to realise any material benefits. So plenty to aim at, plenty of territory left to be charted and plenty of competitive advantage and profit-building still to be gained and won!

8 Streamlining through knowledge management

According to recent Delphi Group research, 88% of knowledge held within an organisation is currently not searchable or retrievable, and on average 20% of employee time is spent finding answers to problems that someone else has already solved. 55% of senior managers of Fortune 500 companies interviewed in a survey felt that knowledge and intellectual capital were *not* being effectively captured in their companies.

Most agree that one of the main assets of an organisation is the knowledge and experience that's contained in most people's heads alongside the information stored on databases. Capitalise upon that knowledge, know-how, insight and expertise and the business must surely become more effective, be able to do things more quickly, be more customer responsive and generally be based on a more sustainable business platform.

This sounds straightforward but in practice it's proved harder than most had expected. Problems have been encountered around the sharing of data. People complain about "initiative overload," "unwillingness to share data," "too busy to share data," "data cannot be shared because it's confidential," "too much data to know what to share." And problems have also arisen around using the systems or tools that have been put in place: "inadequate training," "system difficult to access," "only half the company use the system," "I can never find what I want," "the search engine doesn't work" etc.

Because many early initiatives in this arena have therefore foundered (an IDC report concluded that poor knowledge management was costing Fortune 500 companies a total of $31.5bn in lost revenue), there's now developing a second wave of interest. That's been encouraged by the widespread adoption of the Net as the major communication and information sharing tool within companies. In addition, the open Net standards allow easier participation by different business units and even outside partners, irrespective of their different legacy databases.

As this second wave grows in force and effect so those "riding it" are looking for new ways to describe the concept and to define a process that works and *does* lead to results. At BP, we will learn later about "T-shaped managers"; ChevronTexaco and Dow Chemical for example refer to their "intellectual capital" management. Unilever talk about "learning + innovation". PA Consulting describe their intranet-based system as "KnowledgeNet," others refer to "business intelligence" and some, like Dell and British Aerospace, talk about virtual learning or their "virtual university." While many put different emphases on their knowledge capture environment they're all after one thing: "turning information into profits."

In fact it's often been pointed out how the stock market value of many companies is several times greater than their actual book value. While a number of factors may contribute to this, it's readily acknowledged that it is the intangible assets of the company that can be shown to make up much of the difference. It's the brands, patents and copyrights, the leverage of intellectual capital and know-how that makes companies more valuable and is reflected in the price of their stock.

Robert Goizeuta, the very successful former CEO of Coca-Cola once commented: "all our factories and facilities could burn down tomorrow but you'd hardly touch or hurt the value of the company. That value actually lies in the goodwill of our brand franchise and the collective knowledge in the company."

Figure 8.1 Profiting from human capital

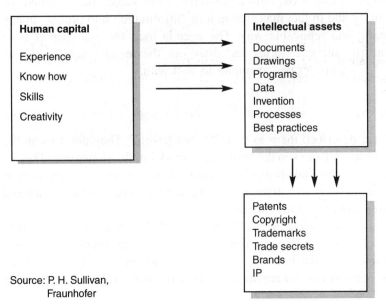

Source: P. H. Sullivan,
        Fraunhofer

105

We are also increasingly finding that competitive advantage is shifting towards knowledge. Information flows used to be all physical, typically on paper, catalogs, invoices or cash. Now all that's being converted into bits on the information highway. As Peter Drucker, famed management guru, has pointed out:

> "the traditional factors of production – land, labor and capital have not disappeared. But they have become secondary. They can be obtained and obtained easily, provided there is knowledge. Knowledge has become a utility, the new means to obtain social and economic results. Knowledge is becoming the only meaningful resource."

Other commentators share Drucker's view:

- "Knowledge is now the crucial factor underpinning economic growth" (Secretary General of OECD).
- "Intellectual capital is something you can't see, you can't touch but it makes you rich!" (*Fortune* business article).
- "A modern company has to face the changes that come with a knowledge-based economy if it doesn't want to miss its connection to the future" (US Securities and Exchange Commission report).

Most organisations do recognise this challenge but, as with much of the experience in this book, only a few have really successful exploited the opportunity and in fact managed to turn "information into profits" in any systematic and replicable way. The agenda then for this chapter is to examine the success stories and draw out the lessons that have been learnt. Let's consider two examples to start with:

Ford

Ford have described them as their "crown jewels." They don't mean the original Model T or even the hottest new model in the showroom. They're referring to the half-million product design resources, production management tools and strategic information assets that are now captured on Ford's company-wide Intranet.

"The internal web is the backbone of Ford's business today," CIO Bud Mathaisel said in a *Fortune* article. "It's even more important than our mainframe infrastructure. We've had to learn how to make it work because we can't afford anything less than top performance." Connecting all of Ford's employees did require significant investment. One not surprising but early lesson has been that without support from senior management this was never going to work. But from the CEO down there was a series of commitments. For example Ford held a weekly "CEO chat room." There was also a push for "web-only" publication of business plans, engineering best practices and product development specs, all intended to send a clear message: "we communicate on the Intranet."

What also contributed to the success of this knowledge Net push is that people can find what they want. So typically 80% of employees access the Intranet daily – not just for e-mail but for the tools to do their job. Every truck and car model for example has its own internal project web site to track design, production, quality control and delivery processes. People can test out various scenarios, examine the effect changes to the spec would have on other departments and on the critical path timetable, find out when key components will be available, who's done this stuff before and can contribute best to the project. Instead of weeks of delay, or reinventing wheels or making changes without reference to the impact on others, now all these things can be managed real time online in collaboration with colleagues all over the world.

To manage the huge amounts of data already available, Ford has insisted on a set of web publishing standards, and crucially there's been an efficient data indexing process from the start. Each department publishes material therefore in standardised formats, a central IS team tracks what's being put on, the search engine is being continuously refined and the different web applications and servers are maintained round the clock. Like a finely-tuned production process!

British Telecom

BT provide some valuable examples of how they've turned a more efficient knowledge environment into bottom-line results. A key part of their knowledge management program is "keeping BT staff up to date." This involves an online library providing news, research, data, feeds from leading telecommunications commentators and market/company reports from analysts and consultants. It's divided into 100 topic channels. Importantly, it is also customisable to individual or department needs. As an example of a simple but early payback, rumors on the Net one morning that a rival telco was in financial difficulties enabled a BT account team to get in promptly and win over a new $2m customer.

Complementing the library topics, BT also have an "ideas system."

Any employee can log on any new idea for business improvement. Ideas are filed and tracked and, if adopted, their effectiveness is assessed leading to bonuses up to £50k.

One BT business unit (BT Ignite) claims one idea on how to reroute web traffic saved the company nearly $100m in infrastructure costs and resulted in a new product launch for BT's internet access product "Surf Time."

BT are keen on incentivising their staff to use the intranet knowledge base and in another area they have paid employees up to £100 a time for every sales lead or tip or piece of advice they entered into the system. The incentive is deliberate as the company found it especially difficult to otherwise get sales people to share leads and market information. Sales prospects in the business unit concerned are now up 12%.

Overall BT have invested very substantially in the system and the view is that "it's more than paid for itself and delivering benefits we hadn't even expected."

What is actually included in "knowledge management"? By some definitions it appears to include everything a company does, every communication made and every piece of data anyone creates or discovers. A helpful survey from the Fraunhofer Institute shows what companies are rating as most important as they roll out their "KM" initiatives (see Figure 8.2).

Figure 8.2 Knowledge management priorities

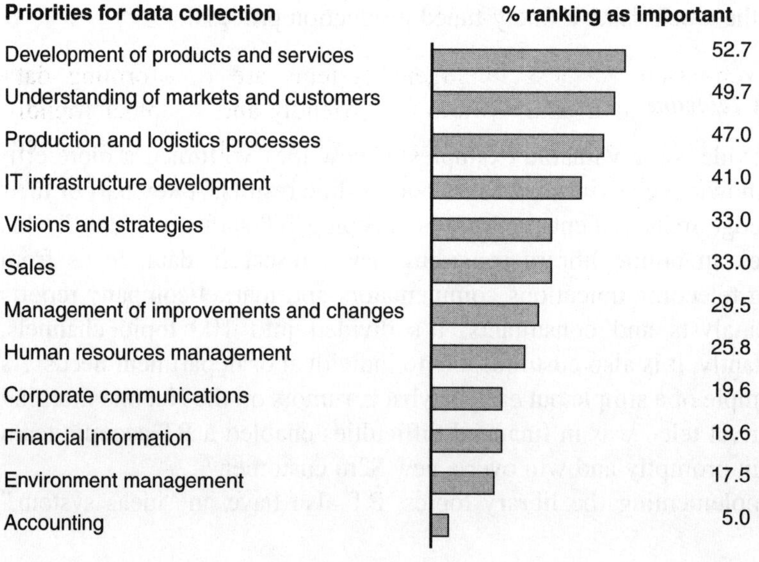

Priorities for data collection	% ranking as important
Development of products and services	52.7
Understanding of markets and customers	49.7
Production and logistics processes	47.0
IT infrastructure development	41.0
Visions and strategies	33.0
Sales	33.0
Management of improvements and changes	29.5
Human resources management	25.8
Corporate communications	19.6
Financial information	19.6
Environment management	17.5
Accounting	5.0

Even with these priorities defined it emerges that there's still a wide range of high interest areas where people see leverage. In today's competitive arena, finding ways to constantly improve a company's core operating platform is key, and turning information into tangible assets that contribute dividends is crucial. Every company in the world will have stores of raw data and real world experience found (or buried) in different databases, document warehouses, e-mail chains and sales reports, and among all of its workforce from the most junior clerk upwards. The challenge is to define what's important and access it – quickly! But it can't be done without some aggregation and filtering system in place.

Because of the increasing attention KM has received in recent times, there's been an outpouring of different technologies and tools that can produce the basic reports but can also provide the capability to drill down into hard core data sources ("data mining"), searching across all the different databases (the "data warehouse"). Report engines and report-building software, ad hoc query tools and use of online analytical processing technology (OLAP) have typically been implemented in most companies' KM systems. Now the Internet has come along and "online knowledge" is changing what can be done and how it can be delivered:

- Simple, cheap open standard connections mean accessibility for all.
- Anytime.
- Anywhere means global reach to all parts of a company's business, including:
  - mobile connectivity to employees on the move
  - e-mail, data, documents, images, video streams, webcams.

New web-based business intelligent systems are transforming data mining and customer analysis into user friendly and customer friendly services. These document management systems are two or three-tiered, aiming to preserve integrity and classification and enabling user-friendly

Figure 8.3 Evolution of knowledge management

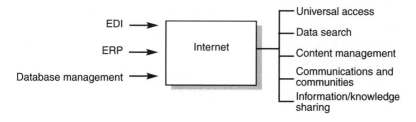

search. The first layer in their architecture is usually a basic file server containing, for example, the documents and the relevant information. The second layer will consist of client software for accessing the system handled by the web browser, and the third layer contains the business logic behind how the documents are first put together and routed to appropriate individuals.

When these web-based systems first arrived, the established "document management" companies were slow to web-enable their products. This has allowed a raft of now well-known software specialists to seize a lot of this territory. This includes newcomers like Autonomy and Verity through to Broadvision and Vignette plus a host of others. These "new players" have been especially web-smart, gearing their solutions to fast intranet implementation, providing automatic translation of content to other languages, providing web-hosting services and the further development of employee portals (see later).

These software houses focus on solutions that enable a workforce to create and access web-based content through a variety of front-end tools, including word processing programs and web authoring. They focus less on data warehousing and data mining, though that too is changing as "content management" becomes an increasingly important part of any intranet/KM implementation.

Nowadays it would not be unusual to find an array of software tools involved in a knowledge management system and it can be the linkages and integration of these that are the most challenging. This is especially the case as the various components may have been introduced over a period of time and may not be immediately compatible or interoperable. But the basic components to consider are:

- **Intranet technology** – presenting a unified environment and access to various sources of information.
- **Electronic document management** – contains procedures for using and maintaining documents, such as checks on updates.
- **Information retrieval** – solutions for text searches and automatic categorisation and summation of documents. Advanced search algorithms can use text mining techniques to discover contexts not available through simple queries.
- **Workflow management** – helps identify referable pieces of data and learning and feed them into KM retrieval.
- **Data warehousing** – data mining techniques (together with OLAP) capture information and show where it is stored.

110

- **Help desks** – complement "information retrieval" as an important application area for shared learning on an individual basis.
- **Agent technology** – software or avatars or "e-bots" based in the essentials of artificial intelligence provide user-friendly applications and guidance.

One company that has put considerable effort into developing this technology environment, and also ensuring its people take advantage of it, is BP Amoco. This organisation with over 100,000 employees in more than 100 countries across nearly 50 different business units has been on a five to six year journey now, gradually instituting processes and the supporting mechanisms to ensure know-how is efficiently captured and shared.

The BP Intranet now provides a unified portal for its employees. There is a range of developed functionality from e-mail through to desktop video-conferencing and an electronic "yellow pages" that identifies experts in different areas and referral points for shared learning and best practices. There is an "ask Sir John" spot (Sir John (now Lord) Browne, the CEO) and it's instructive to see a recent response from him on "how BP uses and values knowledge management."

> "The effective management of know-how is central to delivering today's performance and to the future success of the company.
>
> In my view, the key to real success in being a knowledge-based company is the way we organise it and the behaviors we exhibit.
>
> Our experience shows that an organisation based on a federation of self-standing business units is good for financial performance but not so for transferring know-how. For this reason we have created a number of so called 'peer processes.'
> - Peer groups are established to share know-how around specific communities.
> - Peer reviews expose specific business unit behaviors to the challenge and scrutiny of others.
> - Peer assists are used at the professional, specialist level to make sure the right know-how gets to the right place at the right time."

John Leggate is BP's vice-president for digital business and he's been instrumental in pursuing John Browne's vision of a "knowledge-based company." He's committed c. $250m on initiatives to network employees. Everyone's been equipped with Net-linked laptops, and the web-based employee directory "Connect" has become the principle means for information sharing. It contains not only a "who's who" of experts around the world but detailed data on their projects and lessons learned.

BP executives now point to a number of examples of cost reduction *and* revenue gain due to effective knowledge sharing, and it would seem the investment payback for the company is substantial. Examples include engineers in the Caribbean saving $600k by adopting a drilling process developed in Norway, reducing drilling costs on a new well by an estimated $45m by identifying the key BP experts right at the start of the project, and speeding up project management by coordinating teams virtually instead of flying people in from all over the world.

Aside from the obvious commitment of the CEO and his whole group, the BP case study provides many other examples of how to make a knowledge-sharing exercise work.

- Direct personal contact is needed to effectively transfer the implicit knowledge within people's heads.
- "Moving documents around" is necessary but by itself won't engender the subsequent team collaboration that builds human capital and makes innovation possible.
- In the early days, appointing people accountable and responsible for making the sharing work is important.
- Allow time and provide budgets for "peering" for cross unit knowledge sharing activities; some BP execs reckon they spend c.15–20% of their time doing that.
- "Pass the torch," engender a culture where there's a feeling of obligation to keep this environment alive, pass on learning and ensure others can continue to access it.

Inside BP there are a large number of peer groups and communities sharing knowledge. One such group is the health, safety and environment (HSE) team. There is an HSE web site that now provides a focal point for all issues in that area. On the site is an "HSE Toolbar" available to all the staff. It provides details of good practices. It identifies the network of staff responsible for each management process. There is a self-assessment tool enabling different sites to check how their performance compares and identify what they might do to improve it. New lessons leaned from any incident are drawn out in new reports with the aim of immediate cross-company communication.

Some commentators have extrapolated from the BP story and have coined the term the "T-shaped manager." The essence here is simple. It's about an organisation that demands functional expertise and specialist skills but at the same time wants its experts to step out of the silo and share, meet with peers, be part of a community and take responsibility for building a knowledge company.

Let's take one further illustration from a completely different environment and with a very specific KM application. The company is Torex Meditel. It's a small but highly profitable UK-based company designing, supplying and supporting computer-based management systems. Its Meditel team focusses on hospitals, doctors and the health care arena generally. It supports over 3000 doctors' surgeries across the country with a range of patient record systems and link ups with the National Health Service's NHS Net.

As Meditel grew the sales/marketing director Dominic Monkhouse realised he needed more information. He had a field-based sales force and tech team across the country but he could not easily get information on where the teams were and what they were doing. In addition, any knowledge about the customer was randomly collected and not reliable. People complained about not having enough data to do their job but the organisation was still relying on paper-based records.

Meditel decided to build a customer information web portal and used an Onyx Front Office solution to provide an enterprise-wide, customer-centric e-business application. Alongside the new system was a detailed reworking of the customer information processes, defining what information was needed in what form and how it should be shared.

A first step was to get the sales and tech team to share their customer knowledge.

"What got them to do this was the ease of the online environment. They suddenly realised that instead of printing off and lugging around three-inch thick reports, they could just access the customer's entire history online. Once they began to get the benefits out for themselves they became really quite enthusiastic about regularly updating the data, creating a one-stop knowledge base."

Meditel are getting significant value out of this initiative but Monkhouse emphasises:

"while the technology is really easy to use you can't just throw a computer in front of people and expect them to change the way they work. Particularly when you're asking them to share information. We had to involve the whole sales force in the process from the start, build ownership, make it easy and be sure there were clearly defined benefits."

As these case studies show, there is a way to go about knowledge sharing to be sure to capture the benefits. This learning can be distilled into a simple four-step framework that any organisation could adopt (Figure 8.4).

Figure 8.4 Four steps to knowledge sharing

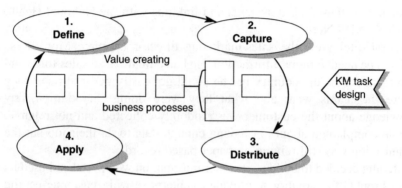

Source: Fraunhofer, Blumberg

Step 1 is to define what knowledge is required, what's actually going to be helpful from the platform of data and information that could be potentially captured.

Too often this step is overlooked as organisations rush to build knowledge management systems to share apparently anything and everything. There is real payback from investing time and effort at this early stage in defining the priorities. No reason of course why eventually the KM system will not be totally comprehensive but recall BP's five to six year journey and recognise, as Dominic Monkhouse discovered, that there's significant training and support required to change processes and behaviors, get the system used and kept alive.

In fact some argue that even before this "definition" step there is a more general awareness-building about "information literacy." This not only gets the organisation aware of the possible value and benefits of sharing knowledge but also checks the extent to which people have the skills and competencies to participate and contribute. Some will struggle to see the wood from the trees and may need general training and guidance around what's important and what's not. To be "information literate" a person must recognise when information is needed and have the ability to locate, evaluate and use that information effectively.

To facilitate that process appointing a CKO, a Chief Knowledge Officer, or equivalent to take the lead can be important. It invariably needs a relatively senior individual in the company in the early days to be the catalyst and enabler, to identify where the company is on its KM journey and what initiatives need to take place to gather interest and momentum.

CKOs themselves have been a fragile group in recent times. Many were appointed in the e-hype and have since departed or been reassigned, but those who have survived acknowledge the big challenge of getting this whole area of opportunity high enough on agendas to merit enough attention. Survivors also talk about the need to be sensitive about the words "knowledge management." In some companies, projects were started on KM when it first came to attention in the mid-1990s, but they have since failed and so the opportunity needs to be reintroduced carefully and sometimes with different labels and descriptions as we read earlier. Pilot projects, small teams, early wins, effective metrics to stimulate interest e.g. comparing new product time to market with that of rivals are all necessary ingredients for getting the program launched successfully. "Getting people to think about it on their own terms and realising how it could help them personally is the trick."

Step 2 of this knowledge management process is also crucial, for it's about locating and converting indispensable chunks of knowledge that can directly help the company work more effectively. Some "chunks" are going to be more difficult to capture than others, and again it will be important to evaluate the value of the knowledge against the complexity of capturing its essence in a meaningful form. One way of assessing this is to plot out all the possible areas of knowledge capture (see Figure 8.5).

This sort of analysis can help the organisation map out a sequence that can deliver some early wins before embarking upon some of the knowledge management topics that are more valuable but at the same time much more challenging to capture.

Step 3, "Distribute," is getting the right knowledge to the right person at the right time. The Internet has helped enormously here because it's providing a common language that's therefore in principle distributable to everyone.

Companies like Toshiba and Dell have very much embraced this "right knowledge right time" philosophy and a good example comes from Toshiba's component assembly lines. As employees in each cell assemble

Figure 8.5 Prioritising knowledge capture: example

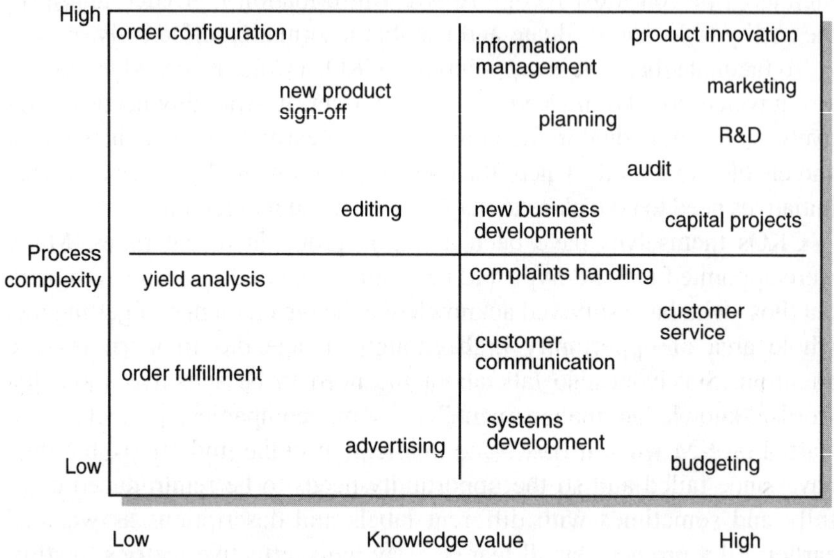

Source: Fraunhofer, Eppler

computers, an easily readable screen pushes perfectly timed step-by-step instructions, tips and advice out to them. Such timely information is critical for productivity and Toshiba instituted a lengthy program of studying the assembly process for possible knowledge gaps where workers would need guidance to carry out the task most efficiently. The resulting system is updated both by technicians and also by the employees themselves who are encouraged to add further tips (though the system is then edited). The result is an assembly line that moves without delay and one of the most productive company processes.

Other organisations have implemented "help desks" online that are geared to provide interactive help just when the employee needs it. For example Microsoft continues to develop its Office Suite of products and the software is tuned to identify triggers (e.g. delays, errors) when the help option might be required. Sometime it's a bit too helpful! but the principle of getting knowledge when it's most needed is the right one and Microsoft developers have dedicated teams continuing to study user profiles and experience so as to fine tune its help.

One other example here is to examine how Southwestern Bell, the US telco, manages "right time" knowledge distribution. The company recognised it had lots of customer data but it only became valuable if it could be available to their call operators immediately they needed it. In an effort to go further and anticipate the need, the company set up a process to match customer data to incoming customer calls. Now when the call is received, the system automatically retrieves the caller number, matches it to a customer ID and puts all the customer data on the call operator's screen: payment history, bad debts, call patterns, phone options etc. This gives the impression Southwestern Bell is in command of its customer services and improves the whole customer experience.

Applying the knowledge once it's defined, captured and made available or distributed is the fourth and final step in the process. For many this is about training. It's about showing people how to access the knowledge and where it can be applied to add value.

Dell starts with its employees even before they've formally started their job. Its aim is to send people as much information as possible so they can learn and hit the ground running once they do start. Taking advantage of the Net, Dell has established a series of interactive training courses which enable people to self-learn and self-certify. It's optional in the pre-start period but not surprisingly an increasing number take advantage to give themselves a head start.

The Limited, Inc waits till employees start, but to get them thinking about applying the available knowledge the Limited has a series of "fun" training programs. Examples include "Lingo Bingo" to learn relevant buzzwords and company concepts. There's also an adapted game of "Jeopardy" to learn and test knowledge of financial and other performance metrics.

"We want to build a deep understanding of our business. For example there's a lot of learning we've built up on merchandising and layout and we want everyone to apply it. We find it takes less than a 2% increase in productivity to generate a 100% return on knowledge training."

In looking at organisations that have demonstrably gone through the "Define, Capture, Distribute and Apply" framework, IBM provides an excellent illustration. It has worked hard to engage the workforce in knowledge capture and ensure its exploitation.

At the last count IBM had around 300,000 employees and was divided into a number of different business units all over the world. Over the past three years it has gradually established a knowledge-sharing infrastructure.

- An Intranet site for fast news flow, document sharing, distribution of "white papers" for comment, presentations available etc.
- An Internet site drawing specified information from the intranet and representing that for clients.
- A quarterly hardcopy newsletter providing company-wide news, list of achievements, announcements etc.
- Newsgroups where shared communities of interest can share learning online.
- Set conference calls built around functional grouping or business units for Q&A and news sharing.
- Global "ShareNet" forums, again for specified communities of interest, where participants meet semi-annually in two or three-day conferences. The aim is to share experiences and ideas, get in outside speakers to stimulate developments on certain topics and capture learning.

In building this infrastructure, IBM first of all went through a process to define what information was critical to drive and improve the company's competitiveness. Initially they found it difficult to get people to participate and contribute. They found themselves in a situation which Peter Drucker has described: "in the knowledge economy we want everyone to be a volunteer, but we are forced to train our people and we end up with conscripts. The real issue then is turning these conscripts back into volunteers."

For IBM this meant they had to complement their definition process with some structured planning around how to encourage knowledge capture, how to ensure that knowledge was distributed at the right time and how to train people to use and apply it consistently. This led to the establishment in the early phases of the work of a core team in each "community" area who would take responsibility for structure and maintaining the knowledge base, making it available, developing methodologies for ongoing experience capture, and constantly communicating to users what was available and how it could be applied.

The goal has been to get knowledge sharing institutionalised. In so large a company it's recognised that use and application will vary and IBM has experimented with a number of incentives. The one that has proved to work best is an "awards program" that offers up to $500 for more active users.

IBM staffers will say it's not always easy to claim that a particular cost saving initiative or new customer win for example only came about because of the knowledge sharing infrastructure. But a recent internal survey showed that on average it used to take five days to discover existing intellectual capital within IBM, while now it seems that's down to a "matter of hours and sometimes minutes."

Technology literate companies like IBM and PA Consulting have been leaders in capitalising on their own learning in putting together effective knowledge management systems. One idea that both organisations have developed – and they've been joined by many others now – is that a company starting down this path should think about the opportunity in terms of a "corporate or employee portal."

On the one hand this is just a simple concept, but on the other hand it recognises both the attraction of the Internet as the place for sharing information and also the value of building a place or "portal" for people with common interests to visit and belong to. As "corporate/employee portals" will become increasingly popular as the "knowledge management" vehicle, the concept is worth some further explanation.

Think of it as an in-house Yahoo! with embedded links to all the company's various applications. It's a web site for employees but importantly each employee can receive or create a customised view as well as use the portal for routine e-mail and data transfer. Typically these portals do start with that basic functionality and then expand to include additional features, e.g. desktop procurement. They also recognise that particular community groupings will be a powerful force to encourage usage. Using the Internet, the portal can provide an integrated single point of entry to all business applications with single sign-on and consistent user interface. It can also of course incorporate the necessary search, retrieval, storage and application tools to establish a knowledge community with all the appropriate links.

Novartis, the global pharmaceutical company headquartered in Switzerland, chose this approach to provide its knowledge management solutions. It wanted to create a "Strategic Knowledge" system for its senior executives as an immediate priority with a web-browser based interface. That would enable it to draw from a wide range of data formats but the system also had to be "user friendly" for senior execs who weren't necessarily using their PC every day!

Novartis used a software solution from a leading knowledge management firm, Autonomy, and chose their "portal-in-a-box" solution. This provided an automated infrastructure for the handling and personalisation of the complex sets of information that needed to be drawn on. The information consisted of both external research and market intelligence as well as internal reports. The system had to aggregate and personalise an enormous amount of content, without incurring large labor costs. The relevant data would need to be "tagged" so it could be captured, but also constantly updated to provide timely insights.

The "portal-in-a-box" was therefore set up to deliver:

- automated content aggregation and navigation
- automatic categorisation of content into specific channels, e.g. "Novartis in the Press", "Competitor News"
- personalised content based on profiling users habits
- identified community of interests: "did you know Joe has also asked for that information recently?"
- information alert which tells users when information of a particular type is being delivered to them (it doesn't rely only on search).

Novartis say that until this solution "handling vast amounts of information cost us a great deal of time and money. Now the process has been automated the costs are way down and we seem to be getting the information we want."

So is your organisation ready to take advantage of what appear to be the substantial benefits available through an *effective* KM program? Drawing on the lessons learned from the case studies described here and elsewhere, we can set out an audit check and questionnaire on the state of the organisation.

There are ten key questions. The basic answer is yes or no but the answer can be scored out of 10, where 0 is a very firm negative and 10 a very firm positive. If the organisation score is less than 35, the implication is that it needs to start right back at the pre-definition stage and examine the "information literacy" of the company, its general attitudes towards KM and its ability today to extract any benefits from investment in this area. In such circumstances it's back to the lessons set out in the chapter on "Getting started," and may even require some significant awareness-building, networking and "champion-building" before any significant exercise can begin.

If the score is 65 or more, then that would suggest the organisation knows what knowledge sharing is about, has had some good experiences to build on and is keen to leverage that and achieve a more systematic and institutionalised solution.

Scores between 35 and 65 imply there are still some roadblocks around and, while the program can begin, prioritising what "knowledge" to capture and establishing a sequence of early wins before tackling the hard stuff may be important steps to build the necessary momentum.

The ten key audit questions are:

Knowledge Management – Audit	Score 0–10
1. Has the company had any success with knowledge sharing in a formal way?	——
2. Has that success been clearly quantified in terms of cost savings or revenue gains?	——
3. Do people recognise that company performance has improved from knowledge sharing?	——
4. Do people want to share their knowledge?	——
5. Are there established community groups that regularly get together to swap info/insights?	——
6. Are there in place formal mechanisms for sharing best practices and lessons learned across the company?	——
7. Is there a unified intranet environment (as opposed to each business/function having its own)?	——
8. Is the intranet used consistently and regularly by more than 80% of employees for things other than simple e-mail?	——
9. Is there a big enough group of people across the organisation who want to take KM to the next phase?	——
10. Is the company prepared to invest at a reasonably significant level in funds and resources to secure those potential KM gains?	——

To add further perspective to this score, it's possible to start benchmarking the scores with those of others. At a simple level this could be a comparison across business units in the same corporation. But perhaps even more enlightening would be a comparison with rival companies. Even a guesstimated score can be revealing in suggesting where your organisation may stand. For example both BP's and Shell's KM successes have been written up and it's at once possible for other energy/oil and gas companies to compare where they are and examine the extent they are ahead of or behind the leading players. Such straightforward analysis can be the initial rallying cry; the company needs to push it on to the next stage of development and progress.

Another tool is to examine the organisation's strengths and weaknesses in various KM areas and use that as a diagnostic tool and catalyst for change. Here you might score 4 for strong, 0 for weak. 4 is the outer band, 0 is the inner. You might find a pattern as illustrated in Figure 8.6.

Figure 8.6 Organisation KM strengths and weaknesses

This simple snapshot can be used as much as anything as a communication device to show people in one frame that for example "new product development" information sharing may be excellent (score 4) but access to relevant "strategic information" (see Novartis) is at best average (score 2) while "project knowledge" sharing (score only 1) is weak.

These sorts of audits and diagnostics might be required to kick-start an organisation into effective knowledge management. For all the case studies described here, these "better practice" companies remain the exceptions rather than the rule. Most will either pay lip service to the concept or be struggling to get people to actually use the system. It's important to emphasise, like many of these e-business transforming/streamlining examples, that success does not come overnight, that it is a journey, that it requires piloting and testing and careful program management to build up momentum, bring on the doubters and skeptics and start establishing KM as a corporate-wide asset that demonstrably delivers value.

We'll end this chapter with a reminder of the benefits and also describe one of the more innovative solutions for knowledge sharing. The benefits recap is drawn from research on capitalising on knowledge by David Skyrme.

- **Faster access to knowledge:** for example American Management Systems estimates its consultants now find the info they need eight times faster using the firm's knowledge centers.

- **Better knowledge sharing:** Xerox estimate that their web knowledge sharing has generated 5000 useful tips per month from its field engineers.

- **Cost savings:** ChevronTexaco credits knowledge sharing as an important contribution to saving $200m in energy costs.

- **Cost avoidance:** Texas Instruments reckon to have avoided building a new plant (cost $500m +) by sharing best practices to improve line utilisation.

- **Increased knowledge:** Chase Manhattan claim better customer knowledge has resulted in stronger relationships and more profitable customers.

- **Productivity gains:** BP reduced a refinery shut-down time by nine days saving c. $10m by sharing of lessons learnt from different projects.

Netherlands Police Agency

Finally, the Netherlands National Police Agency. This organisation has made dramatic strides in nabbing lawbreakers, finding stolen cars, intercepting potential troublemakers and having immediate access to information on people and vehicles. They had information in many different databases; how could it all be captured and better exploited?

The key for them lies in a mobile technology solution using an e-network wireless gateway. It's been developed by IBM to give the police real time access to all the key enforcement databases. It works directly from a "ruggedised" laptop installed in the police car. Within seconds they can access all the information on criminal records, drivers' licenses, car tax, ID papers, vehicle registrations etc.

Before this the Dutch police had to phone in their requests into a dispatch room and it could easily take ten minutes or more to get an answer on any given query, and even then information was incomplete and often found to be inaccurate. This meant, for example, that each patrol car could perform just ten vehicle checks per shift. With the new system this has gone up ten-fold to 100 or even 150. The increased capacity has led to a corresponding rise in arrests and a much more effective border control.

At the police end, radio modems are used to link police cruisers with the wireless network. At the host end, software has been used to enable the disparate databases on the police mainframe to understand messages conveyed over the Internet in the standard Net TCP/IP language, meaning no need to rewrite all the legacy applications. The middleware solution performs the critical function of linking the web interface while at the same time providing secure identification of users. It also includes software to compress data, reducing "packet size" and so speeding up transmission. There's also a live technical back-up so that if there are any communication problems they can be quickly resolved.

This initiative was never described as "knowledge management" but its key was information and data access and effective use. It first started out in test in 1997 but it paid for itself within one week by identifying motorists who hadn't paid their road tax. Because of its real time application, police were given power to extract fines and payment on the spot and this brought a "flood of funds" into the police treasury.

Today the system is widespread but it did require a programmed roll-out: "equipping the cars and then training the police officers did take investment but we are converted data users – we've put a lot of effort into defining what was needed, making sure it worked and teaching how to apply it and now we've got the results."

9 Streamlining in CRM

Customers now expect! They *expect* things to happen quickly and they *demand* high levels of service, attention and care. They want things now and there is close to zero tolerance for delays and mistakes. If one company can't provide then usually there's another round the corner only too willing to snap up the business and quite often at a lower price.

These expectations and demands have been fueled generally by developments in technology and particularly by the Internet. The fact of the matter is that in most industry environments now there is at least one increasingly streamlined player who has raised the game and set a standard in customer service. Not only does that become the benchmark in that sector but it spills over into all others.

Take Amazon as an example. They reckon they've had over 35 million shoppers across the world. These people have experienced "one-click ordering," fast processing, personalisation and recommendations, e-mail responsiveness, 24-hour delivery and a business service that's reliable, user-friendly and works. And that's 35 million people who now expect this, and they expect it not just on books but on any other packaged good they might choose to buy virtually anywhere else. And they expect this not just on the Net but also through a physical store. Once good customer service is built people quite naturally want that repeated time and time again.

Similar customer service trend setters can be found in a variety of industries: among airlines we get Southwest Airlines and Easyjet – it's fun, it's simple, it works; in transportation, we've seen the significant initiatives taken by Fedex and more recently UPS; in retailing, companies like Nordstrom and 7-Eleven (in Japan) have set standards in service and fast response; in software development, Microsoft continues to push ahead in terms of reliability and frequency of upgrade; in service to OEMs on parts and components, Grainger has stolen a lead with its breadth of coverage and customer responsiveness.

While these may be some of the leaders today their market position is constantly under threat. No company anywhere has yet got customer service to such a consistently high standard that it can rest on its laurels (always dangerous!) or be regarded as uncatchable. There's continuous development by all competitors looking to undermine the leader, take share or develop new approaches.

We've already discussed such breakthrough pioneers as Progressive Insurance (20-minute roadside settlement), Herman Miller (two-week custom-built furniture), Dell ("build to order"), Moen (new products to market down from six months to six weeks), Tesco (same day grocery delivery at a pre-planned time); we're seeing governments like those in Singapore and Finland serving their "customers" by committing to a 100% wired-up economy and "always-on" internet environment, and organisations like WellsFargo, Citi and First Direct lead the way in 24/7/365 financial services delivery.

Now the new buzzword is "CRM": customer relationship management. With the advent of the Internet we are told that there are now many new ways to forge customer relationships, beat out apparently better placed rivals and secure that long term customer franchise and contract. New software developers (there are by some accounts nearly 500 in the CRM arena) have come onto the scene promoting the latest piece of software that will bring all these benefits and provide the "in-the-box" solution that seems so attractive. And there are as many firms of system integrators who believe they can do all this quickly – but not yet cheaply!

So what's the underlying reality here? Organisations have been looking to build customer relationships for years. Does the Internet in fact enable new things to be done and done better, and is there something to CRM that is indeed worth considering and evaluating? These are key questions because talk of CRM has to be set into a particular context: that is, that most CRM implementations since its commercialisation in 1999 have failed. They've just not yet delivered the promised benefits. So if there is something around Net technology in this arena then we need to understand its application carefully and look to identify the lessons learned from those implementations that have failed, as well as those that have been successful.

To set the scene for this chapter, we'll examine then a number of areas:

- overview of what is going on
- the benefits that *are* being achieved
- the proper strategic context
- technology impact
- vendors and tools
- key ingredients for success.

Overview

Despite the apparent implementation difficulties (Gartner estimate more than 50% are seen as failures!), such is the need to try to strengthen relationships with customers in these competitive economic times that it's predicted that spending on CRM-related software, hardware and services will rise from around $20bn in 2002 to as much as $60bn by 2005! (The $20bn appears to be a realistic figure as it's been estimated separately by a number of research houses and consultancies.) So this level of activity may be spurred on by hype but it looks set to continue at a significant pace.

One of the reasons why the spend is so high is that CRM can encompass many things. At one level it's simply the direct front-end interface with the customer and so it may be nothing more than a simple solution to help the sales team collect market data. But at another level it can involve almost the entire go-to-market process and go back into sales department admin and support, marketing, stock movement and availability in warehousing and transportation, order processing and go forward to include activities such as billing, query handling and after sales service and contact.

Figure 9.1 CRM value chain

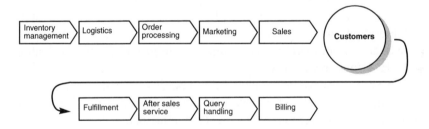

Because of the sheer scope of CRM, one of the growing recognitions is that it is inappropriate to tackle the whole value chain in one go. Far better to do something we've already advocated here, which is to evaluate areas of leverage and define priorities. Start with a piece that can deliver some quick win:wins before tackling the meatier and more challenging chunks.

We'll consider a number of case studies on how companies are getting started in this space and where they are focussing. But research is already highlighting a few areas of greater potential. These would include:

- personalising service and contact
- putting customers in control
- capturing info to support the sales call
- segmenting customers, e.g. into most profitable/least profitable
- putting together a single real time view of the state of the customer relationship.

Before we go further, let's consider a few examples where organisations have started off with relatively simple CRM solutions:

- Provident Central Credit Union is a 50 year old west coast US company providing credit, lending and financial services to some 100,000 members. It has assets of just under $1bn.

  The company wanted to build its market share but needed to do so with relatively limited investment funds. The company also already had a good customer service reputation but wanted to strengthen that. One of its problems was that its legacy transaction system did not give it a holistic single view of its current members. There were two call centers each recording information separately, and there was no means to identify easily past customer transactions and potential new services to offer.

  This was a relatively simple case. It was clear that the solution lay in consolidating the two centers to provide a single point of contact for new and existing clients. While this involved some legacy system integration, it was built around a Microsoft Windows NT-based phone/web communication system and used CRM software called Front Office from Onyx.

  Now as soon as the member ID number is captured on the call, the Provident service rep has screen access to member information, account data and the *complete* transaction history.

  Provident took a step which is fairly straightforward and focussed, but that simple call center consolidation and real time information updating has enabled the company to revolutionise customer service. "We now sell $12m of loans each month, up from $3m, real estate loans have also increased and there's been a 30% drop in the admin costs."
- Nantucket Nectars, the "juice guys," are soft drinks manufacturers with a quirky reputation for innovation and packaging. They have come a long way since their early days and now distribute around the world.

However with that have come problems. "We'd reached a point where we were in desperate straits. Our customers, who are mostly small beverage distributors, were getting very upset. We just couldn't get them the information or the products they needed. We had great manufacturing and a fantastic sales/marketing team but customer order management was a big problem."

After considerable review, Drew Farris, the company's IT director, decided that their current IT environment just wasn't up to it and they decided upon a Net-based solution on top of Oracle database management.

Nantucket Nectars now have in place "Nector Net." Both the sales team and customers can log on via the net. Customers can check on order status, while the sales team can see exactly what's been ordered. Everyone in the supply chain has access to the information on when it will be delivered.

"Our legacy system was an older tool and just stopping us moving into a more customer friendly Internet.... It was a difficult decision to move to a completely new IT environment but in our case it's worked."

- Moray Council is a local city council in Scotland. It's situated in the north-east with some 85,000 residents, covering a large area but with a fairly small population. Like all councils, it's responsible to its residents for services around housing, education, health, environment, social benefits, roads, leisure etc.

Moray wanted to know what services it was offering to which resident and how well it was doing. "We've some residents getting services they shouldn't be (e.g. social welfare abuse) and we've others not receiving services they should." If levels of service were appropriate and if it had one view of all its "customers," how much more efficient could it become? Could it reduce costs for example by having one common customer record instead of employing different people in each department to maintain separate records?

Moray turned to Siebel's e-service applications to help capture the customer data and consolidate it into one customer record accessible to all. Now when there is interaction by phone, web, by mail or in person, there is a multi-channel single customer view. In addition there is a web-based "self-service" environment where residents can submit planning applications, update their own records and track where their communication is in the system.

"Basically we've transformed things here; customers know who to contact, know where they are and so get the best service/response; we can process more enquiries and do it more efficiently, we can monitor our service levels, allocate resources to demand.... And all because we've captured a single view of what's going on with our customers."

CRM applications are now being found right across the value chain. As we arc sccing in the case studies, it's quickly become apparent that the web is an ideal medium. It enables those integrated communications to take place as described at Moray and Provident and at Nantucket Nectars. It enables one to one communication and therefore more personalised interaction (discussed later in the chapter). It provides lower cost solutions, for example encouraging investment in automated FAQ (frequently asked questions) procedures online to take pressure off call centers and reduce costs there. It provides a universal medium to gather and share information about customers that can be analysed to provide insight and identify future call/sell opportunities. It can link frontline staff operating in different locations and with wireless applications give mobility and as well connect up travelling sales people (see Figure 9.2).

While managing customer relations, building loyalty, improving communication and service have been around since the birth of commerce thousands of years ago, CRM in its current guise began around the early 1990s when companies such as Digital, IBM and Wang variously set up projects to get better information exchange between the field technicians and the sales team. They began to move out of exchanging bits of paper and into e-mail and automated reports. This early form of "field sales support" is still a very important area for CRM-type initiatives. But it has now, like other early-form automated customer links, migrated into things like browser-equipped phones and laptops that can integrate with large database systems via virtual private networks.

As all-encompassing as CRM appears to be it is nevertheless quite feasible to start small and in one area. While many of the software vendors will talk of big investment costs (*Business 2.0* magazine esti-mates set-up costs in a call center can run as high as $40,000 per salesperson!), nevertheless with the level of competition amongst suppliers it is possible to start much less expensively (see later case studies). Certainly pilot and test is the key watchword at this stage and it will be vital for any program to be able to identify the benefits and see them coming through. It's also worth emphasising here that the software by itself is of course not the answer. It's everything that will have to go around it – the people training, the processes, the behaviors – that will distinguish the success stories.

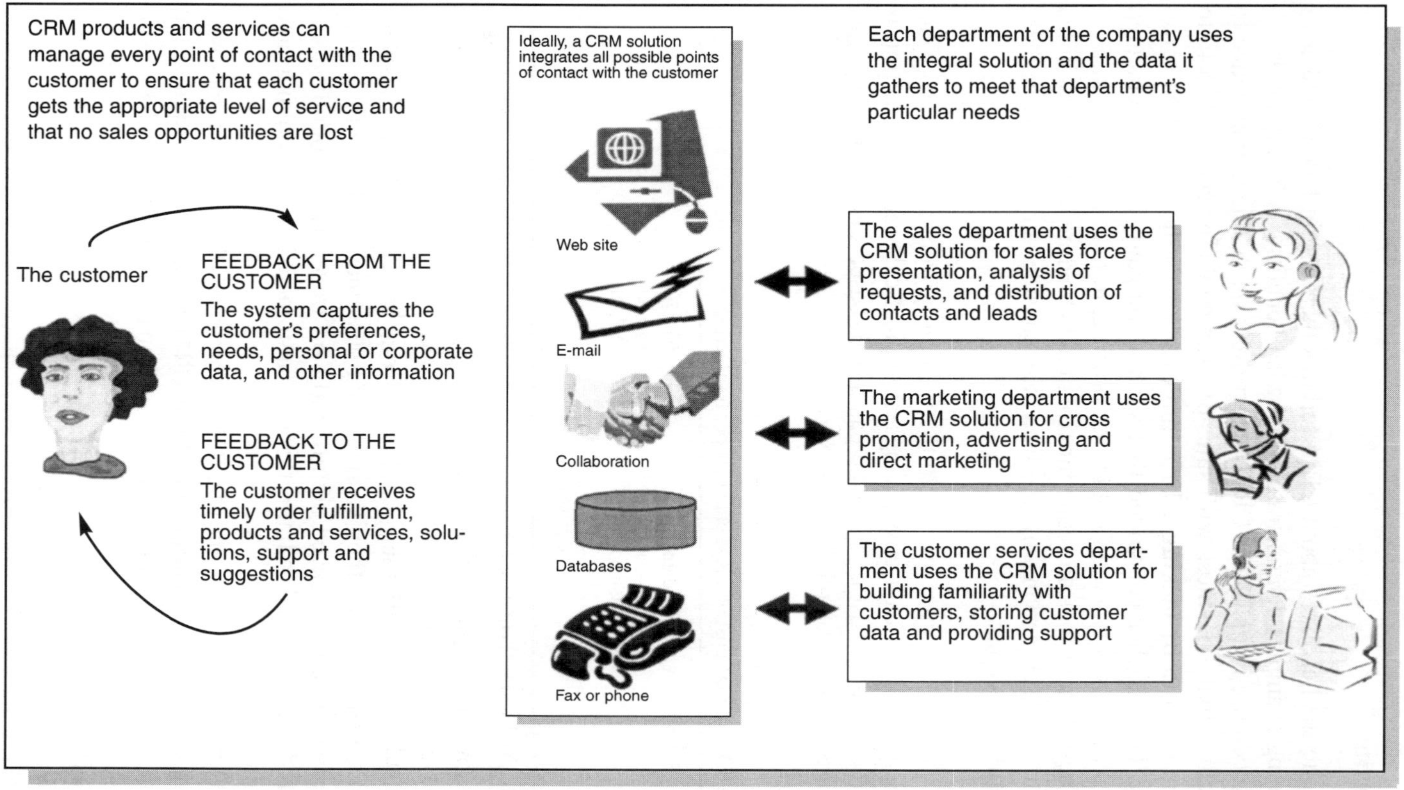

CRM products and services can manage every point of contact with the customer to ensure that each customer gets the appropriate level of service and that no sales opportunities are lost

Each department of the company uses the integral solution and the data it gathers to meet that department's particular needs

The customer

FEEDBACK FROM THE CUSTOMER

The system captures the customer's preferences, needs, personal or corporate data, and other information

FEEDBACK TO THE CUSTOMER

The customer receives timely order fulfillment, products and services, solutions, support and suggestions

Ideally, a CRM solution integrates all possible points of contact with the customer

Web site

E-mail

Collaboration

Databases

Fax or phone

The sales department uses the CRM solution for sales force presentation, analysis of requests, and distribution of contacts and leads

The marketing department uses the CRM solution for cross promotion, advertising and direct marketing

The customer services department uses the CRM solution for building familiarity with customers, storing customer data and providing support

Figure 9.2 CRM in action
Source: *PC Magazine*

Benefits

Despite the headlines about CRM failures there are in fact a number of winning examples demonstrating just what benefits can be captured.

Accenture in its recent CRM report drew on its client experience to conclude that a business with sales of $1bn could expect to add $40 to $50m in profit by making a 10% improvement in the core CRM activities. They further concluded that such a company, if it implemented CRM aggressively, could treble that profit gain to at least $120m.

These conclusions do sound far-reaching but before they get dismissed as further "self-serving hype," let's just consider in what areas these benefits can come:

- Moving customer queries to the web away from the call center can lead to significant cost savings. A typical call center interaction is reckoned to cost c. $35 whereas a web-based one might only cost around $2 (research by Gartner *et al.*).

Table 9.1 Average cost of CRM channels per transaction

Telephone	$34.70
E-mail	$10.00
Chat	$7.80
Message board	$4.50
Web self-service	$1.77

Source: RightNow Technologies

- In migrating all their bookings from travel agents to the web, Easyjet reckoned they've improved customer service with a more direct interface, saved significantly on travel agent commissions, reduced internal admin through automated web booking and increased sales.
- Oracle give the example of CRM investment as the source of improved direct marketing campaigns. "Pre-CRM we had a 2% response but now we build customer profiles based on our interaction with them on the Net and our response on direct marketing is up to 20%. We get more sales and our 'cost per customer' falls correspondingly. It's down from around $2 to 25 cents."
- HMV, the CD/DVD retailer, reckon to have a 20% rise in repeat orders

over the web due to better customer knowledge following a CRM exercise.

- McAfee, the virus protection software provider, put effort into migrating call center calls to the web and reduced the number of call center requests by 50%.
- A survey by research house Doculabs studied over 3.5 million customer service requests made to 202 companies over the Net and found that those who had deployed automated CRM systems saved more than $100,000 on average per quarter, and that 86.9% of "self-service" web calls were handled satisfactorily without the need for follow-up through alternative channels.
- Reichheld and Sasser, pioneers in research on loyalty-building, have shown that customer service initiatives that build loyalty can have a dramatic effect. They found that a 5% increase in loyalty could lead to 25%plus increase in profitability. A similar study by PriceWaterhouse Coopers suggests that as little as a 2% increase in customer retention can have the same impact as a 10% reduction in overhead!
- Ford estimate that each one point gain in owner loyalty/repeat purchasing is worth $100m in profit.
- Gap found that its repeat customers online spent on average 57% more than first time customers.

There are plenty of examples then that suggest CRM initiatives must be worth exploring. What's worth emphasising is that there's plenty that can be done however even *before* the organisation gets to the technology solution.

Figure 9.3 Retaining customers

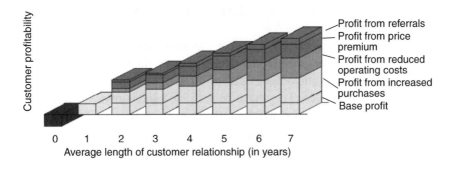

The strategic context

Few would argue about the "importance of the customer," about "putting the customer first," about building "customer intimacy," "locking the customer in," "building loyalty" etc. But for an organisation to really capture advantage and benefit out of more effective customer relations, that organisation has to be "hungry" to win that customer's respect and commitment. Before it gets to the technology it's got to have a deep-rooted passion to deliver levels of customer service that courses through every employee. It's after all the front line staff who deliver.

Anita Roddick, when founding the Body Shop in the 1980s, best captured this need:

> "I want to create an electricity and passion that bonds people to the company and to our customers. You have to find ways to grab people's imagination. You want them to feel they are doing something important, that their own actions will make a difference to how customers feel."

Walmart is another organisation that right from its early days has put the customer first (and second and third!). Sam Walton famously used to gather groups of his employees together and together they made the "Walmart promise":

> "Now I want you to raise your right hand and remember what we say at Walmart – a promise we make is a promise we keep and I want you to say after me: 'from this day forward, I solemnly promise that every time a customer comes within 10 feet of me, I will smile, look the customer in the eye and greet that person, so help me Sam.'"

It's still just a handful of organisations that have really broken through the complacency and lip service that often surrounds customer service (Figure 9.4). They have turned it into something exciting where the basics are in place, product and delivery are reliable, and they're looking to genuinely exceed expectations.

The companies that are reaching out to "delight their customers" are realising they also have to create a culture among their staff where each individual recognises and believes that his or her own personal contribution can make the difference. They have been trained and convinced that what they do and how they do it will directly result in extra growth and profitability. Each customer kept happy is likely to stay loyal; each customer lost is revenue and profit out of the door.

Figure 9.4 Developing customer services

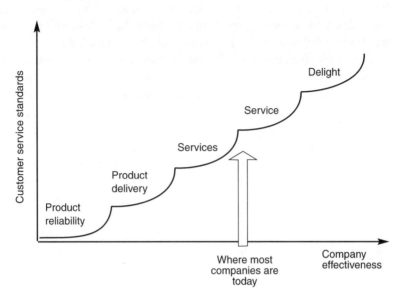

Turn to a company's annual report. Does it mention the customer? Some organisations (and it's especially retailers) like Nordstrom, Walmart and Tesco are sufficiently customer-centric that their reports talk loudly about employee and customer service. Amazon.com will say that their success ultimately will be nothing to do with their Internet-based business model. It will come down to how good their service is. Amazon deliberately encourage a culture of going the extra mile for your customers. Employees who demonstrably do that are recognised, talked about and rewarded.

It's against this kind of strategic commitment to customer service that any CRM initiative must be set. Without this hunger, passion and commitment, the investment and initiative *may* pay back but will never deliver the type of benefits people like Reicheld and Sasser identify.

Many dot.coms failed because they talked rather too grandiosely about building relationships with customers that would deliver "lifetime value." They built their business models on the back of aggressive assumptions not just of how many customers they would win but also about how long they'd keep them. The concept of "customer lifetime value" or CLV took on new resonance during that Internet boom period:

(1) Number of customers x (2) average $ purchases per year
x (3) number of years as a customer

Of course these three key components were highly sensitive to driving up business plans, returns and valuations. Even Amazon now quietly concedes that some of the more high-pitched assumptions – which justified a $40bn market cap – were probably unjustifiable.

This CLV formula nevertheless is useful because it forces a CRM ambitious company to think hard now about these three areas and review just how many customers it can realistically hope to attract, how many it can keep, and among those loyal ones just how it can go about boosting levels of spend. This means researching and understanding customer behavior, customer likes and dislikes and customers' reasons for buying and for switching supplier. It means doing some analysis to segment the potential customer universe and to identify just which ones can be targeted, and indeed which ones are worth going after.

In every market environment it's invariably the case that up to 80% of prospective customers are barely profitable and not worth pursuing while the core 20% or so are the most desirable (Figure 9.5). Identifying that 20% is a useful starting point!

To illustrate let's consider how the airline industry reacted to recent global turmoil. Post September 11 2001, many airlines were forced to contact their customers quickly to explain and reassure. From a purely

Figure 9.5 Customer portfolio evaluation: example

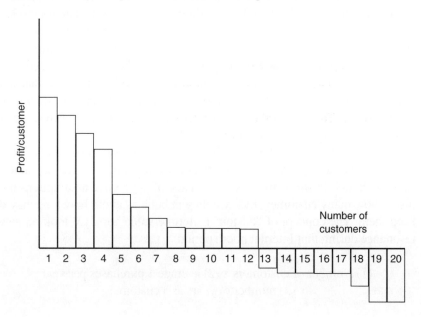

business perspective it was also important to identify who were the frequent flyers and from which airports, so travelers out of Boston say might need very different messages from travelers out of Paris.

A McKinsey report just after September 11 concludes that most airlines in fact have no idea of the value of an individual customer to them, and often have limited profiling information of any real commercial use. On the other hand a few, such as British Airways and Air France, could identify to a 60–70% accuracy level the lifetime value – up to date – of their customers, what their travel needs were and so how best to communicate to them. The report pointed out that an effective "Customer Relationship" system would identify for example those who were brand loyal, price switchers, service switchers, regular flyers, even those who were nervous flyers or had special needs.

British Airways appears to be the leader here. It has an integrated worldwide database with details of all 8.5 million of its passengers. All customer records are being consolidated and so customer profiling, profitable versus unprofitable customers and tailored "one to one" marketing and communication are all becoming even easier. But BA still has some way to go to get the full leverage out of the CRM initiatives. It has tended to focus so much on its high paying customers that others with potential have been neglected. For example regular Concorde passengers get letters and promotions from the Chief Executive whereas those who have travelled on Concorde but only done so occasionally have been ignored. In addition regularly servicing all 8.5m customers effectively is still regarded as taking too much time, cost and effort and the company prefers to plan around "demand occasions" when it will target groups of people with promotion schemes. But it's identifying the right group for the right promotion that's still key, and that sort of segmentation is vital for effective CRM.

Technology impact

There is no doubt that technology is having a major impact on this area. The Internet in particular has given rise to a host of new software tools and applications. It's encouraged the shift from client server, ERP forms of CRM to new web-enabled ones. It's forced organisations like Oracle and SAP to revisit their entire software suites and update them to make them 'e' or net-enabled. Many however have rushed in too quickly and there was concern about early e-CRM offerings from Siebel, Oracle and SAP.

Pre the Internet, solutions focussed mostly on automating and standardising the internal processes associated with managing customers and capturing information about them. Early initiatives ranged from sharing information on customer contacts through to preparing scripts for all call center operators (soon renamed "customer service officers or representatives") to ensure a consistent approach.

But with the Internet in place horizons and ambitions have been stretched. It's now quite possible to configure an architecture that deals uniformly and integrates all forms of contact: telephone, e-mail, voice-enabled web site, personal visits and any other type of customer contact.

Figure 9.6 Integrated IT for seamless customer experience across channels

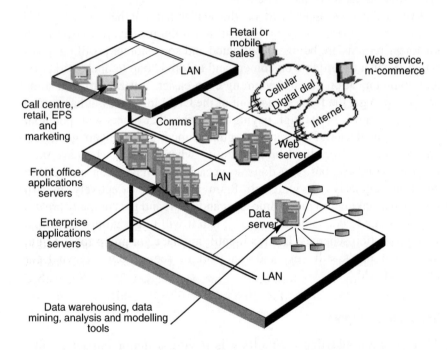

The architecture can now manage and deliver business and customer information to where it's needed, when it's needed. It can automatically trigger the work required across different areas to fulfill a customer request and it can monitor response times and service levels to ensure quality. And it can all still be tied into corporate ERP and database applications.

Companies like Siebel, Clarify (now part of Amdocs), e-Gain and

Oracle are vying to improve their software products and are upgrading to a fully web-based architecture. But these more major players each require significant investment from their client companies to get going and there are smaller, alternative software suppliers with relatively lower cost solutions. Their more basic functionality is offset not just by lower price but also by much quicker implementation. Companies like Commence, Goldmine and Saleslogix (from Interact) can provide a good "test/pilot" start for any size of company.

Goldmine has a product aimed at teams of 20 to 50 users who want to track, refer and take action on telephone and e-mail contacts from customers. It enables users to connect even if they're not on a local network by using a web-based system. Goldmine offers templates for specific industry sectors and includes rules on workflow processes (what can be shared to whom).

Though the software from the smaller vendors is not customised to an individual company's operation, a company can nevertheless get online and start taking advantage of the system within weeks, instead of months. And costs are down to c. $1000 per person (versus the $40k we talked about earlier). Indeed some of the smaller specialists such as salesforce.com will provide even more basic "in-a-box" packages for as little as $50 per user per month. No customisation and no integration but potentially still value-added in terms of customer insight.

Unsurprisingly most of the software houses are US-based and there is some uncertainty among Europeans and Asian-based companies as to the applicability of software in this sector written for a US market. It's left around 30% of European businesses in a recent IDC report uncertain about how to proceed with CRM and uneasy about some of the solution packages available. Companies like Pivotal, a Canadian CRM vendor, however have focussed more on the European market. They've launched versions of their product in French, German, Spanish and Swedish and on the back of what appears to be a more tailored solution have been more prominent as a provider.

One area where European solutions are in growing demand is wireless CRM, where Europe has for several years now been taking more of a lead with its higher rates of usage, penetration and universal communications standard. Now software vendors like eWare, based in Ireland, are emerging as niche vendors in that particular space. They're working hard to configure their offering so it works even with the current GSM technology, but see greater opportunity as 2.5G and 3G bandwidth roll out.

Much of the focus is on the software because that is typically the larger part of the CRM investment. Hardware should be less of an issue. Even the biggest CRM systems do appear to have comparatively modest incremental hardware support. Clarify for example will demonstrate that it will operate quite effectively on a Windows NT Server with its Front Office solution supporting the equivalent of 5000 concurrent users. So while systems need back-up and availability assurance nevertheless it shouldn't need a full room of equipment to run them!

It's also possible to reduce upfront costs further as well as have access to the best possible solution by considering outsourcing. A good illustration comes from Servtek, a division of the plastics, processing and networking manufacturing company Milacron, and interviews and research done at Servtek featured in *PC Magazine*.

- During 2001 Servtek was facing a CRM crisis. The company is essentially a logistics servicing group for Milacron providing warehousing, inventory planning, shipping and order processing for Milacron customers. Servtek services however were failing: "when we bought our call-center system in the mid-1990s it was state of the art, but it required lots of manual intervention, we had no way of recalling customer history without running lengthy reports which took hours and then there was no order tracking. So we employed a lot of people who took a long time to answer lots of basic questions."

  Servtek decided it had to get rid of the call center system and now find a way to use the Internet as a customer contact channel. It also decided it would let someone else figure out the technical requirements for implementing this. So Servtek decided to outsource and looked for companies with CRM Net-based solutions in its sector.

  For Servtek once this decision was reached there was some relief as the new technology was unfamiliar and there was no question from their research that the outsource provider would get them up and running faster to start making improvements to its customer service.

  Now customer history is captured on one screen. "Often we'll have a customer talking separately to five different people in different locations across our company. We used to have people running around doing the same work – now that's all eliminated. We're working better together and our sales team can access the same tracking information. What's more the outsource company – Syncrony – keeps adding functionality and improving the software so we can do more and more things such as sending advance shipping notices."

140

"CRM for rent" is now being offered by a number of ASPs (application service providers). This can be just for the software but can include an entire hosting solution. While this is potentially a highly attractive option, care needs to be taken in selecting the service providers. Issues of reliability, sustainability of the provider's own business and commitment to the software are all critical in deciding who to work with. Unfortunately, because the big software providers still prefer the upfront license fees to monthly rental they have not encouraged or supported the ASP environment. This has been exacerbated during the slower economic environment in 2001/2 when short term revenue gains and upfront license fees are an even greater attraction.

Other words of caution are to check that the software being deployed by the ASP is fully web-enabled. There were early problems when software that hadn't been effectively migrated was crashing and causing any number of reliability/customer information problems. And while there are solutions "in the box," many feel that CRM does need some customisation so it is tailored to a company's own customers' needs. This challenges the ASP economic model, which in its early days is relying on "one uniform solution to many" rental services, based on a single remotely hosted and maintained application (e-mail applications are a good "one to many" application that is typically straightforward and works easily in this environment).

While it's proper to add a cautionary note, nevertheless there are a growing number of ASP providers for CRM catering to all different sizes of company with different budgets and different customisation requirements. One example is Aspective run by former IBM execs which provides Siebel CRM.

> "We formed to operate in the high-end large enterprise market. We have the effective network solution with full back-up and disaster recovery. Because we've done nearly 100 implementations we work more quickly and over a three year contract we probably save clients anything up to 30 to 40% of what it would have cost to install the CRM themselves."

Another company in this space is Norkom Technologies who work on a campaign-specific basis. "Many companies have a skills shortage in-house because market analysts and data mining experts are not available. We offer the expertise on one-off campaigns and provide that almost immediately, no need to wait 12 months to implement a new system."

Salesforce.com are probably the best geared to SMEs. For example they offer sales force automation (customer contact record updating and sharing) for c. $50 per user per month with a one-off implementation fee of $7500. They are backed by Oracle and Gateway so they are probably a reliable provider. There's no customisation but they can modify workflow rules, for cxample to reroute sales leads, and they will adjust templates to reflect a company's own look and feel.

In this section it's also useful to reflect on some of the additional tools available that can be added to a CRM systems environment with the potential to enrich the customer experience and relationships.

One of the main areas for development is linking the web experience to call centers to provide that critical element of human contact and support (good to know it's still valued!) at key points in the interaction or at sticking points in the transaction. The tools include call-back, voice over IP, text chat and page push among others.

Boise Cascade provides a good illustration here. Its Office Products subsidiary has invested c. $20m to "distinguish ourselves in an increasingly competitive industry by collecting and using data about customers to deliver an integrated 'call center web' service." So if customers get lost on a web site they can click on "Need Assistance" and a pop-up screen asks whether they want help by message or phone. Choose message and a contact center rep will be on screen immediately. Choose phone and the rep will call "within 30 seconds." Dave Goudge, the Boise Cascade exec in charge, says that "when customers finish placing an order with us I want them to say, 'God, that was slick.'"

Click2talk is one of the pioneers in voice-enabled web site services. Its HTML code is embedded into the web site. The code is associated with a screen icon. When it's selected, a Java applet initiates a phone call from the PC through to the call center. It's potentially very simple and enables a customer to use the web while talking to an operator at the same time. However there are roadblocks that make this not widely available. The PC must be equipped with a sound card, IP telephony software and some integrated handset (for the voice). Bandwidth for most existing consumer lines is unlikely to be sufficient without at least a DSL connection. However for business to business there should be no technical reason why this cannot develop easily in the future.

"Voice over IP" gets over some of these technical difficulties. Here when a customer clicks on the appropriate "livetalk" icon, a small piece of voice client software in the VOIP engine auto-installs onto the customer's browser. Text chat is more straightforward. Communication can be real time but it's done in an e-mail exchange. Customers can type in questions while still browsing the web site. Companies like Zapdata provide this sort of service but their costs are high: c. $250 per month per user.

Another alternative to this, and currently the most popular, is call-back technology. When a customer clicks the "call me back" button, a window appears on screen that lets the customer request a company representative to call back on a particular number and to state a preferred time for that to happen. Several companies are experimenting with this type of solution but software costs are also remaining obstinately high in these early days of development and market penetration.

Key ingredients for success

In this final section on CRM, the aim is to capture the key lessons learned in how best to ensure a successful CRM implementation. There's examination of how to win the confidence of the workforce involved and also how to make it personal so it "sticks" and delivers the improvements in customer service that are being targeted.

Any implementation must first as we've discussed explore the general backcloth to customer service in the company. What's worked so far and what hasn't, what are the attitudes to customer service, is there a "passion and hunger" to go the extra mile? If not, then it's important to understand why. Step 1 must be to establish the right customer orientation in the company and build awareness of the short-falls and gaps that exist today.

By itself that's not easy and there's no overnight fix. But some simple customer research, captured say on video, that tells the company's staff exactly what the situation is, what customers want and how they rate and compare current services can be a very effective catalyst to wake the company up to what needs to be done.

If there is the appropriate platform in place then examining the more specific CRM initiatives and opportunities becomes a valid and lever-aged exercise. At this point step 2 must be to involve an effective cross-company team. Ensure there are people from sales, from the call center, from marketing, from ops, from IT and any other relevant environment. Any change is likely to impact a wide range of people. CRM implementations have notoriously failed because of this failure to involve all the key stakeholders from the start. It seems that especially the sales department are for various reasons reluctant to adopt new technology tools until they've seen the win:win. This often leads to the provision of new systems which don't get used, information is not updated and the whole exercise falls into disuse and disrepair. Here's one company's path through those hurdles:

- At Staff Leasing, a US employment services company, the CIO Lisa Harris reckoned she was facing near rebellion when CRM was first introduced in the company.

  The initial CRM component was to provide web-based FAQ automated query handling as an alternative to call center operators. Call center employees felt the software threatened their jobs and they began discouraging customers from using it. "Some of us even started deliberately encouraging customers to call us up for a more personal service," one employee told *Business 2.0* in an interview.

  Harris was convinced that a significant proportion of call center calls were routine and could be handled automatically, so to encourage the CRM initiative along she changed the job spec of the call center people. She put a focus more on general relationship building (proactive "hi how's it going" calls, rather than data entry and reactive query handling).

  It took time but eventually the efficiency of the web-based system has emerged. Customers were not unhappy. In fact research was done showing most liked the new approach. And the more proactive selling has started to identify new leads.

Research by Xchange, a CRM software provider, has shown that 74% of companies interviewed felt "culture" was the key barrier preventing more effective CRM implementation. That's an extraordinary statistic. Part of it is due to simple technophobia. But another is fear of redundancy (though when CRM *is* properly implemented, the job actually becomes even higher value add as routine call handling, for example as described at Staff Leasing, turns into a much more leveraged role). Another reason appears to be lack of senior management commitment to the project and therefore inadequate resourcing, funding and general support for the project.

This is worth highlighting as a separate step 3. We often read about initiatives needing CEO or senior officer commitment. CRM, because it does cut across different functions (it's rarely confined to just a change in call center job spec), does require each department to treat the project with the same degree of priority. If it's not important in the sales department, for example, it of course just won't get the support. Given its cross-company nature it will therefore need a group-wide manager to set the agenda and get agreement to the priority.

Because of these challenges, step 4 is about piloting and testing before full scale roll-out. This gives the champion the chance to get things going at lower investment, and therefore lower risk, and if managed effectively to deliver some quick wins to spread the word and gather momentum.

Step 5, which supports the "don't rush into it" theme, is to ensure that the infrastructure is reliable. Customers will expect the same levels of contact; in fact with the Net they'll expect increased levels of availability and support whenever they want them. So it's vital to ensure the software is already proven (avoid being the first to deploy a new release!), any outsource provider will still be around in years to come and there is sufficient capacity and back up for the web-based and other communications.

This means checking for possible bottlenecks at any point from the site through to the servers and out to the storage systems. Typically now web-server equipment is externally hosted and there should be in place adequate redundant network connections, server power supply back up and clusters of servers to ensure things will keep running despite component failures and system over-loads. In addition, a common feature of networked solutions is "load-balancing," which controls the workload going to each server. This is fairly straightforward and in widespread use. It's also easy to test out this equipment and check it can handle possible peak loads and the back up, "disaster-recovery" units will pick up the data processing automatically.

If we've established then an effective platform for CRM, how can we ensure the customer communication *is* more effective and more personalised and that it does build a relationship more firmly? One of the keys for this lies in personalisation, and the Internet environment has created a number of significant new ways to go about achieving that.

Jeff Bezos, of Amazon, has commented that having a million customers is like having to provide a million local newspapers and a million "shops around the corner." People expect an even more personal experience on the web and the challenge is to deliver it. The concept of "mass customisation" has arisen but it simply means how to get one to one even though there's hundreds or thousands of customers to be contacted and managed.

An e-analytics engine is the first requirement. This collects specific data about who are the site's visitors, what pages they access, what information they request, what they buy. It then analyses that data and generates a report to try to explain how effective the web proposition and site is. The report can of course help identify who are the best customers and more specifically how the site could be improved.

The next step is to instal a rules-based personalisation engine. This will customise a page's content, not by determining the personal interests of current site users but by reference to a set of rules that have been predesigned. A typical rule is "show product A to a customer who's bought product B." Even without analysing the customer it's possible to tailor the site and that customer's experience.

For the more ambitious, a company could next implement collaborative filtering. This does investigate a user's preferences, it identifies other individuals who have similar preferences and then serves up to the user additional content enjoyed by members of that same preference group. Mainly this software tool records the pages accessed and the products bought and simply watches what's being clicked on.

The most effective form of personalisation is to tailor the experience from the first visit. Software tools now exist for example that identify which city/country you're accessing the site from and so offer location specific information (nearest local branch is .....), news and promotions which might have a more relevant appeal. The software also stores information about the individual user, previous visits and even other sites visited using the same software, so a big information database builds up about the user's interests and preferences.

Here's an example of one organisation that's captured this:

- Hallmark have been effective users of personalisation techniques on the Net. The greetings card company has quickly established a popular web site as people seem to intuitively enjoy sending greeting and other cards and to use the Net to do so.

  To build on this, Hallmark explained in a *PC Magazine* interview their decision to employ Broadvision personalisation software. Their aim was to keep customer interest in the online environment and develop better relationships.

  Broadvision software enabled Hallmark to capture information about a web user's specific activities online, such as buying habits and preferences, from the moment they logged on. That enabled Hallmark to personalise the web site visit, offer related products of likely interest and generally encourage the user to "stick around."

  As a result of this data capture, Hallmark has initiated its "e-reminder" service to e-mail users about upcoming birthdays for example. It also set up a "free e-card" service allowing customers to design their own card.

These and other services are reckoned to have transformed the number of repeat users and repeat purchases. An average of c. 500,000 cards a week are being ordered and distributed. "You have to be ruthless in establishing a focus on the customer's needs and you need the customer history to do that. Doing it online means using good personalising tools."

The final point to personalisation is privacy management. It's all very well collecting all this information, but for the business to be sustainably successful it has to have an ethics code which will assure visitors and buyers that any information is going to be kept confidential. Opt out/opt in boxes are now common and certainly banks and insurers have been at the forefront in adhering strictly to data protection and personal privacy regulations. Many companies now go on to highlight their privacy policy and will put as much effort into communicating and maintaining that as they will in using what information is accessible to target and personalise and "e-remind" as much as is feasible.

* * * * *

Once again we see examples of Internet technology as enabler or automator or innovator. It's a catalyst to encourage companies to appraise just what can now be achieved to take the business forward and to achieve different levels of effectiveness and, in the case of CRM, relations with customers. The basic idea of getting closer to customers, building loyalty and locking in relationships is not new. Good companies will have been doing that for many years. But the new technology has upped expectations and raised the "best practice" threshold. It requires organisations to push out the boundaries of what they're doing in this CRM arena and be much more effective in delivering true customer service.

10 Wireless interactivity: Internet on the move

Fidelity Investment's Joseph G. Ferra is a pioneer. He's Chief Wireless Officer of Fidelity's e-Business unit and he's convinced that wireless web financial services will become a major part of Fidelity's customer service proposition. He sees the growing number of people with mobile phones, the demand for "connectivity on the move, anytime/anywhere communication." He sees the number of people who already do some of their banking online (42% of US people and 33% of Canadians) and he sees research from groups like the Henley Centre who have found that 80% of 16 to 24 year olds expect to do all their banking and shopping via the web.

Ferra also recognises just how tough it is for financial service firms to differentiate themselves in today's very crowded and highly competitive market places (a recent Cap Gemini E&Y study describes the market as "increasingly commoditized"). He knows that companies such as Fidelity have to keep searching for new and innovative ways to reach out to their customers. He's also done the research that tells him that his target "wireless customers" are among the more affluent of his customer base and the more loyal. "Giving them options in the way they do their banking is going to help us keep these kinds of existing customers."

Fortunately for Fidelity, Ferra is also a realist. He's not about to bet the farm on wireless banking, not right now.

> "We recognise that the reason wireless has not taken off yet is that we haven't made it easy to do. There have been technology limitations. Access devices with Internet connections have been high price, geographic coverage has been limited, bandwidth has been constrained and there's still work to be done on security and encryption. These are not trivial issues but we are way ahead of where we were even two years ago. Look for example how online financial services via a PC have been transformed since they first appeared in 1996. The key is we need to be there as these limitations get worked through. And they will. And when they are we want to have the platform and experience in place to take advantage."

Ferra's mantra is "evolve with the technology." His view is: "as you get better so you establish your brand in that space." Even as he encourages industry colleagues and demands common open standards to improve nationwide access, Ferra has continued to develop Fidelity's services. Recently he landed a tie-up with General Motors to incorporate wireless devices and services in GM automobiles. He's after the captive audience of drivers and wants to develop interactive voice response services for them.

Ferra is not alone in pushing down this path. WellsFargo has also been a leading player in providing wireless banking operations. "Wells wireless" was the first such service to be launched nationwide. It lets customers transfer funds and monitor balances and transaction history using Palm PDA handheld or Sprint PCS mobile phones. WellsFargo is also realistic about the immediate potential of this service.

> "While it's only via a small mobile phone screen we're always going to be limited. But as technology improves the screen will get bigger (as e.g. batteries get smaller), pocket PCs with Net access will become more widely available, graphics will go to color and 3G bandwidth will make communication fast and efficient!"

Fidelity and WellsFargo have been joined by Bank of America (piloting with private banking customers in three major US cities), Chase Manhattan (customers will be able to transfer information from any WAP–enabled cell phone, laptop computer or PDA via any wireless carrier in the US), Wachovia (offering real time account information through web-enabled digital phones to view pay, transfer or cancel), Citibank (launched first in Asia, enabling customers to perform transactions by sending SMS text messages on a GSM network), Charles Schwab ("we want to provide integrated and seamless buy–sell services of stock via retail branches, e-mail or over the phone – that's what real time trading is all about") and Nordea Bank (e-banking via ATM, phone, GSM mobile, PC, interactive TV and WAP phones to provide "the richest access mix in the world").

While most of these financial services firms have been focussing on consumers, Wachovia has also gone on to provide wireless services for its corporate customers. Wachovia's "Connection Plus" enables corporate treasury personnel to create a variety of cash management reports and initiate transactions in domestic and foreign currencies.

> "Wireless access is an important step in providing customers with convenient flexible means for tracking financial activity. Our

149

customers can use the service 24/7 through Web-enabled digital phones. We found in our research that our customers were asking for this kind of anytime/anywhere service. That means they are no longer tied to an office computer for the ability to make critical financial decisions."

Wachovia has been committed to expanding this wireless service and has more recently added a "proactive notification" alert that enables corporate treasurers to receive immediate warning or notification when reports or data are available or when currency movements, for example, require an instant decision on hedging. With this determination to develop these services as fast as technology allows, Wachovia has been receiving top marks in management surveys and is ranking high on customer perception lists (e.g. the Phoenix-Hecht Cash Management Monitor) for performance and relationship management service.

Wireless communications for data as well as voice are now becoming part of our everyday lives. Their rapid development and penetration was unforeseen even a few years ago. SMS text messaging has taken root (estimate of 250 billion text messages globally for 2002) particularly among teenagers and young adults, such that no "self-respecting" 16 year old will be without a mobile. A whole generation is growing up not just Net literate but mobile literate too. Quick use of the thumb to "type out" the message is now a developed skill that the younger generation are comfortable with. For them there are no barriers. The challenge is now for business generally to explore what applications it wants to develop to help drive its communications network with customers, suppliers, partners and employees onto the next platform.

By end 2002 it's expected there will be 200 million wireless devices (mostly phones or PDAs) in use across the US. While only around 5% of these will have Internet access, that is expected to grow to some 40% by 2005 according to the most recent IDC research. By 2003 it's expected that 70% of all people over 15 in Western Europe will have a mobile phone and a third of those will be surfing the Net. In 2006 forecasters reckon there will be more wireless data users in Japan than people because pets and cars will have subscriptions as well! Motorola and Nokia both estimate up to a billion users worldwide by 2002–3 and 1.4 billion subscribers (again according to IDC research) by 2005. By then there will be more mobile phones than TVs in the world! The use of web-enabled cell phones and PDAs is also expected to exceed the number of wired (PC) Internet accounts by around 2005. Sun Microsystems president Edward Zander has

Figure 10.1 Universal Internet access

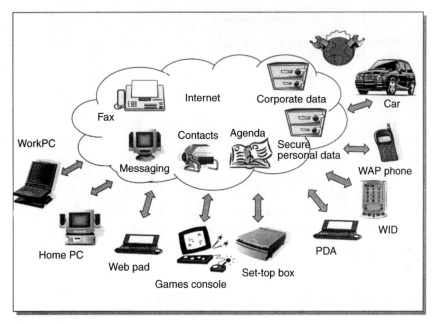

Source: Psion

commented: "most people won't have their first experience on the Internet through a PC, but on a wireless device."

In the context of these sorts of growth and penetration rates, it's hardly surprising that telcos in particular all over the world have been eyeing this market opportunity. At the last count European carriers alone had invested a staggering $116bn to license spectrum for speedy 3G mobile systems. And that investment will be in addition to an estimated $150bn required over the next three years to build the networks and capture this market potential. They are seeing substantial business opportunity and are shaping up to take advantage of the increasing switch they expect from desktop to mobile Internet access. Given that Europe is already one of the most developed cell phone markets this will certainly prove to be a realistic testing arena – and likely to be a bloody battleground too as the various license holders go on to fight for market share.

But investors in the wireless sector are worried, for now they see the hype that accompanied the launch of WAP services in 2000 turn into disappointment. Current technology and bandwidth especially have limited what could be transmitted, and reliability/availability has proved

Figure 10.2 Mobile Internet access

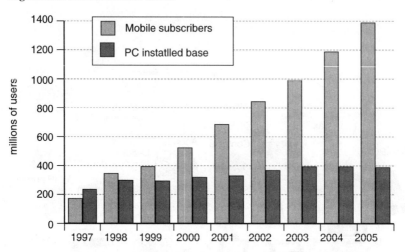

Source: EMC Dataquest, IDC, Psion

Figure 10.3 Wireless and Internet penetration, % of population forecast 2005

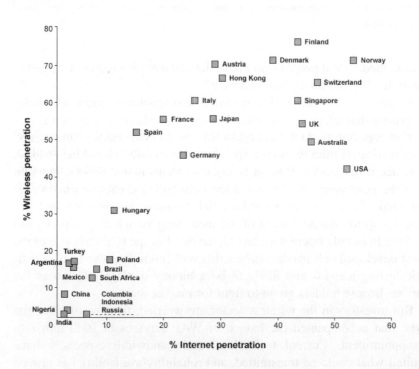

Source; McKinsey, IDC, Business 2.0

disturbingly low. What's more some doubt whether these telcos, who carry the hopes of the entire mobile access community, will be able to deliver. And even if they can, will they deliver on time or in full? They've taken on substantial debt in acquiring the licenses. BT, France Telecom, Deutsche Telekom and Netherland's KPN are among the most burdened and they're struggling to realise their vision, with timetables already being delayed by 12 months. Forrester researchers reckon the huge 3G expenditures will add an average $5 a month per subscriber to the cost of providing mobile services for up to the next 15 years! Some telco consortia will make it – those in Spain and Norway for example were awarded licenses on ability to roll out schedules rather than on how much they were prepared to pay – but others will not. It's already reckoned that Group 3G in Germany will have to merge with another large partner if it's to remain viable.

For the US, the license fee burden may become less of an issue. Observing what is happening in Europe, the US, unusually behind in this technology race, has the chance to learn the lessons of others and adapt its business model accordingly. Right now most US carriers are rolling out their wireless Net services with the radio spectrums they have, and it's expected that CDMA 3G licenses won't come up for bidders till winter 2002 at the soonest. Commentators expect development in the US to be more led by business and consumer demand rather than telco anticipation. And with market research suggesting that there *is* going to be strong demand for that mobile Net connectivity, it is expected that the US scene will gradually evolve through 2003–4 as carriers begin to roll out local 2.5 and 3G networks.

It is useful to contrast the US versus Europe scene for mobile phone/net access development, as it helps determine the reality behind some of the market forecasts. The key for Europe is that it has a uniform technology standard for digital mobile communications whereas the US does not – yet. Europe landed on GSM (global system for mobile communications) and as companies headquartered there have reviewed improvements in technology there's been a commitment to keep that same single standard. Critically that provides the universal anytime/anywhere access that really drives advantage and convenience for customers. It also provides economies of scale for operators and service providers who can roll out their products cross-border. It's this "total region coverage" that has enabled Nokia and until recently Ericsson to lead the world in equipment manufacture and act as gateways for mobile commerce development.

In contrast the US is hampered by incompatible networks and standards, meaning many phones just cannot be used outside a specified region. Furthermore there are regulatory and other hurdles that need to be resolved if the US roll out is really to reach critical mass. These hurdles include subscribers still having to pay for calls they receive. That's unlike their European counterparts. There's also a much more developed cable and broadband PC Net access infrastructure which means "plug 'n' play" wherever you are is more feasible (though still far from ubiquitous) thus, some argue, limiting the demand for mobile phone access on the move.

In Asia, mobile phone usage has been growing rapidly. This is partly due to having less developed fixed wire networks in place. So rolling out wireless access is enabling countries like China to leapfrog the high cost of laying cable and instead provide alternative bandwidth faster and more flexibly.

In South Korea for example, 3G style services were rolled out during 2000. Usage is high; walk down the street in central Seoul and people are tapping away at mobile phone keypads, surfing the Net, playing online games, downloading music and even sending video clips to friends. The three key local operators, SK Telecom, KTF and LG Telecom, have all been heavily involved in these new Net services and are excited about the fresh revenue streams they're generating. It's reckoned that 75% of the country's 30 million mobile customers use wireless Internet services (that compares to the world average in 2002 of c. 5%).

South Korea's global lead in mobile technology is a sign of its government's commitment to information technology and online services. It's been determined to establish a high speed broadband network as a way to catapult its economy forward.

> "The government's role has been to build the new economy. We've linked schools and other public institutions to the Net because we were determined not to be left behind the developed world in the industrialisation process. Using wireless technology has enabled us to catch up and in some ways overtake the rest!"

As South Korea has pioneered, so rivals in other Asian economies and especially in China have looked on anxiously and determined to try to follow the same path. Because of South Korea's innovation, tech companies, ISPs, economic companies, software houses, media and entertainment groups are all setting up headquarters there and expanding rapidly. "We're now ready for business to be done," says Kang Yeown-Sun, a member of the country's Ministry of Finance.

In this global tour we can't leave out the developments in Japan. If it's estimated that the US wireless industry is 18 months behind Europe (according to an *Economist* survey), then Europe is 18 months behind Japan. A recent government survey there showed that by end 2000 the number of mobile phone subscribers in Japan had already surpassed that for fixed phones. Even with the significant take up in Europe, Japan by itself is reckoned to account for more than 10% of all wireless devices in use in 2002.

The leading Japanese mobile phone company is NTT's DoCoMo (meaning "everywhere" in Japanese), which has more than 35 million active subscribers. While the phone is switched on so is the Internet. This "always-on" access is what is revolutionising usage. It's meant that browsing is free and the operators do everything they can to price usage attractively. E-mails cost about 4 cents and even the monthly charge is less than $5.

Given its market strength DoCoMo has rolled out its 3G service – a world first. It gives transmission capability of up to 2 mbps (megabits per second) and that's around 200 times faster than current generation phones! It's encouraging people to use their phone for a range of new services including paying utility bills, buying tickets for events, receiving favorite cartoons (one of DoCoMo's top attractions) and even getting driving directions while travelling to their next destination. It's also forced practically all the Internet-via-PC HTML sites to repurpose their format so page lay-out and content can be viewed more easily via the mobile phone.

Add what's going on in Japan to developments in Korea, China (especially Hong Kong) and Singapore and we find Asia itself is proving a hotbed of wireless activity.

These leading Asian economies have some advantage over Europe and the USA as they race to build their high speed high bandwidth mobile networks. Aside from limited regulatory and other hurdles, they've not been encumbered by widespread and established "older" access technologies. That "encumbrance" has been another factor delaying European roll out. The fact is that straight phone access works, and works well, on the existing mobile phone technology so the need for basic change is reduced. In addition operators are faced with replacing that technology and managing the migration from one to the other on a mass volume scale. It's a technical challenge but also, after the WAP 1.0 disappointment, a customer challenge as well. With all that investment the last thing any operator or service provider wants is disruption or diminution in the basic service levels. Those hurdles mean things are just moving more slowly.

GSM, the current technology, was designed for voice calls. SMS, short message services or text messaging, is one of the few additional functions that does work well enough over the same network. At typical speeds of 14 kbps however, it's hardly surprising that trying to send reconfigured html pages of data has proved slow, clunky and frustrating and led to the general dissatisfaction with WAP 1.0 on GSM as an architecture for Internet access.

Yet GSM can be used for specific business Internet access *provided* the pages are configured carefully. That means black and white, no color, limited amounts of text per page, certainly no "flash" links. Within these constraints, it has enabled companies to pilot Internet access tests for mobile workforces. For example, PA has reconfigured its "Knowledge Net" so that consultants on the move can discover certain key pieces of information about clients, current projects, any queries and complaints, last contacts etc., and so be more immediately productive in serving customers. PA has worked with Compaq's IPAQ and Palm Pilots to connect up these devices to the Net via GSM networks. Soon these devices will have the connectivity built in, but for now the Net connection is achieved via specially designed clip on inter-face cards. That sort of handheld access development is one of the early pilots. There's no "always-on" connection; the user must dial up and download and store data and that requires strong message-oriented middleware to complete the connection between the mobile web browser and the client server.

Other organisations have been testing out applications looking to sensibly leverage the existing technology framework. So Direct Line, the insurer, sends SMS messages to policy holders when a policy is due to expire. As the message contains a phone number, the receiver can press "call" and be put straight through to the Direct Line call center. Reed Recruitment alerts job seekers to openings with a free SMS service, and Heineken in China and Singapore is also using SMS, this time to extend its online Brand to build a loyalty program.

While companies are experimenting with GSM, moving on to the next generation, 2.5G is expected to be available in Europe by end 2002. It eases the bandwidth problems with the introduction of GPRS technology (General Packet Radio Services). It's seen as delivering three distinct advances: (i) it increases transmission speed to around 50 kbps which is equivalent to today's modem-speed data rates; (ii) it can provide "always-on" connectivity and (iii) bandwidth is sufficient to make voice calls while still logged on the Net.

2.5G is seen as a breakthrough for a number of reasons. On the technology side it moves away from GSM circuit switching where a circuit connection is set up between the caller and the other party. In such an environment the circuit switch connection is dedicated and is held open for the duration of the call so the caller is billed for the use of the airtime during the call connection. GPRS uses a packed-switched transmission, where information is split into packets of data that are routed independently through the network over different paths to the final destination. Therefore there's no dedicated circuit switch held open for one specific call. That means any user cost is determined by amounts of information or packets "consumed" or sent during up and download. So users can be "always on" without that by itself incurring any cost or charges. It becomes a free connection that you pay for only when you use it!

Given that 3G, though much faster, also exploits this same "packet-switching" technology, many are wondering if 2.5G won't be the immediate solution for faster internet mobile access and some have even challenged the value of the 3G migration. As we'll see in a moment, 3G will bring many distinct advantages but in the meantime 2.5G is beginning to generate its own advance publicity. Merrill Lynch for example has predicted 2.5G will be the "choice for cell phone users for the next few years." They go on to argue that as the system costs to roll out 2.5G are so much less than 3G it further undermines the business case for 3G roll out.

GPRS is cheaper to roll out because it does make use of existing cellular telephony networks using current base stations and antenna, but both parties need to have a GPRS compatible handset for this to work. With only Nokia at present committed to making those handsets there could be a shortage which could once again undermine the potential of this new technology implementation. Encouragingly a number of handset manufacturers have expressed more recent interest in adding capacity, and the likes of Siemens, Alcatel, Mitsubishi and Philips are all, they say, investigating this area.

Business is being persuaded to look hard at what 2.5G could deliver. Ericsson's business development director Paul Salusbury believes:

> "GPRS can be a meaningful start for organisations who want to improve the effectiveness of employees who are out of the office as it does now provide access to work-related information quickly. Real time data updates are also a possibility and we find a number of financial institutions, broking houses and ISPs are looking hard at the possibilities."

Billing methodologies are also now being reviewed as there is no legitimate charge for the "always on" access. As Salusbury says:

> "you and I as end users aren't necessarily interested in how many kilobytes of information we're sending – we're more interested in content and the usefulness of the applications that we use. What will probably happen is that you will be billed at the end of a month on a lump sum maybe with different tariffs for 'light use' versus heavy use or there may be charges for 'premium access to the high bandwidth.'"

Change in billing structures may by themselves encourage change in behavior and levels of business use but GPRS is certainly going to make a fairly short term impact on mobile Net access.

All these improvements through 2.5G have made the 3G operators nervous. Even the chairman of Sony, Nobuyuki Idei, has publicly voiced his disquiet commenting that "2.5G will meet most of the needs of users. We expect great interest in music and games. MP3 files can be downloaded in minutes." So what are the advantages of 3G and why did UK telcos, for example, invest nearly $35bn (against a forecast $10bn) for the five UK operator licenses? The particular benefits are:

1. Vastly increased speed – we're talking here a step change in data transmission times up from the 50 to 150 kbps with GPRS to 2 megabits per second with 3G.
2. The ability to provide real time streaming of video, film, news (instead of just getting the latest sports updates, with 3G you get the live action).
3. "Always on" with integrated voice and data.
4. Color, graphics, music allowing much better and personal interactivity. For example a small camera could be incorporated in the handset allowing voice *and* video to be exchanged at the same time.
5. Perhaps most crucially, 3G is designed as a universal global standard (it's been the subject of intense worldwide research and development). That means literally anytime anywhere faster connections, eventually all over the globe. It means local network operators won't have to support their users overseas. It means consistent access based on a standardised environment. It also means the same set of services will be available anywhere. And all that's encouraging 3G operators to talk about "virtual homes" where users will always feel they're on their local network.

6. Alongside the introduction of 3G we will see the implementation of WAP 2.0. Among a number of changes, WAP 2.0 is based on xHTML, which is a version of the standard programming language on the Net, and it will run over the TCP/IP (the internet protocol), which is the standard delivery system for packets of data. This means a mobile device could connect directly to a content provider's web server, without having to go through a WAP server as it does today. That will speed up transmission and further improve network reliability

As 3G does get implemented, the universal standard and access (known also as UMTS – universal mobile telecommunications system) is going to make wireless communication as easy as using a phone in an office or in the home today. We don't care who is the provider, we don't worry about availability, communication is instant, it's reliable, it works, it's cheap and we can contact anyone in the world in seconds whenever we want to.

3G in effect delivers that same "ubiquity" for data transmissions as well as voice. That's why 2.5G may meet most short term consumer needs, but 3G will become the faster delivery tool for business and the long term solution. It will enable employee knowledge management portals, for example, to really empower people wherever they are with instant access to files (however large) and to an organisation's entire intranet data base. It will enable vertical industry portals such as Asite.com in construction, INTTRA in cargo shipping, 24/7 in steel, quadrem.com in metals and precious stones all to function with much greater effect. It will enable

Figure 10.4 Growth in wireless data speeds

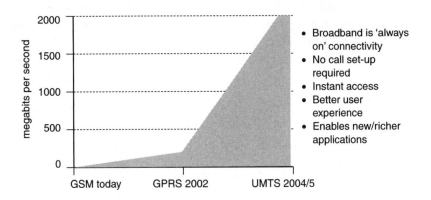

Figure 10.5 Improved bandwidth

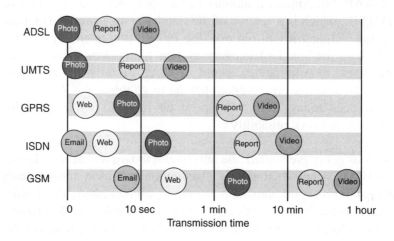

Source: Psion, David Levin

video conferencing and online project assistance ("talk me through it"), and it can connect up disparate communities and teams in remote locations. It provides the Internet on the move.

Alongside these mainstream technology advances, work has been going on around the infrastructure to ensure the network is accessible, and accessible as easily as possible. This is not just about building new base stations for transmitting the radio signals for 3G, it's also about enabling people to use wireless as conveniently as possible and to help business install and use the networks quickly and competitively.

One infrastructure technology that's received a lot of publicity is known as "Bluetooth." This enables a truly wireless communications environment to be established and it's personal. It provides cable-free connectivity between your mobile phone, PC, handheld computer, printer and other devices. It effectively means that provided the PC is plugged in, all devices in an office or a home can automatically talk to each other. It uses a short range radio link to exchange information and operates on a globally available band, allowing you to use Bluetooth-enabled equipment worldwide. It eliminates the need to carry numerous often proprietary cables. Equipment need not remain within line of sight and can maintain a connection while on the move and even when placed in a briefcase (Bluetooth can transmit through solid, but non-metal objects). Its range is from 10 to 100 meters and it can support up to eight devices at a time.

Bluetooth has been developed by a consortium led by Nokia, IBM, Intel, Toshiba and Ericsson. These companies could see how wireless technology was developing and wanted to personalise it: bring the advantages onto a personal platform to improve the workplace and further facilitate the "Internet on the move." After the initial burst of interest in 2000, project delays and differences among consortium members led Intel at one point to declare Bluetooth "dead." But products are now coming on to the market and there is renewed interest among the various hardware manufacturers in incorporating Bluetooth chips in their devices. There are a range of "adapters" already available such as a clip-on card that creates a Bluetooth enabled Palm PDA, and 3Com have a Bluetooth PC card for laptops. However it is only when the chips are fully incorporated into the next generation cell phones that we'll begin to see the benefits.

Automatic data exchange between people carrying Bluetooth-enabled equipment will be one of the more obvious and attractive applications. Two people could meet in a room and exchange business cards or other data without even a click of a button. A mobile phone can be synchronised automatically with a PC to update e.g. contact data, without taking the phone out of the case. The synchronisation would start as soon as the phone is in range of the PC. A digital camera could be wirelessly connected to a phone or PC to send images or video to other local devices while the sender provides a commentary over the phone on the film.

One software developer, Nicholas Knowles, who among other things has won the Queen's award for technology development in the UK, has talked in visionary terms about Bluetooth in a recent McKinsey interview:

> "I think wireless will become a sort of telepathy. Things like Bluetooth will allow you to break the device down into a body area network so you won't have to hold an object. You'll have something in your ear, something in your eyes and something listening to you, and the actual electronics will be in your back pocket and you won't even touch them. So it'll be coming straight into you and you'll have in effect this telepresence: you can communicate with someone at a distance and see information from afar. The technology is giving you superhuman powers to see and assemble information at a distance."

That vision may well be a few years away but it's important to recognise that the technology *does* exist, it's being improved, it's being commercialised and it will gradually infiltrate our environment. And just as Bluetooth gets personal so other technology developments have been looking at the total office environment and exploring how best to make that work for people, how to connect a "fixed" location up to a wireless infrastructure so it can take advantage of that cable-free communication.

The idea is that if you can have wireless at home, why not have it at the office as well? A wireless system can be installed at lower cost and in less time. It provides mobility for employees – they can be sure to get their "desktop" call wherever they are in the building or its vicinity – and it should therefore increase productivity. Also by using a wireless PBX (private branch exchange), a user in the US can eliminate local telco phone charges to calls in buildings in the same area, thereby saving potentially thousands of dollars in phone and data link changes. These "in-building" systems are being looked at with renewed interest as we roll out to the more universal 3G standard and "wireless office" services are being developed. AT&T for example are promoting products in this area, claiming the average employee spends 677 hours during work time over the course of a year away from his or her desk, often at present without immediate means of accessibility. That's around one-third of an average work year, so improving connections here could have considerable benefit.

Several organisations have already taken advantage of "in-building" wireless office solutions. Ron Schneiderman, editor of *Wireless Systems*, in his extensive research in this area also expects significant take up of these services. Kmart, for example, uses these systems in its supermarkets to enable managers and staff to connect up and respond to calls on price checks or in-store customer service needs. The Georgia Hospital Association also uses this approach to enable staff to link up more easily, and it's become the standard tool for nurses trying to reach doctors to respond to patient questions. And conference centers like the Jacob Javits Halls in New York have installed a wireless PBX so that conference delegates can make and receive calls anywhere within the facility.

From "in-building solutions," telcos and others have also been developing WLANs – wireless local area networks – which extend the in-building solution to wider areas, e.g. college campuses, business parks, large shopping malls etc. A WLAN is intended to expand the fixed-line local area network, but uses wireless rather than laying more cable. It's garnered plenty of interest because it uses a part of the radio spectrum that allows for high speed data transmission. "WLANs are emerging as a superior solution for providing next generation wireless services to indoor and campus hotspots. They can handle large volumes of data at significantly lower cost" (Frost & Sullivan research).

To date WLANs have been pioneered by specialists such as Mobilestar and Wayport in the US, and by smaller European telcos such as Telia in Sweden and Sonera in Finland. There is also some rivalry between these companies and 3G operators. The 3G committed companies not unexpectedly are claiming 3G will provide all the solutions a WLAN can deliver so you don't need both. The counter argument from the WLAN teams is to point to delays in 3G roll out and the lower costs of developing WLAN environments. It's likely however that the two will in fact coexist, with 3G providing the more universal solution and WLANs operating in confined environments like airports, campuses etc. providing lower cost local solutions.

While referring to alternative and facilitating infrastructures, it's worth also mentioning wireless local loops (WLL). The local loop is the connection between the phone on the desk or at home and the central telephone switching office. A *wireless* local loop can be an attractive and cheaper alternative to installation of fixed wire fiber-optic cables. It's emerging as a strong low cost solution for resolving the "last mile" problem of getting high bandwidth into homes or offices which do not yet have fixed cable access.

While the western world can perhaps more comfortably debate the various "last mile" access options, the developing world sees WLL as a "no-brainer." As a result countries from China to Mexico are starting to invest in WLL telephony systems. It's expected that there will be the equivalent of 100 million WLL lines installed by 2003 and it's being seen as a significant opportunity to connect up remote rival areas. While there are concerns about congestion in the low frequency spectrum typically being employed, there is no "standard WLL" and so local operators are using whatever spectrum they can license to deliver higher bandwidth and ensure these sorts of solutions can connect up businesses and consumers in particular areas in the way they want.

Whether we're talking 2.5G or 3G, WLANs or in-building systems, Bluetooth in the home or the office, one thing is certain: wireless communication is here, it will increase in bandwidth and penetration, it will become pervasive. And as it develops so the application and possibilities of using it will grow and develop. There are already a number of case studies and e-examples and it's now possible to review a number of them. The most progressive illustrations to date fall into these main categories:

- sales force
- CRM
- tracking
- location specific
- micro-transactions.

Sales force

Using wireless technology to connect up the sales force is already big business. We've discussed some of this in the chapter on CRM but with an estimated 30% of the US workforce estimated to be travelling out of the office at any given time, that's nearly 40 million people on the move in the US alone, and many of these will have some sales responsibility or function tied into their job. The days of simply equipping these people with a laptop to plug in next time they hit a fixed wire connection are fast disappearing as the technology evolves.

Figure 10.6 Internet-enabled PDA

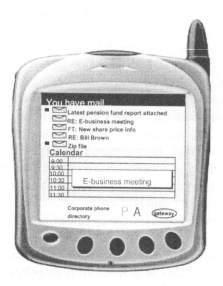

Hewlett Packard are among a number of enthusiasts in this space. As described by Frederick Newell in *Wireless Rules*, they've enabled their salespeople to go into their web site from a PDA, check customer files, update a database and get new information. "There was no additional software, middleware or hardware necessary and our payback in new sales was phenomenal." Singapore Airlines is installing equipment on its flights to enable passengers to receive and send e-mails. Every 15 minutes during the flight a server sends a radio signal via satellite, transmits incoming and outgoing e-mail and updates web pages. Passengers can access the system from any Internet access device. Field Centrix, a US heating ventilation service company, has linked its field team to suppliers' inventory availability so they can real time check on spare parts and lead times for their customers. And companies such as NTL, Xerox and NCR are linking staff in the field via WAP or SMS-enabled mobile phones or PDAs. They are finding that doing something as simple as sending an alert to an engineer if there's a parts problem or a customer call can produce much better service. NTL for example reckon on an 84% return on their investment in just 12 months by implementing a job dispatch system via the mobile network.

CRM

While the above initiatives all empower and enable the sales force, CRM involves a much more extensive examination of the customer relationship and encourages many more wireless applications.

Selling the proposition to the customer can be strengthened by equipping the sales force with a PDA as an "unobtrusive tool" (it's nothing like getting out and cabling up a laptop) with wireless Net connections. It can help the salesperson respond immediately and accurately to questions like: "when can I get this?" "what price if I buy double the volume?" "can you change the spec?" etc.

Such a mobile device can also help the sales and tech. teams stay in touch with customers so they can provide immediate responses to questions and check back via their Net link for more data and expertise. Some companies are pushing down this path as much for cost-saving reasons as enhancing sales. They've calculated the admin and time delays associated with the more traditional phone, fax, or fixed wire downloads and can see how establishing an online office environment can only but improve productivity and cut out head office admin once mobile workers can access the information for themselves.

Going further, the more adventurous are actually empowering their *customers* in this way by equipping them with PDAs or pocket PCs to access information for themselves. So Chubb Insurance is providing mobile communications for its brokers, giving them access to Chubb product details, running customer queries past the Chubb FQA system and enabling competitive quotation comparisons.

Getting to this level of interactivity and making it work with customers has taken time and companies like Chubb will have been on a wireless exploration journey, checking out and testing a number of different applications before assuring themselves of the reliability, usefulness and payback of equipping customers in this way.

Tracking

UPS and FedEx "track 'n' trace" have already been referred to so, we can consider a slightly different example here from a case by Frederick Newell on wireless applications.

Landstar is a Florida-based company that manages information for thousands of truck drivers, using the Net to post available freight and other critical road transport data. Drivers used to need a laptop for access and that was obviously often difficult to use on the road. Drivers are Landstar's customers so, as wireless solutions become available, it was one of the first companies to test out a new proposition. Now using the same Net database, drivers can access it via a cell phone or PDA to track what kind of loads are available and where they are. They can also find out what a job is worth and get route directions. Landstar estimate their investment will deliver a ten-fold plus return. For example, they get commission on each job fulfilled through their system so every extra load they "sell" lands them extra revenues.

Location specific

All cell phones since January 2002 will likely have been equipped with GPS (as distinct from GPRS) technology. That's the Global Positioning satellite System that locates where the user is. The main reason is not "Big Brother is watching you" but to ensure calls made to the emergency services are trackable to a location, as existing landline calls already are.

While GPS will therefore be a considerable aid to the police and other services, it's also started businesses thinking about how they could take advantage of this same location technology. It means that if you switch your phone on in a shopping mall, for example, it could automatically register you with the retailers present in the mall and you could be simultaneously e-mailed or "alerted" to promotions, discounts and other deals available in the various shops, almost as you walk by.

It also provides additional services to the mobile user, for example providing instant information about the neighborhood you're in, giving access to a local directory of restaurants, providing "step-by-step" directions, and enabling you to locate and then "click and order" your take-out meal even while you're still a few blocks away.

While there are important issues of privacy here that do need to be carefully managed, many organisations exploring this area are making sure for example that users have opted in for "permission-based marketing" and

Table 10.1 Leading mobile applications, 2000–5 (ranked by number of users)

2000	2003	2005
1 PIM*	PIM	Navigation/location
2 Entertainment	Entertainment	PIM
3 Financial services	Navigation/location	Entertainment
4 Internet browsing	Financial services	Financial services
5 Navigation/location	Internet browsing	Internet browsing
6 m-commerce	m-commerce	m-commerce
7 Intranet	Intranet	Intranet

* Personal Information Management
Source: ARC Group research survey

have formally signed up either with the merchant or the mobile phone operator to participate in this sort of extended online commerce.

Micro-transactions

Combine this GPS wireless application with a mobile wallet, and business can begin to really maximise the use of wireless Internet connections. The mobile wallet essentially enables you to buy items using the mobile phone, with the bill coming through at the end of the month alongside the standard telephone connection charges. There are a number of ways of establishing this wallet; for example Deutsche Telecom enables users to enter all their personal and credit card data once into a secure database. When they make a "micro purchase" for a drink, meal, movie ticket etc., the connected retail merchant simply enters their phone number and the price and the transaction is automatically completed. Alternatively, dial up a specific merchant Net access number, select and pay!

There's a good in-store example of combining wireless, location-specific and microwallet technologies that comes from a US company called Klever Marketing and their "Klever-Kart" product. Klever-Kart consists of a small screen and terminal fixed to a shopping cart. As customers enter the store the cart is connected to the WLAN, activated and a stream of product information and promotional information can then be transmitted over the RF (radio frequency) network. Market research data shows that c. 80% of all purchase decisions in a grocery store are made at the shelf in response to impulses and impressions created there, as opposed to a fixed decision to buy a particular item made before entering the shop. So retailers and suppliers are especially interested in trialling these sort of devices to influence consumer purchasing.

KleverKart is experimenting also with two-way interactions enabling the customer to swipe a frequent shopper card through the cart terminal or type in a PIN number to link to a microwallet infrastructure, along the Deutsche Telecom lines (Motorola has a similar sort of system though billing is still through the credit card rather than the phone bill). Of course information about customer purchasing behavior can then be collected and mined, and more importantly next time the customer comes into the store and swipes the card, more intelligent one to one marketing can be carried through.

Ahold in Europe has been experimenting with similar systems involving hand-held or trolley-cart fixed terminals with wireless connections. The aim of all these sorts of initiatives is to use technology to clearly empower the customer, improve service, provide convenience and generally strengthen the relationship.

Implementing innovations such as those from KleverKart, or setting up microwallets with Motorola or automating the sales force with PDA Net connections is something that's straightforward to describe but it can be hard to do. If each application is considered in isolation then, like the Hewlett Packard sales team, it's relatively straightforward to push through. But most of these applications have to be considered in the broader context. Companies have to consider their total technology architecture, the interoperability of different systems, managing all the different databases, coordinating the various customer relationship connections, ensuring the whole configuration is reliable and meets all the various stakeholder needs. In addition new solutions require new behaviors from the people who'll be involved, and that can require training, incentives and new back office processes and structures to facilitate the initiative.

Driving some of the IT challenges is the need to decide which access devices to support. Does the company truly encourage the anytime anywhere connection and so support phones, laptops, PDAs as well as PCs and potentially interactive TV? To complicate things further, should an organisation get behind 2.5G or wait for 3G, or should it try and bypass all of that and simply establish a WLAN? That would extend fast bandwidth coverage to the near vicinity but beyond that the network will for the short term have its limitations. If we wait for 3G, might we still be waiting beyond 2003–4 because of further unexpected delays and technical problems? And what kind of wireless access do our customers really want and what kind of real time connection is actually required to add the value and leverage the potential?

Bringing that all together is challenging, and while there is no panacea

168

there is encouragement from the companies described here and others who to some extent have "been there and done it." They've inevitably made their own mistakes on the way but have built up a wealth of lessons learned and know-how. What's more, in these Internet and wireless break-through days those companies that have been successful are especially enthusiastic about "telling the world" what they've achieved and those looking to follow in their footsteps can visit, interview, discuss and learn from these case studies. With c. 1.5 billion web-enabled wireless phones and PDAs in use worldwide in the next few years, there's just no question that the "Internet is on the move" and there will be many opportunities for both new and existing businesses to stamp their authority and market presence on this emerging scene.

11 iTV

For Domino's Pizza, the TV remote control has proven to be a "magic wand"! The company runs interactive TV ads especially around *The Simpsons* early evening show. Click the red connection button any time during the program and there's automatic dial-up and ordering. "Cookies" keep track of previous orders and choices, allowing a simple one click "same as last time" option. Sales both through iTV but also at the restaurants have grown significantly on the back of this initiative. Customers seem to enjoy the simplicity of the process and the comfort of not moving from the TV couch! "It's given us strong Brand recognition and a real presence on digital TV."

Interactive TV (iTV) is a part of the recent technology revolution that is often overlooked. Launched principally in Europe in the late 1990s, but now also slowly expanding across North America, it provides a new and potentially vibrant way of conducting business. It's naturally thought of as a mass medium for reaching consumers in new and innovative ways, but as we'll see it could also be used by businesses to communicate, transmit data and interact with employees, community groups and other target markets.

It's being overlooked right now because, like e-commerce generally, it too has suffered from overhype, leading to inevitable disappointment and frustration. It was initially presented as being a superior communication tool to the Internet and a route to instantly transforming business. With European governments committing to digital signals replacing analog (the UK Government is still thinking of mandating this for 2006), in theory everyone will have a digital TV. That means access into every home and to every consumer (plus second and third TVs in bedrooms and kitchens), no need to wait for PC penetration and separate dial-up Internet connections, no need to worry about training technophobes to log on; the all-purpose ubiquitous remote control will lead consumers comfortably down a "t-commerce" path. Indeed respected researchers Jupiter initially forecast that by 2005 iTV would develop such that more people would access the Net through their TV than through their PC.

Figure 11.1 The continuing revolution in e-commerce

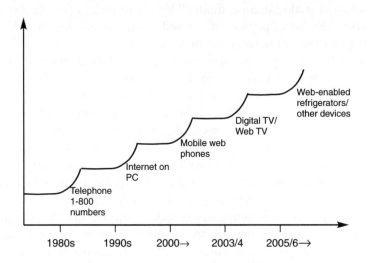

But while digital TV access is growing, 2002 still sees lower than expected take-up rates. The USA leads in terms of number and percentage of households with some kind of interactive set top box (STB) capability. The estimate is around 43 million households, principally on cable and satellite. In Europe, the UK is the most developed market by far with c. 8 million homes with digital TV, and the majority of those have an interactive pathway. This is followed by smaller franchises in France, with c. 3 million, and also in Germany, Denmark, Italy and Spain.

Figure 11.2 Forecast digital penetration rates (UK)

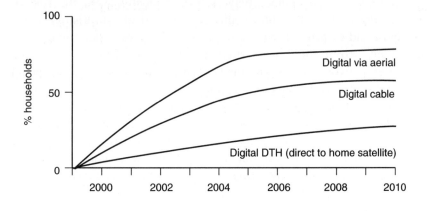

The feature that most people use their digital TV for is access to an even larger array of broadcast channels. In the US, which has long had a multi-channel analog regime, digital TV is nevertheless popular because it also provides better picture quality and a simple route for Pay TV. The most popular content is sport and movies.

In the US, Echostar (now also owner of DirecTV) dominates satellite iTV broadcasting, while companies like Cablevision, AT&T, TimeWarner Cable and others are fighting it out for fixed line access. Microsoft provides a service variously called MSN TV or Web TV or Ultimate TV, which is providing STB software solutions for hardware providers as well as providing interactive TV services (also available in Japan). AOL launched its iTV channel services in mid-2001 with both interactive and internet access features, but marketing and consequent uptake to date has been limited.

A number of media "heavyweights" are clearly in place with platforms but none have seen any meaningful payback yet on their investments. In the other developed market, the UK, the situation is similar but features different companies. The major force is Rupert Murdoch's News Corporation's Sky Interactive. This company deserves praise for "making the market." It has invested substantially, struck breakthrough deals with content providers, especially in the sports arena in soccer and rugby, rewritten the rules by giving away set top boxes for free and further challenged them by insisting every STB installation must be accompanied by a return path (telephone line) connection, thereby forcing through and establishing an interactive environment. As a result Sky has helped drive the market up to critical mass levels and enabled interactive TV to become a reality. "Our mantra is: press the red button!" UK competition has been playing catch up, with Telewest and NTL leading on the cable to home front and OnDigital (now itself known as "Interactive TV") providing simple digital TV broadcasting with an optional return path only.

In all markets, the major players have typically taken the role of content aggregators and informediaries, but perhaps surprisingly have also built and own the distribution network. They've either come at the opportunity from the broadcast/content end, like Sky, or from the distributor network end, as with the US cable companies. But their spread and control over large parts of the value chain is perhaps symptomatic of early form, immature markets. They may indeed retain that span of asset and content control, but it's likely they will focus on what they perceive to be the more value-added parts, e.g. content aggregation and consumer franchise rather than the asset-intensive distribution network.

These early iTV days have also seen relatively little t-commerce activity, and we shall discuss the reasons for that in the next section. Instead the initial focus has been on content and unique programming to attract subscriptions. Set top boxes seem to work, are reliable and are proving simple to use (essentially "switch on and forget"), and while most of the material is still being decoded and seen on an analog box it is expected that integrated digital TVs will begin to reach attractive commercial prices as the market develops further through 2003–4. The next generation of services which is being rolled out across the US and Europe has more interactivity, with near video on demand (not quite real time video streaming), e-mail, in some cases Web access, in a few instances hard disk drive recording features and finally 'e' or 't'-commerce.

While there is some general debate about whether a TV can ever switch from a purely passive "couch potato" medium to a more active and engaging environment, nevertheless the richness of the medium – sound, color, movement – its familiarity and its reach, all keep prompting the view that t-interactivity will eventually become a high profile and signif-icant commercial opportunity. However if that is ever to be realised, then there's no question that the market needs to go through a step-change in the way it's structured and exploited today. While the internet itself has attracted a multiplicity of organisations all investing and innovating hard to leverage its capabilities, and while wireless too is attracting a lot of interest as future operating networks with high bandwidth get built, iTV is still regarded as a "minority investment interest." It's low on corporate agendas, and the big TV media companies like Canal Plus, Carlton, Viacom's CBS and Walt Disney's ABC are all struggling with either a weak profits base or other interests. Companies like Sky can't make national markets on their own and certainly would find it difficult to replicate and afford that commitment in many other countries. Government generally is continuing as catalyst by looking to make the digital signal switch, even if timing is uncertain, but it will ultimately be up to the private sector to sort out the issues.

These are significant and are worth further attention if only to focus debate on what needs to change to get this opportunity fixed and opened up. The main hurdles and issues are:

- bandwidth
- "walled gardens"
- TV vs. PC battle
- "killer aps"
- B2B?

Bandwidth

To date the main problem preventing better take-up, particularly in the area of t-commerce, has been poor bandwidth. For example when Sky, through "Open," launched its interactive shopping channel in 1999, expectations were high. Open's management team showed exciting videos to prospective retailers and banks who were keen to explore the new medium and reach out directly to their consumers. The videos promised movement and sound, suggested 3-D type shopping (e.g. walking up the shopping aisle) and generally presented a hard-to-resist experience and environment. Then back to reality. In practice band-width was limited. It meant 30 to 60 second download times, no movement or sound! retailers limited to only showcasing a few products, and a generally static and lifeless presentation. Not surprising, the stats show that while most subscribers visited, less than 1% bought.

This has all resulted in a vicious circle of frustration and disap-pointment on all sides. It's not what was promised, it's boring, usage is low and as consumers turn off so do the prospective t-commerce merchants. As a result instead of a clamor to participate and a surge of investment and promotion to attract people, there's just dull silence.

Fortunately in the US environment this bandwidth problem has not been so manifest. There, at least 50% of interactive TV access is via cable into the home. Most cable companies already offer high speed

Figure 11.3 iTV: 2002 bandwidth challenge

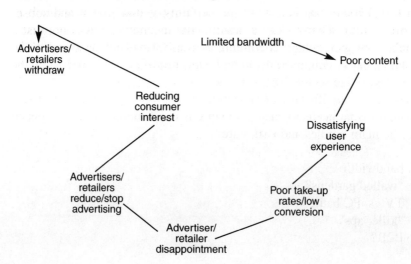

174

internet and so are operating anyway in a hi-bandwidth environment. Many of the cable connections are themselves being upgraded to provide video on demand, and the industry's outlook is to widen scope and compete hard against rival operators and alternative interactive access devices and experiences. Some organisations like Cablevision are spending c. $2bn through 2002 for example, upgrading their infrastructure to provide a full range of digital services: "we plan to dazzle customers with such services as video on demand, e-mail, video games, internet-based telephoning and general Web/e-commerce access."

As a result the US environment is stretching its lead over Europe, creating a much more satisfying consumer experience. That's led analysts at Bear Stearns, for example, to talk up the whole opportunity, arguing that "the prospects for digital TV are extremely promising." The question now is whether Europe will follow suit to any significant degree.

"Walled gardens"

In their rush to make their channels available, and in their fairly short term outlook of let's just build it and get some revenue in, companies like Open and others have established what they call "walled gardens" (see example from Telewest, Figure 11.4).

This means that, instead of being able to access the Net from the TV, subscribers are commonly only given access to a limited number of merchants in a specifically configured and purposed area. For example, Open launched with c. 60 companies represented and cleverly went after an "elite" group, taking the major retail, bank, holiday companies and travel brands on board. At the same time, this elite – and subsequently others – had to pay a price to participate. This was not just a variable cost percentage of the transaction. Instead it was a high fixed cost of entry premium payable to Open, and that was apart from the other costs of set-up and launch. Forrester researchers estimated that in the UK it is currently impossible for an iTV retailer to make any profit. The economics are such that, with the operators (Sky, NTL, Telewest) taking c. 10% of revenues as commission and with annual "tenancy fees," technology and basic marketing costs running at c. 20% of 2002 forecast revenues, then gross margins of c. 25% of revenues are simply not enough to cover the basic cost of being there and doing business.

That has to change of course if the market is to get the level of renewed commitment from the supply side that will be so necessary to restimulate demand and interest. It means the operators will need to review their

Figure 11.4 Telewest Broadband UK Interactive Directory

Shopping	Holidays & travel	Entertainment & sport	News & directories
Argos	1Ski.com	Aloud.com	Autotrader.co.uk
Bid Up TV	ABC Traveltime	BBC Sport	BBC News
Comet	Airmiles	Bid Up TV	BBC Weather
Domino's Pizza	Avis	Blue Square	Birmingham City
Gadgetshop.com	Axa Travel Insurance	Cartoon Network	Council
Iceland.co.uk	BBC Holiday	Coral Eurobet	Bloomberg
Interflora	Shopping Guide	Discovery	Bristol City Council
Kitbag Sports	Bargainholidays.com	First Call	CNN.com
Lastminute.com	Board-It.com	Heart of Midlothian FC	Fish4 Directory
Marks & Spencer	British Airways	ITN Sport	Fish4 Jobs
QVC	Co-op Travel	Kitbag Sports	Improveline
Scene One	Cosmos	Ladbrokes	Interactive
Screenshop	First Choice	Lastminute.com	Exchange & Mart
Shop!	Going Places	Littlewoods Bet24/7	ITN News Channel
Telewest Keyboard	Hertz	Living	ITN Weather
shop	Lastminute.com	MUTV	Job Channel.tv
Tie Rack	More th>n	Nickelodeon	KIC TV (Knowsley
Valuedirect	Online Travel	Paddy Power	Only)
WH Smith	Company	Popcorn.co.uk	Loot
	P&O Cruises	Rock & Pop Tickets	Mersey workplace
	Teletext Holidays	on TV	Newcastle City
	Telme Flights	Scene One	Council
	Telme Hotels	Screenshop	Teletext National
	Thomascook.com	Simply Food	News
	Thomson	Sportingbet.TV	Teletext Weather
	Travel Choice	Sportinglife.com	Yellow Pages, The
	Travel Deals Direct	Teletext Sport	Garden Centre
	Worldcover Direct	Trouble	
		Turner Classic	
		Movies	
		Tweenies	
		Two Way TV	
		William Hill	

pricing, perhaps open up the "walled garden" to others, and charge less rather than more. It also means that the advertisers themselves will need to cooperate in some way to put more pressure on operators – who currently act as gatekeepers – to respond to these challenges.

TV vs. PC

A further "distraction" in the development of the iTV arena is the PC. Many have seen the two as alternative access devices to the world of e-commerce, rather than complementary. While Microsoft has hedged its bets by pushing on both fronts, others have chosen to play down TV as an active medium. The "war of words" among retailers, suppliers, hardware and software

176

Games & learning	Money & property	Motoring
BBC Bitesize	08004homes.com	Autotrader
Discovery	1st Quote Insurance	BBC TV Top Gear
Dorling Kindersley	Abbey National	Shopping Guide
Gameplay	ADVFN Asserta Home	Exchange & Mart
Jamba	AXA Assurance/AXA	Fish4 Cars
Leisuredistrict.net	Insurance	Loot
Playjam	Bloomberg	RAC
Tweenies	Bristol & West	WhatCar
TwoWayTV	Cahoot	
UpRoar	Cheltenham &	
WH Smith	Gloucester	
	Eagle Star Interactive	
	Fish4Homes	
	FTYourMoney.com	
	Hot Property	
	HSBC	
	Lloyds TSB	
	Marks & Spencer	
	More th>n	
	Net Windfall	
	Newcastle Building	
	Society	
	Northern Rock	
	Norwich Union Car	
	and Home Insurance	
	Norwich Union ISAs	
	Pearl	
	Property Channel.TV	
	Prudential	
	TD Waterhouse	
	Teletext Finance	
	UK Invest	
	West Bromwich	
	Building Society	
	Yorkshire Building	
	Society	

developers and distributors, and the wide spread of the PC in the dominating US environment, have also been reasons for iTV to get less attention.

What most expect to happen is that the two will emerge as complementary but inevitably will have different appeal. It's expected that in the long term commercial activity will segment. The PC/Internet access will continue to prevail for home-surfing and family investigation of major one-off purchases such as a mortgage, a car, a high ticket appliance or piece of furniture, where information searching, "digesting" and discussion will form part of the decision making process. The mobile phone/PDA will prevail for those transactions which are impulse, relatively small scale and require on the spot ordering. TV commerce will more likely succeed in areas that are the domain of the house person –

Figure 11.5 Interactive t, e and m commerce

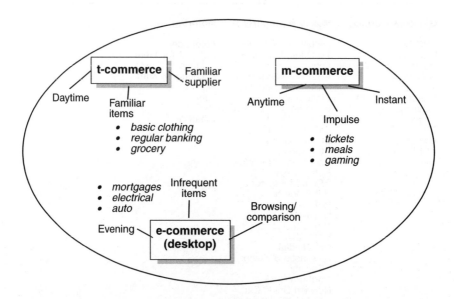

wife or husband who is mostly at home – with children or perhaps elderly dependents. Here, where things are daytime and familiar, TV will be a comfortable easy environment. It will also develop some specific program and advertising killer aps which we'll come to next.

Killer aps

What will kick-start the next wave of interest in iTV? Clearly bandwidth needs to be sorted (especially in Europe), and operators need to become less possessive and elitist, open up their walled gardens and make the economics attractive for companies to participate, even in test mode. But what can also crystallise interest and force the pace are new applications that provoke and stimulate interest and consumer participation.

The quirkily-named Wink TV could be one such application. In a nutshell it provides interactive TV advertising. As the ad unfolds, a specific icon appears in the corner of the screen; viewers with iTV access can click on the remote and automatically get sent a free sample of the product or more information on the holiday, an application form for the insurance policy or a subsequent call from a salesperson providing more detail. Wink is a start-up US company but it already reaches 4 million US households (three-quarters by satellite and the rest by cable). Cable and

178

satellite operators can very easily download the Wink system into existing set top boxes and there's no need for any special equipment. The download can be free and it's easy to use.

Since launch in early 2001, many major advertisers have been trialing this. Procter & Gamble, J&J, Ford, Disney, Glaxo and American Airlines especially have all been experimenting with this interactive advertising, and getting good rates of response. They've trialled "interactive ads" as well as embedding products in sponsored programs and having the interactive icon appear on screen during the program itself. The cable networks like CNBC, CNN and Bloomberg are all beginning to promote this as a new service to subscribers, as are the major broadcast networks. And while there are rival companies in the field such as RespondTV, they have been focussing on STBs that integrate with the Web, and for various technical reasons they've been stumbling on their own market implementation plans.

Advertisers seem ready to pay Wink for its services at 25 cents per click and as much as $1.50 for details of the interested subscriber: name, address etc. Even with just typical low direct marketing response rates, Forrester estimate a 10 million impression media buy could generate a minimum 8000 clicks and 3000 leads at current Wink charges of c. $7000. That's low cost and attractive, and it's just that sort of innovative pricing and simple technology provision that can transform both supply side investment and demand response.

It's expected that Wink will appeal especially at the basic and familiar grocery/drug store product level providing "send me a sample or a coupon." It's also anticipated that the likes of Coca-Cola will use the medium to establish games or contests, while financial services companies are said to be investigating how to work with Wink to generate sales leads for call center or rep follow-up

As one example, Wink has linked up with Lifetime Television to add interactive capabilities to that channel's programming.

> "With a few clicks of the remote control our viewers can now access additional information on products and services that improves the whole viewing and entertainment experience. They can get a daily health schedule with detailed instructions, recipes, personal horoscopes and it won't cost them anything extra."

Aside from Wink's innovations, there are a number of other possible "killer aps." E-mail is one, and certainly that's the most commonly used interactivity among iTV subscribers. Video on demand/video streaming is another

Figure 11.6 Wink's strategic relationships

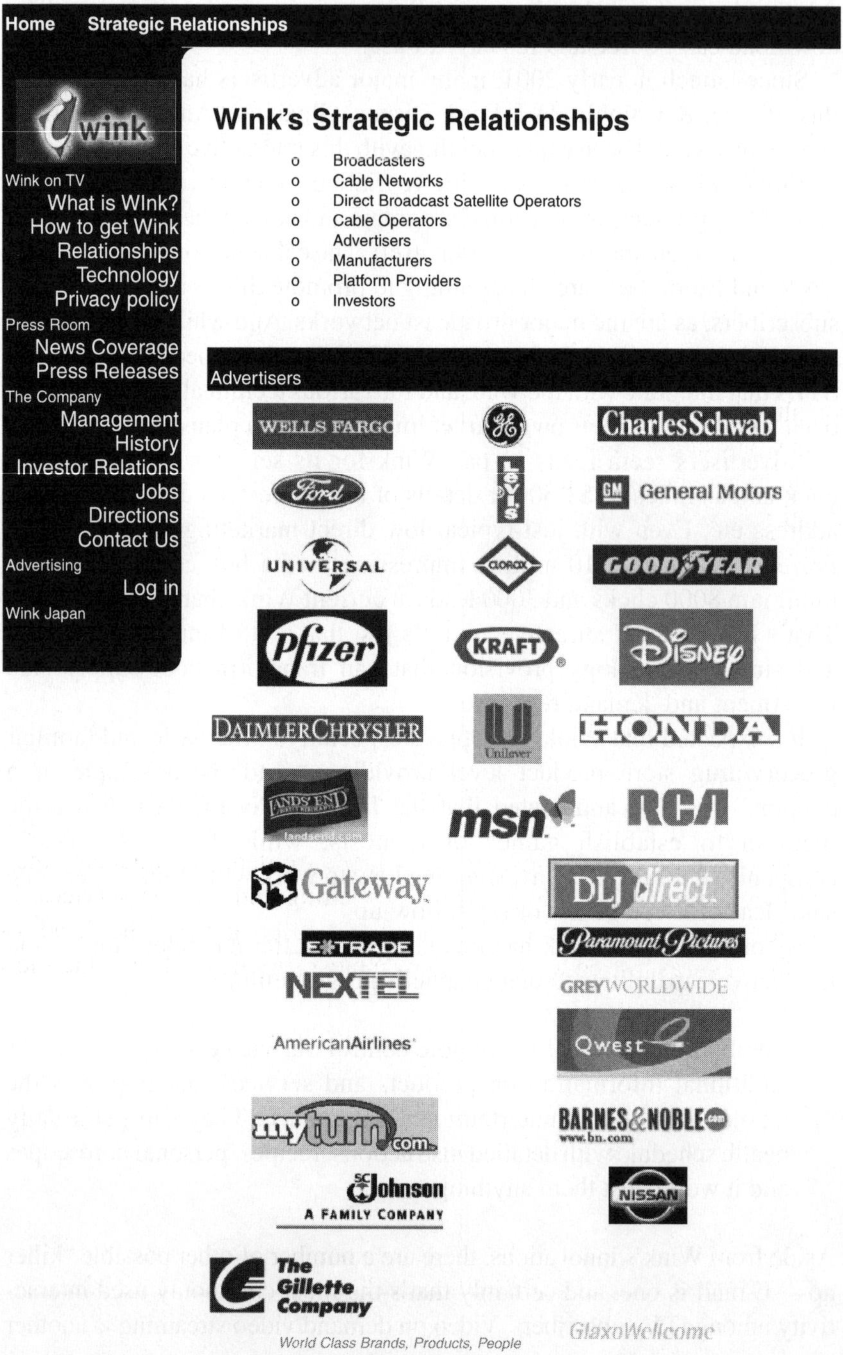

but the technology and bandwidth aren't yet in place, even among the volume cable TV operators. A third opportunity is around "kids," and ideas have been explored of evolving walled gardens from general mass merchandise malls to safe, secure, restricted access, approved-only merchants and services, all aimed exclusively at children. Parents can let their children "surf" and experience e-commerce but without the risks inherent in searching the whole world-wide web where it's still possible innocently to access adult sites for examples. Given kids' ready interest in anything TV-orientated, such a development may have strong appeal.

One other application which is already showing signs of "killer ap" potential is emerging in the UK around betting and gaming. According to leading betting company Ladbrokes (part of Hilton Group), 12% more adults would start betting if they could do so easily over the TV. In the UK that would add at least 2 million potential new customers. Other countries or states where betting is unlawful may be off limits for now, but "off-shore" betting is already a proven formula (UK betting companies successfully set up such operations till tax laws changed). In that mode some companies are even looking at places like China where betting is still forbidden "on-shore" yet there are nevertheless a relatively high proportion of what would be called compulsive gamblers potentially accessible from "off-shore" sites.

In the more developed UK environment, Sky's gambling service has already been used by nearly 70% of the subscriber basis. "Incremental costs of launching this service are minimal and it's encouraging people to use some of our interactive services as well. It's expected that betting could make up one-third of our other interactive revenues as this medium develops." Ladbrokes themselves are equally excited. In announcing their own joint venture with Sky to provide betting and gaming services, in particular on horse-racing and popular soccer games, the head of Ladbrokes was moved to say "this is the most significant deal in the short history of interactive TV."

Research and initial take-up suggests this bullish view will prove realistic and if it does it is the sort of initiative that will both boost UK interest and also further encourage other players in this space to initiate their own investments and initiatives in exploiting iTV.

B2B?

iTV is usually only ever considered as a mass consumer medium, reaching into the home both to entertain and also potentially to sell. Is it foolish then to consider whether there are any meaningful B2B type applications? It's unimaginable that one business would communicate to another through the TV set, but might businesses use this medium to communicate to employees, to members or in other environments where they're trying to reach a large number of people? Might states or governments use iTV for elections and referendums, where viewers can see the various points of views being put forward and vote with one click of the remote? Might businesses use the medium to showcase new corporate initiatives, or hold press conferences and shareholder meetings?

Fact is iTV is not used today in any of these business contexts. The opportunity is not being explored, mostly because people think of TV as expensive broadcasting requiring high infrastructure costs and the need to provide continuous content and information. But it's not impossible to imagine a scenario where, for example, an iTV "Business Channel" is established that would "rent out" space for a day to, say, broadcast GE's or BP's annual general meeting. Not all shareholders can attend in person but they could watch through their TV program, from the comfort of their couch, yet also have the opportunity to interact.

While all this could also be done through a PC once home bandwidth issues are resolved, in the meantime TV provides a potentially ready and attractive alternative. Indeed cost could be kept low by using regional cable TV companies, especially available in the US, to support local business initiatives and communication opportunities to their staff. It could even encompass distribution of the Xmas "thanks and good luck" message: Bill Ford (Ford's CEO) on TV at 11.30 am Xmas day with the year-end thanks and goodwill video to all 350,000 Ford employees accessible by satellite or cable link?

Such initiatives are as yet untried and untested, and in the short term iTV is in danger of becoming an overlooked opportunity for this type of communication and interaction. Those who argue its value can only hope that the likes of Sky and a few other dedicated "big guns" will continue to pour in investment to "make the market," stimulate demand and generally agitate for a more streamlined infrastructure that will make it easier for companies to consider this medium for business communications.

While B2B then may represent some further as yet untapped potential, no doubt the main areas of leverage moving forward will still be predominantly in the whole B2C arena. As companies variously consider whether or not to invest in iTV, there are at present a few new technology initiatives which will at least facilitate some further progress and development.

Return path bandwidth – probably the major stumbling block for those with satellite access – may improve as companies continue to explore "last mile into the home bandwidth solutions." One simple solution which is already being rolled out is to use DSL technology to enhance the existing telephone copper wire. However, telcos continue to price this high (in UK it's a £100 installation plus c. £30 each month line rental), making it unaffordable for the mass market. Alternatively, premium rate fast bandwidth connections by satellite are being trialled by Sky in Scotland. More innovatively fixed wireless internet access solutions may emerge as alternatives in this area but there's been little testing of this possibility to date. In the meantime, cable providers are hoping that their already embedded high bandwidth return path will deliver the fast and reliable access that will encourage further consumer take-up.

Another improvement on the way is plans to upgrade the set top box to incorporate its own higher capacity hard disk. This could be in the stand-alone STB or integrated into the Digital TV. Doing this means games, videos or other content can be downloaded and then used again without going through the waiting time to order up and get the content on screen. Gartner see this as an inevitable development: "'thick' clients will be more successful because they give consumers control over programming, recording and storage."

With improved set top boxes comes the opportunity for personalised marketing and selling. Greater functionality should mean the TV can be used more easily in the same way as the PC to identify, through cookie-like systems as well as voluntary registration, who the customers are, their profile, their location, their other purchasing habits and their history, and thereby tailor future marketing campaigns, e.g. using e-mail to the TV receiver.

Finally there are also plans to try to standardise the operating system so that, no matter which iTV platform provider is being used, advertisers only need to reconfigure content and communication once. Inevitably the lead for this is coming from the US rather than the even more fragmented European environment, and at present two of the leading software providers in this space – Microsoft and Liberate – have the backing of large parts of the US digital cable industry to write a specification for an open standard which is cable-compliant to all STBs in the USA.

If these various improvements do take place at some reasonable pace then iTV will no longer languish as a poor cousin to the PC, and interactive t-commerce may begin to meet some of its early forecasts and predictions. In the meantime of course the PC and developing wireless environments will continue to facilitate widespread Net and commerce connections and, despite TV's familiar appeal, will no doubt dominate future interactivity.

12 e-learning

People at Dell will talk about the Internet as being "part of our core value set." The company has created an environment where there is widespread understanding of what the Internet is about and recognition of its importance to the company. Employees have been trained generally in "e-awareness" and when they've passed the relevant courses and programs they get a certificate that reads: "Michael says I know the Net." (Michael Dell is the CEO.) It's got to the point that senior management no longer need to encourage the workforce to use the Net or think of how the Internet can improve productivity and performance; they think of it for themselves.

Dell has established a "pull environment" rather than a push. They've built an e-learning organisation which is on a roll. It's built up a momentum and an enthusiasm that involves and engages each and every employee. They can see how the company has used the Net to establish an extraordinarily powerful low cost business model. They can see how Dell is continuing to innovate in that space and they want to make their contribution.

This chapter is about building that e-learning organisation, establishing that groundswell of interest and understanding that the whole organisation is going to be Net-enabled. It's about taking forward these streamlining ideas in procurement, in the supply chain, through knowledge management and CRM and in wireless applications. It's about doing more than just initiating projects in these areas. It's setting up alongside them a program of education, encouragement, sharing of best practices and lessons and getting people to see the benefits – for themselves. Properly executed, as our winning companies have shown, the Internet can be a powerful and positive force, and streamlining can mean lower costs but also redeployment and retasking and retooling into the more value-added areas, as opposed to just fewer jobs.

"Power to the people" is a mantra that's been invoked from time to time and a few other organisations are beginning to aspire to the Dell model. At GE, Jack Welch often acknowledged that "the greatest

improvements in productivity will come from the inspiration of individual employees.... Any company that's trying to compete these days
has to find a way to engage the mind of every single employee." Since
GE "woke up to the web" in 1999 it's been relentlessly driving a
program of streamlining through internet-enablement and automation.
Gradually the series of top down initiatives ("each manager tasked with
developing an e-plan") is being replaced by a growing number of
bottom-up suggestions and ideas for performance improvement, with
the web as catalyst.

Simultaneously, at Southwest Airlines front line staff are being actively
encouraged and incentivised to "think electronic" and, at suggestions from
its own ticket clerks, Southwest became one of the first to test and pilot e-
ticketing. That initiative has grown on the back of significant cost benefits
and improved times for passenger loading. Passengers like Southwest's
"pioneering spirit," "willingness to try new things" and "being in touch
with what's latest and new," and now a significant portion of all tickets are
"issued" in this way.

Yahoo! has also "empowered" people – this time Yahoo!'s own
customers. According to Yahoo! there is such a strong community sense
among its members, driven by the fact that it was one of the first major
Internet search engines and a survivor from the early day, that it receives
literally thousands of enthusiastic notes and comments on how the site
could be improved and how the company should develop. Yahoo!'s own
customers want the company to become the most e-literate, the most e-
enabled! While for sure many of the suggestions are self-serving, how
many other companies today get this level of positive feedback, advice
and ideas from their own customers – unsolicited?

Another way of thinking about this is that it's about building the
company's "web DNA," getting the new technology scene so embedded
into the company that it's in every fiber, every part, every action, every
meeting, and it becomes natural and part of the way of doing business, not
forced and coercive. Russell Reynolds for example, the employment
search firm, talk about looking for candidates with this web DNA: a set
of characteristics, a set of differentiating skills and traits that mark out
executives as "Internet-enabled" and able thereby to lead companies more
effectively into the online marketplace and build for future success.

A key to establishing this sort of environment is to focus particularly in
the first instance on e-training and e-education. And it's worth doing that
in financial terms as well. Ford estimated the value to date of its "best practice training program" at $1.1bn, and Siemens more modestly reckon that

the value of new solutions to business problems that have been developed through its management e-education courses during 2001 adds up to $11m.

John Chambers, CEO of Cisco, recently described "e-training" as one of the "killer applications of the Internet" and went on to say it's an opportunity that's yet to be fully realised. Research by Click2learn indicates that in 2002 only 8% of companies surveyed had implemented any significant e-training/e-learning, and even among the handful who have it's often without the context of a complete company-wide e-strategy. Roadblocks cited in the research include cost of implementation, but the major reason quoted by 80% of HR officers interviewed was that e-learning is "not yet a top ten boardroom issue."

These roadblocks appear despite an ongoing series of research projects carried out by the American Society for Training and Development (ASTD). These consistently show that there is a correlation between the amount invested in this area and overall company performance. In fact the numbers are startling. Those investing more than c. $1000 per employee outperform the stock market by up to 45% according to ASTD. Those that invest significantly less than this threshold, on the other hand, under-perform the market by 22%.

Whether the size of this over or under-performance is exactly correct matters less than the overall conclusions from the research. Invest in this area, consistently, over time and the company will get payback. Overlook this value-add opportunity and the company risks failing to leverage and empower its staff to make a difference in the marketplace. Facts are that c. 90% of employees in most developed countries now work in offices connected to the Net, that in the major economies of North America, Northern Europe and a number of "Asian Tigers," consumer Internet penetration is often 50% plus, and a whole new generation is growing up Net literate. People therefore want to apply these new skills, technologies and ideas in their workplace and they're mostly just looking for the catalyst to enable them to do that.

E-training tends to develop hand-in-hand with using the Net as a complementary tool and communication device. The goal is to establish a learning environment which is "self-service" and personalised. What companies are learning is that what works best is a mix of continuing face to face training that is combined with using the Net as well. Apart from many other benefits such as remote learning, learning when you want, do it at your convenience, accessibility 24/7, there's also the preference that many have for learning privately. It means they can ask those apparently "naïve and embarrassing questions" such as "what does HTML stand for?" or "what's the difference between HTML and XML?" and can ask in the privacy of their own environment without risking losing face in front of their peers.

Many companies however have only begun to scratch the surface of the whole employee communication on the Net. There's some basic corporate-wide employee information that's already getting posted on a bulletin board, there's the individual sharing of data on request via e-mail, and some peer groups and communities of interest will have organised some voluntary sharing of relevant information, market and project news. Training on the Net, if there is any, will be relatively uncoordinated. There will be access to training modules from software companies, some departments will put some of their training material online, but what's not common is to see a concerted company-wide program and what's still rare is to see that personalised to individual employees who can gain self-accreditation, access training experts, post particular queries and requests for help and get advice on what to train on and how to go about it.

SAP's Managing Director, Hans-Peter Kleay, puts it this way:

> "Tomorrow's employees will have their own personal portals with a customisable menu of interests. We're working towards the intelligent workplace where each individual is empowered and in control. They are technology-enabled, can evaluate the company's and their own performance real time and learn as they go."

Let's consider some further examples of companies who are getting their e-learning programs more effectively under way:

Figure 12.1 Employee learning on the Net

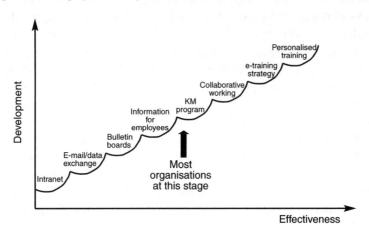

- Bank of Scotland, now HBOS, has built a specific Training Centre on its intranet for its employees. There are 28 topics including everything from budgeting and balance sheets to e-commerce and the WWW. It's a voluntary resource but the Bank is finding that as many as 80% of its employees use it. "As much as anything it's a useful dip-in, dip-out resource where execs can brush up on their skills."

- Cisco, with c. 40,000 employees scattered across the world, has quickly realised the potential of learning tools to drive efficiency into its work-place. Before 1998, 85% of training took place in formal classrooms. "To keep things both economical and actually useful we needed to change that."

  A key motivator in early days was thus cost savings and as a result of putting some 50% of training online the company has reduced costs by a roughly similar amount. But the main objective has been to create a learning environment online that could be constantly updated and made topical (no need to wait for that next training course in a year's time).

  "We've developed learning portals for many different parts of Cisco." For example there's a site that aggregates all the learning resources for account managers, and another one for field engineers. There's access to "learning roadmaps" and information relevant to specific jobs.

  On top of that are a number of other applications. All managers have access to the "Manager Dashboard," describing the various training programs available with links and also general info on HR policies, latest news etc. There's live TV broadcasting delivered directly to the desktop via satellite links to convey e.g. new product briefings, single training sessions and training updates. And there's video on demand to provide "just in time" training, for example for a sales person to get an update on specific product specs or otherwise refresh certain core or new skills.

  "All these systems are to empower our employees to do their jobs more effectively. At first we had to 'push' the system through with a lot of internal promotion. But now, because it is designed to meet specific demands and individual needs, people are 'pulling' the materials and are asking for more."

- Motorola has spent over $500m in two years to build its e-learning capability. "This has been the key to e-enabling the whole organisa-tion. We wanted people to be united in this mission and viewed the training as the most important investment." Motorola University has just a small team but it's used the Net to establish worldwide training

groups. It had all its employees through its e-learning courses by end 2001 and plans to update and refresh the courses on a continuous basis.
- Deutsche Bank also has a University. Like Motorola it has also established an e-learning program. But it has experienced some difficulties in implementing this across the whole company and, unlike at Motorola, employee participation has been patchy especially in the early days.

However, the bank has made new and senior commitments to making this initiative work. The chairman has made a number of public statements about the bank's desire to compile and transmit learning and knowledge electronically. 200 different training modules have been established on the "corporate university portal." But access is not free. Employees have to pay for the online seminar out of department budgets.

Accepting that the "pay for training" might be a barrier, Deutsche Bank reckons that it's still in the first stages of electronic education. "We've started out softly softly and we're learning ourselves as we go. So we'll phase in new features such as 'video on demand' courses at appropriate points as the franchise develops."

This last example is instructive because it does highlight some of the difficulties companies will face as they progress down this path.

First there is an overload of new technologies, new approaches and new information. What needs to be captured? What's important? It's not just a question of translating physical course materials into digital format. That's relatively undemanding and is a straightforward exercise. But the objective here is to go beyond that. It's to create a learning environment where people absorb the lessons, start asking for them and start thinking about where and how they can apply them into their own area. So the training and education that needs to go online has to be not only the key hard facts but also the "how-tos" and "examples" and lessons learned and best practices. It needs to be in a program set by management that's supplemented by face to face explanation and workshops that encourage the culture to adopt these new lessons and examples. People should know that doing this, observing it, applying it will be recognised, that it is important, in fact it's crucial, and will be rewarded. So the first lesson is to sort through the information overload, identify some key insights and approaches, and create a mix of teaching and other events or initiatives that helps employees see the whole context.

The second lesson is to appreciate that this cannot be achieved overnight. Like much of what is described in this book it does not happen quickly. Change is not an instant thing. To be all-embracing and sustainable it needs to win hearts and minds. The same is true for e-learning programs. People need to get used to the idea that a four-day "conference" at Pebble Beach with a "golfing" afternoon for "team-building" is now an exception rather than the rule. It's a "perk" that's earned rather than automatically enjoyed. People also need training in how to train online and how to take advantage of that new environment. All this also means that the initial courses and teaching aids and expert inputs will need to be regularly revised, refreshed and improved as the company learns how to do it.

The third lesson, which we'll return to, is the need to go beyond company-wide education. To really get people's interest it needs to be done in the context of a community of interest and personalised, so whatever's put together means something to the individual.

The fourth lesson is set the whole thing up in a way that delivers early wins. So Cisco for example may now have 100 hours of material online but most of the modules are designed to be completed in 20 minutes or less. At KPMG, an editorial board vets all material on a regular basis to see what's valid, what needs updating and what needs deleting. At Colgate-Palmolive, people know that using the material is regarded by senior management as important and not using it can be a bar to promotion. At Motorola, their Latin-American offices for example insist that training is accompanied by site visits and interviews with outside execs in other companies so people can explore ideas, hurdles, opportunities in real life. At Skandia, employees are encouraged to take their new-found learning and go on secondment to other companies as "consultants" to test out the ideas in practice.

Perhaps the final hurdle to describe in this context is for the company to consider how its employees will want to access the material in the future. It's the same as the general "knowledge management" challenge. People will not want to be "chained" to a desktop to use it. They'll be mobile and may want a skills or an e-news update on a project before going to a meeting, or want to use the hour during a taxi/car/plane ride to catch up on that new learning module on e.g. wireless applications. Deciding which access device to use is important because as we've described wireless can work, and can work well today, even with the bandwidth limitations, provided the pages are formatted purposefully and carefully for that environment. Simply translating a web page into WAP will not work and only causes frustration.

190

Just as there are challenges in the implementation, so equally getting it right can pay back. It's not just Dell, or Ford, or Siemens who are reaping advantage. Companies are finding that three distinct areas of benefit do emerge. These are important because they help underpin and validate any business case that's being promoted to create this e-learning opportunity.

- **Employee loyalty:** Companies are finding they are getting greater engagement and involvement from their workforce, they're creating channels for new ideas to come through and it's leading to reduced employee turnover.
- **Business effectiveness:** People are learning new skills, sharing better practices and, through this, generally improving performance and productivity.
- **Lower costs:** Reduced costs of training by developing alternative pathways online. For example the Creative Learning Agency estimate in a survey that costs could be reduced by up to 90%. Or, more positively, from the same budget, a company could achieve up to ten times as much learning.

Unipart is a UK-based automotive manufacturing firm that has long had an outstanding reputation for its advanced management thinking. It places a strong emphasis on learning and training and was one of the first organisations to run its own "university" material over the Net, link it to specific company projects and skill sets, and tie it all in firmly with the company's whole knowledge management program.

The senior execs at Unipart know that, as a relatively small supplier (turnover is c. $3.5bn but margins are tight at 4 to 5%) competing on the global stage with sophisticated auto customers, the company needs to crystallise every piece of know-how into a learning environment it can share with all its employees. Equally, as it began to see the power of the Net, it was important to do everything it could to get its workforce up to speed and get them to use the latest tools and technologies in the business all the time to improve productivity. As one way to achieve this, Unipart has developed its "Faculty on the Floor" to help workers on the production floor share the latest know-how. The system is intranet-based and has become the tool for advice, problem solving, and product and manufacturing process information. Because of the

Net's easy ubiquity this is shared with employees – wherever they are – all over the world. "We find 'Faculty on the Floor' breaks down all the previous barriers, it's got us sharing and replicating knowledge.... New ideas now travel very quickly."

Unipart has been successful with its e-learning initiatives. So successful in fact that it enjoys and is proud to promote itself as the learning organisation. Its employees have a willingness and enthusiasm to learn about new ideas and share them widely. It uses this platform to go further. First, it involves customers in its learning environment, inviting them not just to visit its facilities but also to share in some of the learning programs. Second, it has realised that this know-how that it's built up is itself a valuable asset. To exploit it Unipart has established an Advanced Learning Systems (ALS) unit. This unit is like a consultancy; it certainly charges for its services! But its task is to train and advise others. Within its sector, ALS is developing a strong niche position as a specialist firm that can advise but also has the infrastructure to pass on its learning and help clients and customers establish their own similar environment.

For an organisation that does want to do more than just establish another e-project, then getting e-learning into the heart of the company, getting the "pull" rather than the "push," is the big opportunity. It may start with an awareness/training program but the end is much more challenging and exciting. It may be getting to the point where the company is so enthused that it wants to tell the world and show them how to do it, like

Figure 12.2 Empowering the e-employee: portal example

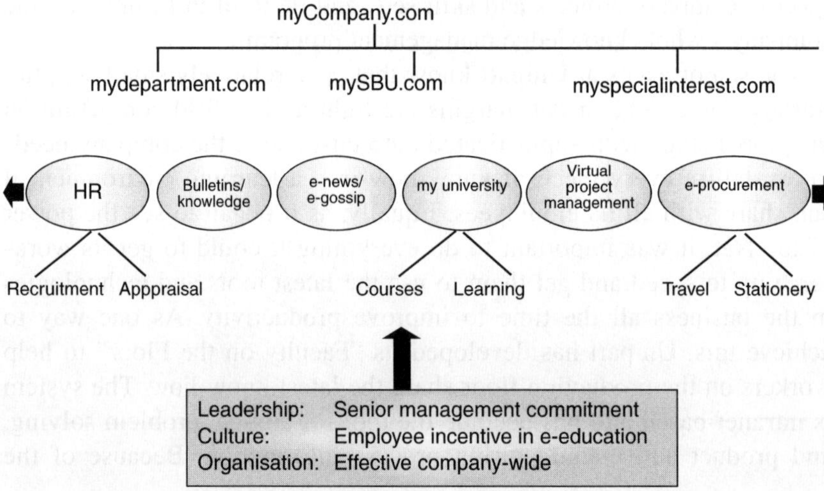

192

Unipart, or it may be more simply that it wants to Internet-enable and automate everything it can, like Dell, so it can compete harder and better on every front end, and that way secure both individual employment and the company's own lasting success.

Companies are discovering that one of the best devices to stimulate and kick start an e-learning program is to build an e-portal but one which can be personalised. It needs to be a place people want to come to and will likely include a range of additional functionality. That might include everything from online gossip and chat rooms through to important project knowledge sharing. But it's all about building up the human capital to boost the intellectual capital of the organisation. As Watson Wyatt, the global employee services company, have commented:

"the corporate sector is gradually waking up to the promise of e-learning or Internet-enabling.... They are realising they can combine online training with other knowledge sharing to lay the groundwork for a more productive working environment. The opportunity is now to develop a careful plan that helps everyone learn and then thrive in the new digital age."

13 Making it happen

The size of the prize is so significant that we are still left with the question why aren't more companies taking advantage of these new e-enabling technologies? Why are there still only a relative small number of "break-through companies" who have discovered this significant profit booster? Does it mean that the rest of business has stood still or is it more simply that others are trying but not yet succeeding?

This final chapter is about summarising the lessons learnt from the winning companies. Others indeed have not stood still but, as we shall see, are sometimes making mistakes in the ways they approach this new opportunity. Let's consider then:

- eight things to avoid
- ten things to aim at.

No organisation is perfect and of course no single company will ever be able to put ticks in every box. But e-business is no longer new. It's been around. People have learned how to do things. The technologies are no longer in their infancy. The new tools have been applied enough times with enough success that we can demonstrate quite unequivocally what can be streamlined and how to go about it. As a result we're not talking about "inventing wheels" or "betting the farm" on new approaches that are untried and untested. We're rather drawing together the lessons that have already been learnt.

Eight things to avoid

1. Doing it haphazardly.
2. Doing it alone.
3. Seeing payback only in the long term.
4. Treating 'e' as "BAU."
5. Bottom up only.
6. Assuming it's only about cost-cutting.

7. Insufficient resources …
8. … Insufficient skills.

1. Doing it haphazardly

After the 1999–2000 hype, lots of companies got so burnt by 'e' fall-out that they cut back, reduced, put on hold, disbanded and generally put a stop on most e-business related initiatives.

However a few typically slipped through the net. What still carried on and persisted depended upon individual passions and enthusiasms. In some instances there'd been early wins or initial successes which were enough to persuade management to indulge that particular investment, while in other circumstances the effort was simply "below the radar screen" – it wasn't of such scope or size that senior management either knew about it or cared enough to intervene.

This has led to a situation where most companies are still carrying out 'e'/new technology initiatives but in a fairly haphazard and opportunistic fashion. This misses out on a critical component of capturing the e-business opportunity. It means the necessary linkages and synergies and required cross-company involvements are just not happening. For by definition the advantage to be gained for example on an e-procurement exercise is to consider all the company's suppliers and its total purchase volume, leverage, and interactivity with each. Doing this in only one division could easily miss out most of the benefit if another division or business unit shares suppliers or products or components. Equally on the

Figure 13.1 "Opportunistic"/random approach

Examples	Division A		Division B		Division C
	Country 1	Country 2	Sales Dept	Purchasing Dept	
1. Web enable basics	X		X		
2. SCM (supply chain management)		X		X	
3. B in B communication	X				X
4. Customer interactivity					X
5. Supplier interactivity				X	

customer side, value only comes from leveraging an organisation's total interaction with that customer, not missing out half of it.

Continuing to do things in an uncoordinated fashion means a vast number of activities end up being duplicated. Information is entered into different systems, the same checks and verifications get done in different ways and the same documents get handled through different processes. It leads to inconsistency and complexity, and that typically drives error, delay and cost. And that typically results in poorer market performance and lost business as well as demotivated staff who see the problem but don't often have the power to influence the alternative solution.

So cardinal rule number 1 is: avoid doing things in an uncoordinated haphazard way. The goal is to benchmark Oracle and others, and find and establish those necessary linkages across the organisation that will drive the resulting synergistic approach to change. And e-business technologies do enable and encourage these boundaries to break down, walls to crumble and opportunities to collaborate to become more visible. It may not mean every link has to be made immediately but there does need to be a deliberate decision about which synergies to go after.

Figure 13.2 Coordinated approach to 'e'

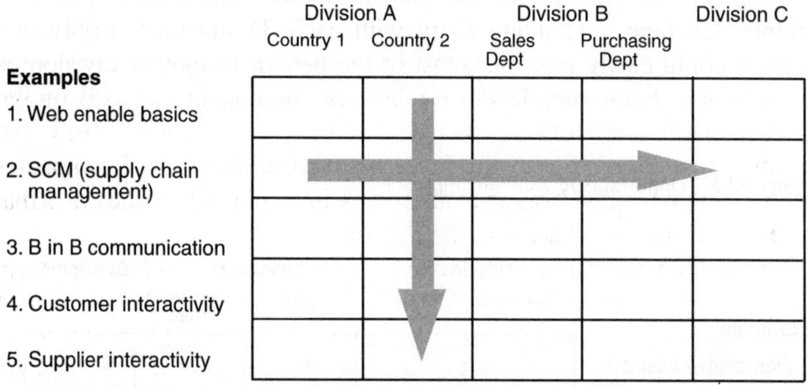

	Division A		Division B		Division C
	Country 1	Country 2	Sales Dept	Purchasing Dept	
Examples					
1. Web enable basics					
2. SCM (supply chain management)					
3. B in B communication					
4. Customer interactivity					
5. Supplier interactivity					

2. Things to avoid: doing it alone

Technology companies like Cisco, Intel and Microsoft have been role models in building networks of alliances, joint ventures and cooperative working agreements. Their aim is to develop a shared approach and thereby access others' methods, technologies and skills. They have set their targets, but they are also farseeing enough to realise they either can't get there on their own or could get there much quicker with the help of others.

The more savvy "e-implementers" nowadays are therefore locking up companies more formally as partners. Often this involves investment and risk sharing; for example Barclays Bank recent $50m contract with IBM is based on a three-year program to dedicate teams and share IP, and payment is contingent on agreed deliverables.

Whether it's straightforward arm's length outsourcing or more formal and intimate partnerships, doing it jointly rather than alone is making increasing sense. Most would now agree that technology and change are moving so fast that it's almost impossible for one organisation, no matter how large, to stay abreast of all techniques and best practices. Despite that, it's extraordinary how many even now eschew the help of experts or the more formal commitment and participation of others. "Value networks" as they're called are offering a much more leveraged alternative and, if some companies like Microsoft or Cisco are looked on as benchmarks, we may expect to see a page in the annual report in future listing for example "our top 20 key strategic partnerships and how they are enabling the business to move forward faster."

3. *Things to avoid: seeing payback only in the long term*

Thinking of e-business as being able to provide only a long term payback can be a major blocker. If the whole arena is considered as only providing gain in three or more years' time, then of course the motivation to pursue this will reduce significantly. If, equally, the cant is that it's risky and requires significant investment, then it's not surprising lots of companies won't get onto the bandwagon at all or only in response to some crisis that forces these sorts of ideas onto the agenda.

In Chapter 5 we specifically looked at the importance of building early momentum and getting some short term wins on the board. A number of companies were highlighted, from big guns like GE and DuPont to relatively smaller enterprises like Herman Miller and Fisher Scientific, who have discovered how to pilot and test their way to success. Doing it step by step is the only way to get skeptics and doubters to join the cause, the only way to get a broad coalition of interest, the only way to get the funding and resourcing for the bigger prizes. Encouragingly there are enough areas of short term opportunity – from e-procurement at one end to CRM at the other – with quick payback features that mean building the momentum should be very feasible.

4. Things to avoid: treating e-business as just "business as usual"

We've referred to this already but a common viewpoint is that: "there's nothing new about 'e', it's just business as usual, it's just another excuse to talk about IT or technology, it's something that's being kept up by the IT department to increase their budgets, all things are 'e' now anyway ..." etc.

Part of this reaction is due to the e-disappointments of 2000/1 but part of it just misses the point. 'e' is different. It is new. There are new technologies. There are new software tools and applications. It enables new things to be done that either could not be done before or were too expensive and time-consuming. Now common language and global connectivity around the Net do enable tasks to be performed differently, more cost effectively and with wider and quicker benefits.

The new technologies have given birth to a host of new tools and applications that are demonstrably different from what was available. They can, if pursued rigorously, deliver a transformation in the way things get done. These new tools do need to be thought about very particularly and there's a need to define the relevant expertise and experience to carry them through.

Figure 13.3 Ten new e-business tools

- Speed up time for response and communication, e.g. real time
- Lower costs, e.g. automated contacts, 'zero touch'
- New forms of convenience for customers
- More information/more insight, e.g. 1 on 1 marketing
- New routes to market/new sources of growth
- New ways to communicate, e.g. mobile, virtual learning
- New software tools, e.g. Xml, middleware
- New software applications, e.g. Broadvision, Commerce One
- Competition, e.g. boundaries blur, alliances
- New forms of outsourcing, e.g. ASPs

- Profit growth
- Performance improvement

5. Things to avoid: bottom-up only

Just as we talked about the disadvantages and demerits of a haphazard/ opportunistic approach, so it's critical that implementation is not done purely "bottom-up" through individual functions, departments and business units. That "bottom-up" swelling of interest and desire for change and improvement has to be met by equal if not greater measures of "top-down" enthusiasm, commitment and passion. Without that combination, there's no chance of success.

Most companies do now operate in a decentralised fashion, delegating power and authority to individual business unit and function heads. But this cannot be an excuse to abrogate power and authority. Where there is a substantial prize to be had in shareholder value, a central team cannot just leave it to others. There has to be a considerable amount of leadership, target-setting, prioritisation and responsibility taken.

Figure 13.4 Central team leadership

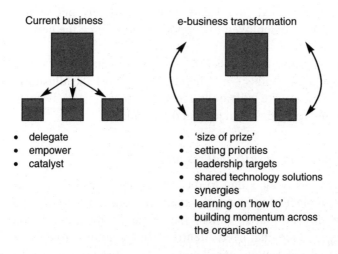

That is not to say that individual business heads are "disempowered." What this is saying though is that they must be enabled and supported and sometimes "encouraged" to take the actions and initiatives that will drive the benefits. Given the need for cross-company links in particular to be made, some of that behavior may have to be mandated. Though once the benefits are articulated and quantified that becomes a lot easier to do.

6. Things to avoid: assuming it's only about cost-cutting

If there's one sure way to kill off an idea when a company's not in crisis, it's to position any new initiative as a cost-cutting exercise. Hackles rise, defenses get quickly built, positions get taken and a hundred and one reasons emerge as to why now's not the right time to make that sort of change here and anyway it wouldn't work, and we've already been cutting costs for the past ten years and if we do more we'll endanger safety, the customer, our reputation … etc.

Sometimes these points of view are indeed valid but to get a more open-minded response it's important to talk about the upside. Streamlining-led change is very different from its predecessor, re-engineering. That was typically perceived as a negative force for change. It became associated with "downsizing" and "rightsizing" and tended to be an exercise about jobs, redundancies and costs.

Yes, for sure, streamlining can drive that way. But its greatest power is for positive change and growth. Because the new technologies enable things to be done differently, quicker and smarter, it means the proposition in front of the customer can be dramatically improved. Jobs can be cut in that context or instead, more effectively and with greater potential benefit, redeployed to support and reinforce the new customer initiative.

Some might argue that this is just "window dressing" but if you consider our "pioneer case studies" in Chapter 3, many of the illustrations, for example at Cisco, were built around redeployment to take advantage of the new opportunities, rather than just cut out people.

7. Things to avoid: insufficient resource

At one level everyone's day to day job is about change and improvement. But the fact of the matter is that everyone's day to day job is full of day to day pressures, things that need fixing, people who need managing, products that need attention, things going wrong, committee meetings that need attending. There's often just no time to devote to change projects. "They don't need doing now, they can be left till tomorrow … and the next day."

What a number of companies now recognise is that change is a specific challenge. It contains specific tasks and responsibilities that are typically additional to the day jobs. In response companies have set up dedicated resources. People are selected as program managers, change agents, they are put on specific projects – all with a view to resourcing up the various streamlining projects. There's a growing recognition that without enough resource the change will never get implemented, the benefits never realised.

Procter & Gamble tell the story of how they embarked upon a recent restructuring. The corporation conducted a review with the help of consultants identifying a number of high potential projects. At the end of the review the consultants' very strong recommendation was that P&G could only achieve its goals if it chose a team of 120 people – yes 120 – who would be seconded full time for up to two years as dedicated change managers. And these people had to be 120 of the best people P&G had, not just those who were "available" or who could be easily released from their existing day jobs. 120 of the best.

At first P&G not unexpectedly shied away from this. No way did they have 120 of their best people available. If they were taken off their current tasks all sorts of other problems would occur. But to their credit the consulting firm involved was insistent. And finally P&G did agree. It did compromise a bit, but eventually some 80 full time personnel were reassigned.

Commentators and insiders agree that it was only in this way, with that kind of investment and commitment and recognition of the resourcing need, that P&G then went on to get the results it did.

8. *Things to avoid: insufficient skills*

If the resources are there, then the skills must be there too. Some people are just better at change management than others. It requires specific skills involving project management disciplines, a talent for handling people, "enjoying" hitting "brick walls" and being the sort of executive who relishes the challenge of finding new solutions, remains enthusiastic and positive despite time and target pressures, and has an appreciation of the power of the new technology tools (of increasing value in today's environment).

It could be argued that every manager should have these skills but we all know how some are just better "project managers" than others. In particular, understanding the new technology scene is also critical. Some companies as a result are now insisting their would be 'e' champions take study visits, going to best practice companies in this arena, interviewing there and discovering and learning how best to proceed along this journey.

Ten things to aim at

We've had the "don'ts"; now let's be positive and examine the "dos." The case histories of companies who've been pioneering internet developments are showing a consistent list of "must haves": things that have got to be in place for any significant streamlining program to deliver.

1. Dare.
2. "Neutralise + co-opt."
3. It is the technology ...
4. Develop a strong "new technologies" team.
5. It's also the processes and the structures.
6. Involve partners and customers.
7. A program of continuous learning and development.
8. Hearts + minds.
9. Align the rewards structure.
10. Continuous "MMR."

1. Dare

The new technology environment is uncertain. Its potential is emerging but there are still many very real questions and concerns. Do these opportunities apply to my type of company, are we ready for this kind of change, are our customers/suppliers/partners ready to respond?

It's against this kind of backcloth that decisions nevertheless need to get made. Companies have a choice of course: do nothing, do a few things incrementally, or carpe diem – seize the day and the time. Take advantage of this catalyst to drive the organisation into the next era of the twenty-first century. Establish a new platform to produce the next round of wealth for stakeholders. Take responsibility for ensuring the long term as well as the short term health of the company.

Company researchers Collins and Porras, in their breakthrough book *Built to Last*, looked at companies who were winners and tried

Figure 13.5 Companies have a choice

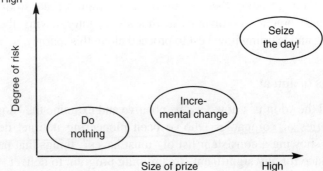

to define their characteristics. One that emerged strongly was the willingness, desire and passion to set "BHAGS" – big hairy audacious goals! They looked at companies from Ford to GE and Procter & Gamble and demonstrated how the vision, the daring, the boldness, the "persistent commitment" set by leaders had driven these companies forward, eventually outlasting and outsmarting competition to achieve significant shareholder value rewards over long periods of time.

Their message, and one echoed by others, is: "be bold, dare!" Of course, manage the risk, no need to "bet the entire farm," but it's only by setting stretching and tough targets that the organisation has any rallying point or set of visceral and tangible goals to direct its efforts.

We're all familiar now with President Kennedy's bold assertion in 1961, "we're going to have a man on the moon at the end of this decade." The vision was just about feasible, just about possible; it was hugely challenging, yet believable enough to motivate the entire NASA staff. Result: eight years later Armstrong's famous words, "one small step for man, a giant step for the human race."

Time frames and expectations may be shorter than an entire decade now – and that's not unrealistic given the various advances that have been made – but the next batch of winning organisations is waiting to emerge and the question remains: who will have the vision to start their organisation along that journey? Here are a few who have:

- Siemens: "50% of our procurement worldwide will be done electronically by 2003 and our savings target is €1bn."
- Misys: "To enable us to compete in the new economy we commit to be among the top three tech investors in our sector."
- Japan: "We will surpass the US in integrated high speed Internet infrastructure by 2006."
- UK (Tony Blair): "The UK will become the best economy in the world for e-commerce by 2006."
- Pearson: "At Pearson we are increasing investment in Internet-related initiatives.... We plan a path to payback within 18 months."
- Cisco: "We see this as the second industrial revolution and we're going to be the dominant force."
- Intel: "We have to keep transforming our company into an e-company, otherwise we won't survive."

2. *"Neutralise and co-opt"*

IBM staffers tell the story of how 'e' first got on their agenda in the early 1990s.

Initially there was just a small group of people who felt there was a substantial opportunity developing. They could see how Internet technology was establishing a step-change in information transfer. An open system by definition meant easier and cheaper connectivity. This small group became evangelical and impatient. They became vociferous, disrupted meetings and started to bang the drum loudly. Unfortunately for them, they were a little ahead of the consensus and were regarded as mavericks. Before long they were forced to move on because they couldn't get any backing.

But behind this vanguard lay a growing number of others. They'd seen how the first group had created some entrenched views and more enemies than friends. So they embarked on a crusade of "neutralise and co-opt."

Figure 13.6 Building company-wide recognition

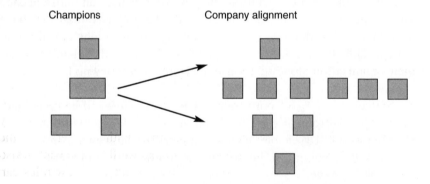

"Neutralising" meant finding out who were the "nay-sayers," the doubters, the critics and isolating them. "Co-opting" meant discovering the enthusiasts, the believers and encouraging them.

This was still a deliberate campaign, but its goal was to quietly find and build a network of champions. The aim was to build this network to such a critical mass that it became an unstoppable force. And of course that's what they succeeded in doing. Now IBM is one of the e-champions, it has committed substantial resources, spends over $100m a year advertising its e-ambitions and credentials, and reckons its 'e'-related work accounts for c. 40% plus of all projects.

The learning process is critical here. Many organisations are still generally skeptical about e-business and uncertain about what it can achieve. Many others are either generally cynical about change opportunities or wary of the implications. Starting to bang the drum too loudly from one corner of the company could be counter-productive. "Neutralising and co-opting" might take a bit longer but might ultimately be far more rewarding.

3. It is the technology

Most people first became acquainted with the Internet when they came across the world-wide web as a network of information and research sources. They were introduced to the Netscape web browser – for free – and once that software was loaded onto the PC, they found instant access to global news, buying and selling, and fast electronic transmission of data.

For many this is still what the Internet is all about. A vast collection of html pages, an open standard, that enables anytime anywhere anymachine access and communication.

But it didn't take long for other applications to develop. If we can e-mail, we can share knowledge for example, and we can store that data on a central server. So this is an enabler for easy and cheap (no interoperability issues between different computer systems) knowledge management. Hence the development of corporate intranets, ostensibly to enable this rapid sharing of intellectual capital. And other applications started developing as well, built around similar processes. Who needs EDI (electronic data interchange) with expensive and time-consuming legacy system integration when we can simply connect with suppliers over the Net? Let them send us an invoice via e-mail and we'll tell the bank – also via e-mail – when to pay. And simple software and workflow rules can automate that process.

Suddenly this simple technology breakthrough is ubiquitous. Easy to learn, simple to implement, quick to establish. It just needs everyone to get onto the Net bandwagon. What stops the more rapid and widespread adoption of this way of communicating? Put simply, it's the existing systems in the company. Having just invested say $20m and three years in building an ERP (enterprise-wide resource planning) system to connect the company, its various functions, business units and employees, you naturally have a vested interest to make that work. But if you're starting from scratch today...?

Typically companies nowadays with established "legacy" systems always approach a situation requiring a technology solution with the same constraint: what information do we have in our systems and how can we best deliver it to help solve the problem or add value? Such an approach seems inevitably to result in a mismatch between what is provided and what users really need.

A better approach has to be to first understand the information needs and then identify the system solution to meet those requirements. This is especially true when the competitive environment is demanding technical solutions that are the most tailored, the most user-friendly, and not ones that have to cross-check complex legacy systems to arrive at just a part of the answer.

The Internet enables these type of user/customer-friendly solutions to be developed much more readily. This is because all employees are now equipped with a web browser giving them Internet access and so the facility to access networks of information. Combine a web browser-based solution with a "middleware" business layer and solutions can now be developed that don't require any material change to the back office legacy environment.

This sort of ever-increasing solution has at its heart the separation of front end users from back office systems. It in effect creates different layers of business process and system solution. The ERP layer is left largely untouched, enabling the company to maximise the potential of those enterprise-wide systems. The "middle layer" insulates the front end application from changes in the back end and vice versa. The front end application is "liberated" from existing legacy complexities and is

Figure 13.7 Internet and middleware to drive business solutions

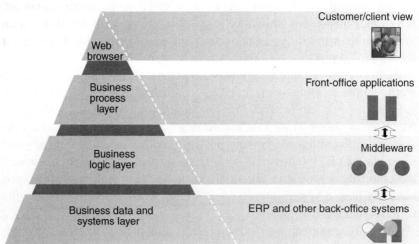

enabled to provide rapid response. It also protects the user/customer from interfacing with lots of different legacy systems. It simply draws out all the information needed and presents it in a single view.

With this sort of approach it's now very possible to build the infra-structure for example to share customer knowledge across the company, with employees, suppliers and customers themselves. Before the Net, the cost of developing customer-facing applications across say hundreds of contact points would probably not have been justifiable. The changes to the legacy systems, increased networking requirements, upgrading everyone's desktop PC would have involved considerable time and expense. There would have been numerous operational issues for the IT department in particular because it would have meant the standardisation of software applications for different parts of the business.

Because of today's maturing Internet technology these barriers no longer exist. The Internet and the developed front end applications that have been built around it provide the "universal transport mechanism" for interchange of data across corporate networks (intranets). But they can also be linked with third parties (extranets), with customers (www) and also with mobile users (internet). This means that the system admin costs associated with a traditional IT system deployment across an extended enterprise are much reduced. It also means one common appli-cation (e.g. written in a multi-platform web language such as Java) can be implemented across multiple devices.

The Internet therefore enables multi-point connectivity and transfer of information in a way that just could not have been done before. As we shall see, it's as much about the software applications that have been developed to take advantage of the Internet backbone as the Internet itself. But it does mean the technology is now a key enabler of change and an organisation must understand this and have people who appreciate this if they are to take advantage of this new environment.

4. Develop a strong "new technologies" team

It's a simple point. If no one in the company has expertise in this new technology arena then it's less likely this area of opportunity will be developed.

An easy way to get started is to get advisers – auditors, bankers or consultants – to set up an "Internet *e·a·i* roadshow," visiting other companies who have already started down this path. This was common when e-commerce first burst onto the commercial scene in the late 1990s.

Gangs of wide-eyed execs from Europe especially would tour Silicon Valley and wander around Palo Alto and Menlo Park interviewing 22 year olds with pony-tails who talked about a revolution.

Well, we don't need to visit the West Coast (shame!) and the interviewees are likely to be older and more sober-suited, but the value to be derived is critical. It's the immersion into the world of Internet-driven change and development. It's listening to people who've "been there and done it." It's seeing first hand how a process works today and comparing it with what one is typically used to. It's an experience based on fact, on what's actually being achieved today. It's not one based on hype and promise and hubris.

One specific example is to visit PA Consulting's Technology Centre in Cambridge, England or Princeton, New Jersey. These centers showcase new technology developments and applications. They demonstrate how these new approaches work. They are especially strong in developing 3G wireless solutions. They'll give you a hand-held pocket PC, connect it to the Net, and illustrate from their own "KnowledgeNet" how "mobile logistics" can be transformed by a combination of Internet and improving wireless technology.

It brings it to life, makes it real with case study and example and inspires teams to review what they're doing and explore how new technology can help.

5. *It's also the processes, the structures*

Reports from Gartner and other research houses have recently shown that in the CRM (customer relationship management) arena most new technology solutions put in during the initial hype period have failed. Around two-thirds of identifiable projects did not pay back. To move forward effectively, it's absolutely critical to take on board the learning as to why.

Part of the failure was simply due to the fact that the investment was made during the early hype years when it was not uncommon to throw large sums of money at new internet-related software providers like Siebel and expect big benefits to materialise automatically. The lesson learned is in fact an old one now being repeated and re-emphasised. Technology by itself won't deliver big paybacks and returns. It's all the stuff that goes with it. Most particularly, as described, it's the process, the structure and indeed the right strategic orientation and targets.

Why is it that so many new 'e' implementations have failed in the early years? When we interview the companies concerned the key

Figure 13.8 Technology in context

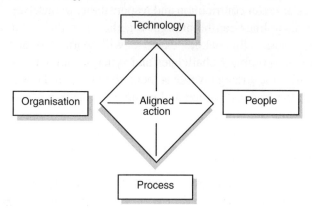

reason coming back is that the old processes, for example around customer management, in fact never changed. So there is a new system, but old ways of collecting and syndicating information on customers still prevail. In effect the "old" costs never got taken out, manual processes with their own costs in delay, error and time are still in place. Training on the new system is perfunctory and inadequate. User support is poor. People may start with the new but unless everyone does it and wants to do it on day 1 and persists with it, it will never be sustained.

Similarly the organisation structure to support and enable the change must be established. The whole point of a CRM implementation for instance is to coordinate, to bring together disparate data about customers lying in different databases with different people. If there's value in having "one consolidated view of the customer," then there need to be structural mechanisms to facilitate that consolidation. Managers of different channels – e.g. branches, brokers, telesales and Internet for a financial services organisation – might previously have worked in their own distinct and discrete channel/business unit teams. Now there needs to be a "multi-channel manager" or some formal mechanism at minimum to ensure effective consolidation and then exploitation of the developed customer knowledge base.

All this needs to be set into a sensible strategic context. If there is no value to be had from sharing customer knowledge (unlikely as that might be), then there should be no CRM program in the first place. If there is, then what is the value? If it's about increased loyalty, extra revenues and incremental market share growth, then let's set those targets and let's cascade them down to individual managers so that they are "compelled" to respond because they've got a clear target contribution and responsibility themselves.

If all these disciplines can be brought together then there is a significantly greater chance this whole exercise will work. No one would suggest such cross-company challenges and synergies are easy to set up. But if the quantifiable strategic value is there, then it has to be worthwhile paying heed to the lessons learned and going after the opportunity in the most effective way.

6. Involve partners + customers

It's said that the Internet breaks down barriers and borders. Where once company A dealt with supplier B or customer C mostly at arm's length, now there is no reason for the divide. Each partner or customer can be part of the same network. Each can access the others' information systems to participate in a real time and intimate commercial network.

Collaboration throughout the supply chain is becoming one of the most important networking opportunities to emerge out of the Internet. It's predicted for example by Gartner that "collaborative commerce initiatives involving web-enabled interaction between enterprises, their customers, trading partners and employees will surpass e-commerce and transaction management as a top priority." They've even sponsored a web site: www.collaborativecommerce.com.

Another research house, this time Forrester, estimate that "in-depth business collaboration such as demand forecasting and joint product development are now getting more organisation interest than areas such as e-procurement." Research suggests the vast majority of execs in a survey, some 63%, were putting this area top of their agenda.

Whether this high level of interest will be maintained is less important than the growing recognition that the new technology tools don't get optimised unless supply chain partners are involved. If we go back to our "pioneers," companies like Moen and Dell have transformed their business model by following a collaboration path. Even older established organisations like Procter & Gamble have long been engaged in these sorts of forward-thinking partnerships and have been among the most aggressive in extracting value. What P&G and others are demonstrating is that collaboration can drive much stronger business relationships, generate growth in sales for both parties, reduce the costs of doing business and generally create a win:win business environment.

7. A program of continuous learning + development

We're still learning about the Net. New applications are coming out with increasing frequency: new software tools, new standards, new common languages such as Xml, new industry initiatives, new collaborations in the marketplace offering innovative solutions. At the same time we're still in that test-bed ground where some ideas are still failing, some software tools are being overtaken by other better offerings providing a better web face, some ventures are struggling financially and others are being "restructured." What's more there are new ways of working and innovations like the ASP model – application service provider – which enable a company to rent rather than buy.

In this environment it's important that every management team stays in touch with experts who are following the scene, not because management needs to be at the leading edge but more to ensure that it does get access to the latest know-how, the most recent market insights. For example, if the team has a range of specific problems would Oracle's integrated e-business suite of solutions offer a better option than picking the best software applications in each area, such as Autonomy for knowledge management, Siebel for CRM and Commerce One for e-procurement? What works, what doesn't, what's proven already and where is there risk?

As already described there are a number of ways to keep on learning. Study tours, using consultants, benchmarking, knowledge-sharing, training, testing and learning, collaborating with others, outsourcing, value networks, hiring in from other companies … these and other devices are all valuable in equipping a company for this e-business journey. Training courses especially (Chapter 12) can now be developed online, where employees can in their own time learn about html and Xml and Java and appreciate what acronyms like DSL and GPRS mean and involve. Some organisations have even gone on to provide a means of self-accreditation to empower people to get internet literate and establish themselves more vigorously as contributors to the future.

8. Hearts + minds

In "Things to avoid," doing it only "bottom up" was described as inadequate. It needs top down management involvement too. But how best put together that "heady mix" of leaders and followers, managers and workforce collaborating enthusiastically to the same end? It's one of the perennial challenges for all companies in all their various endeavors. There are no easy answers but the researchers Collins & Porras have also examined this issue at length, trying to see how a leader's vision best gets implemented. The rub seems to be all about "sharing" (and for more see Chapter 15 of *Strategy in Crisis* by the author).

Most important is the sharing of the strategy and its benefits, the core values it embraces and the facts and information and context that led to its adoption. What are we trying to achieve, why are we trying to get there, what will be the benefits for the company as a whole – and for us, why is it critical we succeed at this and most importantly what's my personal and individual contribution to this whole game plan?

Examples can be cited where this has happened and a critical catalyst in winning hearts and minds is communicating the strategy in a way even the most junior employee finds engaging and exciting. So for example Toyota promote a strategy of product excellence, but as they rolled out their European development program they put their goal into the context of "Beat Mercedes." They wanted to find a simple idea that captured their ambition and yet was instantly engaging to the whole workforce. And as Jack Welch has commented, "if people are to put out the extraordinary effort required to realise corporate targets then they must all be able to identify with them and share in the ideas and goals that they represent."

So it's critical that a plan gets put together which not only reflects "things to avoid" but also, in the context of "things to do," incorporates

Figure 13.9 Sharing for commitment

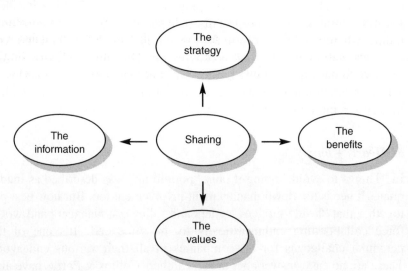

deliberate investment in time and resource to explain, communicate and involve all the employees. And this cannot be just a one-off exercise; it has to be continuous to keep people informed and manage their motivation levels so they reach the right pitch.

9. Align the rewards structure

Very much building on the previous point, the rewards must reflect the contributions. So if there is substantial gain to be had when the streamlining exercise is successful, then the employees should be rewarded accordingly.

When the Internet was in its boom this notion was being reflected in substantial stock option packages. Frustratingly, most of these were soon "under water" as the stock market fell away, but the principle is the right one: a long term incentive plan that reflects increases in shareholder value, properly measured against a basket of rival companies, and at sensible levels so the potential reward remains motivating but is not so great as to appear unfair.

That simple mechanism is very easy to implement. In some cases it goes hand-in-hand with a lower basic salary, putting more of the emphasis in the total remuneration package on the longer term incentive element. But while most companies will have such a reward for senior execs, it often does not extend through to the whole company. This seems short-sighted, and organisations where even the most junior clerk is eligible typically run more highly motivated teams.

This has been borne out by a survey of America's "Most Admired Corporations," an annual survey carried out by *Fortune* business magazine. Among other things they found that the top companies were typically also members of the "Employee Ownership List" (a listing of 1000 companies where employees own more than 4% of the stock).

10. Continuous "MMR"

Alongside all these "must dos," the last and in some ways the most important is "Monitor Measure + Report" (MMR).

Whatever a company does, if the initiative is not effectively MMR'd then there's less chance of implementation success. It's a combination of sound project management disciplines, sharing information, keeping people informed and motivated and at the end of the day ensuring the "P2P" or the path to profitability is followed, is kept on track and does lead to the original targeted return.

Some companies here develop a "dashboard" or a balanced scorecard. This contains the "KPI," the key performance indicators that measure how well a company is doing. Companies will have a mix of core financial performance metrics such as margin and return on capital, but also have measures on aspects such as customer retention and employee satisfaction. While in some companies these KPI get fixed and rarely reviewed, the more dynamic organisation is reappraising them regularly and will often incorporate several tactical measures that may endure for no more than a year or two. But they are introduced to monitor performance on key projects, for example, or key areas of change.

In the early e-days a company might have responded to the hype by introducing notions of "total e/IT investment" or "total number of e-projects" because that was what Wall Street and the City were themselves clamoring for. Now with the more sober reality having hit home, more likely measures might be rather around payback, number of customers interacting 100% electronically, number of processes automated to zero touch or percentage of employees using the knowledge management portal. These sort of measures would indicate not only the financial leverage of any investment but the degree to which the company is getting Net-enabled and working with its customers to do the same.

It's these kinds of KPI that an organisation can develop to monitor just how far its enable/automate/innovate ambitions are progressing and to see just how much streamlining has taken a hold on the company's culture.

* * * * *

Eight things to avoid, ten things to aim at. Of course it's not as simple as "follow these rules and everything will work and will deliver the planned ROI." But there are pitfalls that can be avoided and there are better practices that can be pursued. Each organisation team must select the aspects it regards as the most critical and the ideas that most apply to its situation. The approach needs to be tailored and fine-tuned so that people can readily see the value. It also needs to be "translated" into language and context that all employees can immediately recognise and acknowledge. So it's no use talking about 'e' if the company got so burnt by bad e-investments. Maybe more productive to refer to "new technology"! In the same context, there's no point talking about "Dare" if a management team is still groping its way through early test piloting. But through all this it does need champions, advocates, promoters and enthusiasts who want their organisation to keep learning, keep getting better and be in a position to take advantage of the new business approaches being developed.

Streamlining is nothing if not challenging. But it's also exciting. Quoting Geoffrey Colvin of *Fortune* again, it's potentially the biggest opportunity for transforming shareholder value that management's going to get this decade. There have been plenty of illustrations here of how that can be done and what can be achieved. Options for *e·a·i* change and improvement range across the whole company, involving practically every process where better efficiency and effect can boost profit. Time it seems for the second wave of success stories to emerge in the wake of the vanguard, and time for business generally to seize this unique chance to transform the organisation and its prospects.

Figures

1.1	Streamlining: the new agenda	5
1.2	Internet as catalyst	6
2.1	Streamlining: key points of leverage	7
3.1	S,G&A costs as percentage of net revenue for Dell from 1997 to 2001	22
3.2	Netbanking at Nordea	27
3.3	Fortune brands	29
4.1	The three core new technologies	35
4.2	Key business drivers for adoption of e-business solutions	37
4.3	"e-business" as catalyst	37
4.4	Cycles of Internet development	38
4.5	Stages in technology development	40
4.6	US productivity	41
4.7	Dot.coms digout: total operating income of the 35 companies in the Dow Jones Internet Index	43
4.8	Thus plc: telecomms infrastructure	44
5.1	e-business progress	52
5.2	Three steps to *e·a·i*	53
5.3	The technology fit	56
5.4	e-projects portfolio management	57
5.5	Understanding the new e-business tools	59
5.6	Looking for *e·a·i* priorities across the value chain	60
5.7	Fixing on the priorities	61
5.8	New technology tools/approaches across the value chain	61
5.9	Innovation and immersion	64
6.1	Procurement chain	75
6.2	e-procurement product selection	76
6.3	e-procurement through the desktop	78
7.1	Supply chain evolution	89
7.2	INTTRA: customer driven, carrier sponsored	94
7.3	Order processing	98
8.1	Profiting from human capital	105

8.2	Knowledge management priorities	108
8.3	Evolution of knowledge management	109
8.4	Four steps to knowledge sharing	114
8.5	Prioritising knowledge capture: example	116
8.6	Organisation KM strengths and weaknesses	122
9.1	CRM value chain	127
9.2	CRM in action	131
9.3	Retaining customers	133
9.4	Developing customer services	135
9.5	Customer portfolio evaluation: example	136
9.6	Integrated IT for seamless customer experience across channels	138
10.1	Universal Internet access	151
10.2	Mobile Internet access	152
10.3	Wireless and Internet penetration forecast 2005	152
10.4	Growth in wireless data speeds	159
10.5	Improved bandwidth	160
10.6	Internet-enabled PDA	164
11.1	The continuing revolution in e-commerce	171
11.2	Forecast digital TV penetration rates (UK)	171
11.3	iTV: 2002 bandwidth challenge	174
11.4	Telewest Broadband UK Interactive Directory	176
11.5	Interactive t, e and m commerce	178
11.6	Wink's strategic relationships	180
12.1	Employee learning on the Net	187
12.2	Empowering the e-employee: portal example	192
13.1	"Opportunistic"/random approach	195
13.2	Coordinated approach to 'e'	196
13.3	Ten new e-business tools	198
13.4	Central team leadership	199
13.5	Companies have a choice	202
13.6	Building company-wide recognition	204
13.7	Internet and middleware to drive business solutions	206
13.8	Technology in context	209
13.9	Sharing for commitment	212

Tables

3.1 Pioneers across most sectors   12
4.1 Technology innovation continuing fast   35
5.1 The benchmarking challenge: examples   54
6.1 e-procurement cost savings opportunities   67
6.2 Example of Commerce One marketplace, suppliers included 72
9.1 Average cost of CRM channels per transaction   132
10.1 Leading mobile applications, 2000–5   167

Abbreviations

3G	Third Generation Network in wireless communications will enable a convergence of voice, data and multimedia services with high bandwidth capacity.
ASP	Application Service Providers offer access to applications such as software related services on a rental basis via the Internet.
ATM	Automatic Teller Machine
CDMA	Code Division Multiple Access is a radio transmission format used in North America for wireless or cellular telephone services.
CRM	Customer Relationship Management is a category of business applications, for example call center management, that focusses on the connection between the company and its customers.
DSL	or ADSL (asymmetric digital subscriber line) is a physical layer protocol that supports high bandwidth transmissions (up to 8mbps downstream and up 1mbps upstream). The asymmetrical aspect of ADSL technology makes it ideal for internet browsing, video on demand and remote local area network access.
DWDM	Dense wave division multiplexing separates different transmissions by using different colors or frequencies of light within the same fibre optic strand.
EDI	Electronic data interchange provides for the exchange of information between businesses using wide area networks (WAN). EDI transactions transfer structured data such as electronic payment and related documents.
ERP	Enterprise Resource Planning software is a system with integrated functions for all parts of the business such as production, distribution, sales, finance and human resources.
FAQ	Frequently Asked Questions.

FX	Foreign Exchange.
GPRS	General Packet Radio Service is a "2.5 generation" of wireless technology offered as a standard across Europe.
GPS	Global Positioning satellite System.
GSM	Global System for Mobile telecommunications is the second generation digital wireless communications standard approved and used widely across Europe.
HTML	Hypertext Markup Language is the method used to create web pages and documents.
IP	Internet Protocol is the standard communications protocol for passing data over the Internet.
Java	An object oriented programming language developed by Sun Microsystems. It is designed to be platform neutral and so is used widely for programming web applications and facilitating networking from many types of computers.
MRO	Maintenance Repair and Operations is a term used in the procurement process to refer to non-core inputs.
OEMs	Original Equipment Manufacturers
OLAP	Online analytical processing is a tool to provide multi-dimensional data analysis that looks across different databases to provide a different view of related data.
PDA	Personal Digital Assistant is a lightweight palmtop computer designed to provide personal organiser functions as well as communications.
ROI	Return on Investment.
SME	Small to medium enterprises.
SMS	Short Message Service has become a popular form of message transmission over mobile networks.
STP	Straight-Through order Processing.
TCP/IP	Transmission Control Protocol/Internet Protocol is the set of transport protocols that have become a de facto networking standard. The protocol manages the bundling of outgoing data into packets and the transmission of packets on a network, and checks the bundles for errors.
UMTS	Universal Mobile Telecommunications System is a mobile access network and part of the global family of 3G mobile communication systems providing high capacity transmission.
WAP	Wireless Application Protocol is a worldwide standard for providing internet communications and advanced

	telephony services on digital mobile phones, PDAs and other wireless terminals.
Windows NT	An operating system developed by Microsoft intended to support "high end" multi-tasking environments.
Windows XP	Released in October 2001 it provides an updated operating system as a successor to Windows 2000 with improved networking and home entertainment systems.
WLAN	Wireless Local Area Networks.
WLL	Wireless Local Loops.
XML	eXtensible Markup Language lets web developers create customised tags offering greater flexibility in organising and presenting data and is being adopted as a common language platform in some sectors.

Index

1–800 Flowers 42
2G (second generation network) *see* GSM
2.5G 139, 156–8, 159, 163, 168
3Com 161
3G (third generation network) *ix*, 49, 58,
    139, 149, 153–63 *passim*, 168, 208
  advantages 158–9
  speed of transmission 155, 158
7-Eleven 125

AA (Automobile Association) 47
ABB (Asea Brown Boveri) 13
Abbey National 25
ABC 173
ABN Amro 46
Accenture 132
accounting 15, 19, 20, 24
Acorn 39
Actrade 45
ADSL 58, 183
Advanced Learning Systems 192
agent technology 111
Ahold 168
Air France 137
airlines/air travel 2, 36, 47, 136–7, 179
  booking 2, 42, 47, 132
  in-flight e-mailing 164
Alcatel 157
Alloy Online 42
Amazon 12, 49, 54, 102, 125, 134, 135,
    136, 145
Amdocs 138
American Airlines 179
American Management Systems 123
American Society for Training and Devel-
    opment (ASTD) 186
Ameritrade 42
Amstrad 39
anti-competive practices 30, 73
AOL 42, 172
Apple 40, 101
Ariba 55

artificial intelligence 111
Asia 139, 149, 155
Asite.com 159
ASP (application service provider) *ix*, 73,
    141, 211
Aspective 141
assembly line 116
AT&T 87, 162, 172
Atari 39
ATM 149
ATRIAX 46
auctions 69, 70–1, 73, 84
authentication 75, 79, 81, 93
auto industry, early development of 39
automated invoicing *see* online facilities
automating *ix*, 2, 3, 4, 5, 48, 120, 138,
    161, 185
  of orders 19, 23, 23, 24, 67, 75, 90, 95
  of sales 19, 21, 142
  of tracking 95
Autonomy 110, 119
autonomy 17, 20

B2B (business to business processes) 4,
    17, 34, 45, 49, 71, 92, 142
  iTV 181–3
B2C (business to customer) transactions
    7, 26, 34, 49, 182
Ballmer, Steve 33
bandwidth 34, 38, 58, 148, 151, 154, 155,
    156, 158, 168, 173, 174–5, 178, 181,
    182, 183
Bank of America 25, 46, 149
Bank of Scotland 188
banking 12, 97, 126, 147
  and foreign exchange 46
bar codes 92, 95
  2d bar codes 96
Barclays 46, 197
Bear Sterns 95, 175
benchmarking 53–5, 57, 121, 125, 197,
    211

222

Benetton 103
Beney, Robert E 43
best practices 54, 54, 112, 121, 122, 123, 147, 185, 189
Bezos, Jeff 33, 145
Blair, Tony 6, 203
Bloomberg 179
Bluetooth 160–2
BMW 52
bonuses/incentives 16, 20, 100, 108, 118
  see also employees motivating
BP Amoco *ix*, 12, 54, 76–7, 80, 104, 111–12, 121, 123
Brabeck-Letmathe, Peter 13, 14
branding 25, 149, 170
Bristol-Myers Squibb 67
British Aerospace 105
British Airways (BA) 137
British Telecom 107–8
Broadvision 55, 110, 146
Browne, Lord John 111
BT (British Telecom) 153
Built to last 202
Business 2.0 130, 144
business principles 43, 48, 58, 64, 76
  see also project management
Business Week 42, 46

cable access 154, 160, 162, 163, 171, 172, 174–5, 178–83 *passim*,
Cablevision 172, 175
Cahoot 25
call-back 142, 143
call centers 3, 15, 16, 21, 116, 128, 130, 133, 138, 140, 142, 144, 156
  cost per call 23, 132
  set-up costs 130
Canada 139, 148
Canal Plus 173
Cap Gemini 148
Carlton 173
CAs (certificate authorities) 79
CBS 173
centralisation 19
CGNU 26, 52
Chambers, John 15, 33, 186
champions *see* key individuals
change experts 66
Charles Schwab 149
Chase Manhattan 149
Chemdex.com 72
chemicals industry 69, 96, 103
Chevron Texaco 105, 123
China 154, 155, 156, 181

Christianbank, Norway 25
Chubb Insurance 165
Cisco *ix*, 6, 12, 15–18, 33, 34, 36, 87, 186, 188, 190, 196, 197, 200, 203
Citibank 46, 97, 126, 149
Clarify 138, 140
Click2Learn 186
Click2Talk 142
click to order/connect etc 3, 54, 143, 166, 170, 182
clothing 62–4, 87, 98, 99, 101, 103
CMA 92
CNBC 179
CNN 179
Coca-Cola 4, 47, 105, 179
Colgate-Palmolive 190
collaboration 11, 28, 48, 80, 83, 86, 87, 88, 91, 101, 102, 112, 210, 211
  see also partnership
Colvin, Geoffrey 36, 215
Commence 139
Commerce One 55, 69, 71, 87
Commodore 39
communication 2, 5, 48, 90, 130, 170, 204
  across company 13, 14, 187
  increased need 92
  of Internet software systems 31–2, 104, 110, 198, 205, 207
  networks 37, 44, 45, 85, 92, 98
  of teams 11, 209
  universal 5
  see also knowledge/information sharing
communities of interest 111, 112, 118, 120, 187
Compaq/Hewlett Packard 40, 67–8, 91, 156, 164
compatibility, issues of 5, 13, 19, 20, 52, 54, 55, 56, 67, 68, 70, 97, 128, 129, 141, 154, 157, 168
competition 3, 38, 39, 60, 74, 106, 109, 125, 126, 130, 142, 191, 203, 206
complacency 18
computers, costs in 1980s 34
  see also PCs
Computerworld 34
Concorde 137
confidentiality 104
consultants 65, 100, 190, 201, 207, 211
Cook, Tim 101
cookies 170, 183
cost 24, 37, 50
  of ADSL lines 183
  of "always on" systems 157, 158
  and auctions 73

duplication of 19, 20, 21
of interactive marketing 179
of invoicing 51, 97
of manufacturing 15
of marketing 25
of poor knowledge management 104, 120
of processing transactions 26, 68, 74, 82
of requisition/procurement 23–4, 52, 67–9, 74, 84
reduction 2, 4, 5, 11, 12, 13, 14, 15, 16, 18, 21, 23, 25, 26, 30, 34, 36, 38, 46, 51, 67–8, 69, 70, 73, 74, 77, 80, 82, 84, 87, 91, 93, 108, 112, 120, 121, 123, 128, 130, 132, 133, 139, 165, 188, 191, 199–200, 203, 210
of S,G&A (sales, general and admin) 12, 21, 23, 128, 132, 165
and strategic knowledge system 119
of transmitting data 45
of transport 94
Covisint 4, 73
Creative Learning Agency 191
critical path 2, 107
CRM (customer relations management) 125–47, 184, 197, 208, 209
benefits 132–3
failure of software solutions 55, 126, 127, 141, 143, 208
key ingredients 143–7
spending on software 127
strategic context 134–7
and technology 137–43
wireless 139, 165
culture, corporate 8, 21, 59, 82, 83, 112, 130, 134, 144, 212
Currenex 46
customer
changing behaviour/demands 47, 85, 92, 125, 145
dissatisfaction 3, 20, 102, 129
expectations 62
e-banking 25, 36
extranet links for 16
interaction 85
interactive systems 54
online interface 23
long term/loyal 130, 133, 134–6, 137, 147, 148, 156, 209
profiling 21, 37, 51, 86, 91, 102, 109, 113, 116–17, 128, 130, 132, 136, 138, 140, 142, 145–6, 147, 168, 183, 209
relations/service *x*, 1, 3, 14, 19, 21, 23, 28, 29, 34, 37, 38, 54, 55, 84, 86, 93, 97–8, 98, 127, 132, 134, 144, 165, 168, 185, 192, 200, 210–11
reluctant to use Internet 91
research programs 63
tracking of 2
web experience 23
wireless 148
see also CRM
customisation/build to order 23, 85, 90, 98, 100–2, 103, 107, 125, 130, 139, 145
of portals 119, 120, 187, 193
of web sites 145, 146
cutbacks 1, 200
see also redundancies
cycles of development 38, 40, 41
new technologies 8, 39

data
compression 124
global 2, 35
index 107
problems of sharing 104
tagging 120
transfer 5, 15, 207
see also EDI, transmission speed
data mining 109, 110, 141
data protection rules 147
data warehouse 3, 109, 110
databases
company 13
EMC storage 45, 119
fragmented 19, 20, 37, 76
global 19, 35, 137
speeding transmission *see* transmission
streamlining/consolidating 18, 19, 21
Universal Database 91
Datamonitor 47
deadlines 66, 81, 82
decentralisation 17, 18, 68, 70, 76, 111, 198
decision making 19, 37, 48
dedicated circuit switching 157
dedicated resources 66, 200–1
delay 3, 16, 19, 37, 85, 87, 100, 102, 116, 125, 140, 165, 209
delivery, speeding up of time to market 4, 11, 63, 85–6, 102
see also product to market time
Dell 8, 12, 21–4, 40, 49, 85, 101, 105, 115, 117, 126, 184, 191, 193, 210
customisation 101
Dell, Michael 4, 24, 184
Delphi group 104

demand 22
  forecasting 85, 90, 92, 98, 210
Denmark 93, 171
desktop environment 30, 32
Deustche Bank 46, 189
Deutsche Telekom 153, 167, 168
Digital 39, 40, 130
digital certificates 79
digital TV 170–2, 183
  number of users 171
digital/analog signals 170, 173
Disney 173, 179
distributed computing 31–2
distribution 4, 13, 51
DoCoMo 47, 155
  number of subscribers 155
document management systems 109–10,
domain registers 45
Domino's Pizza 170
dot.com
  boom/bomb ix, 1, 7, 33, 34, 39, 43, 51,
    92, 115, 134, 151, 195, 198, 208,
    213, 214
  revolution, early stage of 33, 41–2
Dow Chemical 105
Drucker, Peter 33, 45, 106
DSL technology *see* ADSL
Dunkelberg, William 43,
duplication 17, 19, 20, 21, 196, 209,
DuPont 51, 197
DWDM (dense wave division
  multiplexing) 45
Dynergy 12

Eastman Chemical 68–70
Easyjet 47, 125, 132
e-banking 25, 36, 39, 42, 47, 148, 149
  see also Nordea Bank
eBay 42
e-billing 96–7
  see also online invoicing
EBP *see* e-billing
economic climate 17, 24, 141
economies of scale 13
EDI (electronic data interchange) 67, 75,
  77–9, 80, 81, 83, 84, 85, 90, 93, 96,
  205
e-enabling, profitability of ix, 12
efficiency 3, 48, 93
  inefficiencies 19, 21, 37
effort, duplication of 17, 19, 20, 196, 209
e-gain 138
Elcom.com 74
e-learning 8, 184–93

Ellison, Larry 6, 19–20
e-mail 13, 95, 98, 111, 125, 138, 139, 141,
  143, 149, 173, 179, 183, 187, 205
  cost of 132, 155
  diversity of systems 20
  "e-mail the expert" facility 16–17
  in-flight 164
e-marketplace *see* online marketplaces
EMC data storage 45, 119
Emerson inc 62, 64, 81
employees 14, 38, 187
  evaluation 16
  motivating 5, 11, 16, 19, 55–6, 60, 62,
    64, 65, 69, 69, 71, 81, 82, 100, 107,
    113, 122, 123, 134, 134, 143, 144,
    168, 184, 185, 188, 189, 190, 191,
    192, 196, 198, 204–5, 212, 213, 214
  response to innovation 57, 144
  suggestions 108, 116, 123, 185
  time at desk 162
enabling ix, 5
encryption 74, 93, 148
equipment performance monitoring 62
e-revolution, time scale of 13
Ericsson 46, 153, 157, 161
ERP (enterprise resource planning) ix, 3,
  70, 137, 138, 206
ethics 147
Europe 14, 139, 150, 151, 153, 154, 155,
  170, 171, 175, 178, 183
EVA (economic value added) program 52
EZOrder.com 14

FAQs 16, 21, 130, 144
fax 67, 165
  cost of 14
Federal Reserve Board 40
Fedex 68, 95, 125, 166
Ferra, Joseph G 148–9
Fidelity Investment 12, 148–9
Field Centrix 164
file server 110
financial services 26, 148, 157, 179, 214
  online 42, 47, 148
  see also banking, e-banking, insurance
Financial Times 34, 64
Findwhat.com 42
Finland 25, 47, 126
firewalls 74
First Direct bank 126
Fisher Scientific 6, 51, 97, 197
Ford Motor Company 23, 38, 95, 103,
  106–7, 133, 179, 185, 191, 203
  Henry Ford approach 85

foreign exchange 45–6, 150
Forrester Research 30, 84, 153, 175, 179, 210
Fortune 31, 36, 49, 62, 104, 106, 213, 214
Fortune Brands 28
Fox School of Business and Management 90, 94
France 171
France Telecom 153
fraud *see* security
Frost and Sullivan Research 162
FTSE companies 34
Future Shock 34
FX Connect 46
FXALL 46
FXtrades 46

Gap 133
Gartner 30, 127, 132, 183, 208, 210
Gates, Bill 31, 33
GE (General Electric) *ix*, 6, 12, 36, 51, 62, 71, 81–2, 184, 197, 203
Germany 39, 47, 153, 171
Glaxo 179
global IT divisions 20
GM (General Motors) 39, 79, 149
GoCargo.com 93
Goizeuta, Robert 105
gold rush 40
Goudge, David 142
GPRS (general packet radio services) 58, 156, 157, 158
GPS (global positioning system) 166
Grainger.com 6, 72, 98, 125
Greenspan, Alan 11
Group 3G 153
growth
    cycles of 38, 40, 41
    economic growth rates 17
    Internet growth rate 49
    knowledge as driver 106
    of online logistics 84
    in productivity 11, 40, 41
    and small businesses 43
GSM 49, 58, 149, 153
    circuit switching 157
    and Internet 156
    transmission speeds 156
Guess? Corporation 87–8

Hallmark 146
Hamel, Professor Gary 47
Harris, Lisa 144

head office remoteness from customers 63
health care 113, 162
health, safety and environment 112
help desks 111, 116
Henley Centre Research 39, 148
Herman Miller 6, 51, 102–3, 126, 197
holidays 47
    see also air travel
Homestore.com 42
Honeywell International 12, 85–6
Hong Kong 93, 155
HTML (hypertext markup language) 5, 142, 156
human contact 16, 142
human resources 19, 24, 112, 200–1

i2 55
IBM 62, 79, 81–2, 117–19, 123, 130, 161, 197, 204
IDC 104, 139, 150
Industry Standard 33, 34
information literacy 114–15, 120, 211
information retrieval 110, 111, 119
    see also knowledge sharing
infrastructure 160, 203, 207
    in place 44–5
    need for reliability 145
innovation *ix*, 2, 3, 4, 6, 59–60, 62–4
    haphazard 195–6, 198–9
    historical 40
    innovation intensive companies 64
    over rapid 55
    practicalities of 63–4
    resistance to 19, 57, 82
insurance 26, 72, 147, 156, 178
    auto 3, 6, 12
    company costs 74
    Tryg-Baltica 25
Intel 31, 161, 196, 203
intelligent chips 96
interface cards 156
Internet, the *ix*, 2, 6, 7, 8, 15, 18, 21, 28, 33, 58, 76, 90, 92, 95, 100, 102, 109, 115, 118, 119, 124, 125, 140, 145, 164, 173, 177, 184, 203, 204, 205, 206, 207, 210
    access 34, 38, 150, 154, 158, 173
    customer reluctance to use 91
    delivering profits 42–3
    development of 35
    distributed computing 31–2
    e-banking *see* e-banking, Nordea Bank
    and foreign exchange 46
    as global database 19, 35

growth rate 49
and GSM
and Microsoft 30–1
and mobile phone "always on" link
155, 156
and new generation of users 39
number of users 154
penetration 39, 186
and procurement *see* procurement
rate of increase 15
volume of use at Dell 22
wireless connections 148
intranet 14, 63, 69, 76, 82, 106, 107, 110,
118, 121, 159, 191, 205, 207
extranet 207
need for single, unified system 55, 121
scale of use 107, 121
INTTRA 92–5, 159
inventory 13, 14, 15, 21–2, 29, 48, 52, 55,
63, 67, 69, 74, 84, 85, 86, 87, 98, 101,
102, 165
in auto industry 90, 95
in chemical industry 96
in electronics 90
management 90–2
investment corporations 12, 148
investment in e-technology
barrier to change 155
controlling 57, 58, 65
in CRM 127
ineffective 55
at Nestlé 13
scale of 33, 139, 151, 175, 197
wireless spectrum licenses 151, 153
investors 13, 14
expectations 40
invoicing 19, 127
IP telephony 142
Ireland 139
ISPs (internet service providers) 31, 154,
157
ISS (Internet Security Systems) 45
IT, decentralised model 17
IT systems 5
communication between 5, 74, 115,
160, 205
consolidating diverse/uncoordinated
systems 13, 18, 20, 37, 52, 77
proprietary 5, 58, 76
Italy 171
iTV (interactive television) 7, 8, 14, 35,
149, 168, 170–83
B2B 181–3
banking 47

economics of 172, 173, 175, 178
interactive advertising/shopping 174,
178–9
killer aps 178–81, 186
minority investment interest 173
and PCs 176–8
renting program space 182
walled gardens 175–6, 178, 181

Japan 47, 125, 150, 155, 172, 203
Java 5, 142, 207
JIT (just in time) systems 85, 90, 102
training 188
JP Morgan Chase 46
Jupiter 170

Kennedy, President John F. 203
key individuals/champions 19, 50, 57, 65,
115, 118, 120, 145, 200, 201, 204, 214
Kingston Communications 97
Kleay, Hans-Peter 187
Klever Marketing 167–8
Kmart 162
know-how, buying in of 31
see also consultants
knowledge management 14, 37, 48, 51,
52, 55, 63, 70, 90, 104–24, 159, 184,
190
access 19, 109, 122, 123–4, 128
audit/diagnosis 120–4
and company valuation 105
cost of poor procedures 104
definition 108
see also knowledge sharing
knowledge sharing 5, 11, 12,
14, 19, 29, 31, 32, 35, 48, 52, 55, 69,
72, 80, 84, 86, 87, 90, 91, 93, 104,
108, 111–14 *passim*, 117–19, 121,
122, 123, 130, 193, 196, 197, 206–7,
210, 212, 213
4-step framework for 114
Korea 154, 155
government policy 154
KPMG 190
KPN, Netherlands 153
KTF 154

Ladbrokes 181
Landstar 166
language
software in different nations 139
translation 110
laptops *see* PCs
LastMinute.com 42

legacy systems 19, 37, 50, 52–8, 69, 76,
    77–8, 104, 110, 128, 129, 155,
    205–7, 209
Leggate, John 111
leverage *x*, 13, 14, 19, 38, 52, 59, 68, 82,
    83, 92, 109, 127, 195, 196, 214
Levi Strauss 101
Liberate 183
licensing 141
Lifetime Television 179
Limited inc, the 117
load-balancing 145
location specific information 146, 166–7,
    167
Lufthansa 79

Maersk Sealand 92
management 65, 66
    accountability 112
    autonomy of managers 17, 20, 198
    chief knowledge officers 115
    commitment 11, 19, 66, 107, 144, 198,
        203, 211
    portals for 119, 188
    simplifying layers of 5
    and web DNA 185
    see also key individuals
marketing 20, 21, 35, 37, 63, 165
    cost per customer 25, 132
    global campaigns 4
    one to one 137
Marks & Spencer 98–9
Mastercard 46
Mathaisel, Bud 106
Mazda 91
Merrill Lynch 157
Meyer, Governor Lawrence H 40
Microsoft 30–2, 33, 87, 116, 125, 128,
    172, 176, 183, 196, 197
middleware 55, 91, 156, 206
Milacron 140
Mitsubishi 157
Mitsubishi Auto 85–6, 90
MMR (monitor, measure and report)
    213–14
mobile phones 12, 26, 32, 35, 38, 130,
    148, 149, 154, 155, 160, 166, 177
    and 2.5G 157
    "always on" internet 155, 156, 157, 158
    compatible networks 157
    number of subscribers 155, 169
    as payment system 47, 155, 167, 168
    see also telephone, wireless
    applications

Mobilestar 162
Moen 28–30, 126, 210
    ProjectNet 29
    SupplyNet 29
Monkhouse, Dominic 113, 114
Monstor.com 42
Moray Council, Scotland 129–30
Morgan Stanley 25
Motorola 46, 68, 150, 168, 188–9, 190
MRO (maintenance, repair and
    operational) items 68–71, 98
Murdoch, Rupert 172
myplant.com 86

Nantucket Nectars 128–9
NASA 203
National Association of Independent
    Businesses 43
National Association of Purchasing
    Managers 67
National Health Service (UK) 113
NCR 165
Nestlé 12–14, 59
Net, the *ix*, 3, 4, 5, 13, 14, 16, 63, 83, 96,
    97, 104, 129, 198, 211
    and EDI 77–8, 81, 205
    penetration 186
NetBank 42
Netherlands Police Agency 123–4
Netscape 30
networking 7, 39, 45, 85, 98, 111, 120, 196
    value networks 197, 211
new technologies *ix*, *x*, 1, 3, 4, 7, 18, 34,
    45, 62, 65, 84, 125, 140, 198, 201,
    205, 207–8, 210, 211
    haphazard introduction of 195–6, 198–9
    historical development of 8, 40, 41
    and training 58–9, 72
    tried and tested 11, 40, 145
Newell, Frederick 164, 166
Nokia 150, 153, 157, 161
Nordbanken, Sweden 25
Nordea Bank 24–7, 149
Nordstrom 125, 134
Norkom Technologies 141
North Sea 4
Norway 25, 112, 153
Norwich Union *see* CGNU
Novartis 119–20
NTL 165, 172, 175

OECD 106
OEMs (original equipment manufacturers)
    4, 100–1, 125

oil and gas operations 4, 86, 112, 121
    boom of 1860s 40
OLAP (online analytical processing
    technology) 109, 110
Olson, Ken 40
OnDigital 172
online, number of people 49, 154
online facilities
    betting 36, 181
    credit 45
    currency exchange portals 46
    directions to drivers 155
    experts 17, 21, 86, 160
    invoicing payment/settlement 45, 51,
        67, 72, 77, 85, 90, 92, 95, 205
    marketplaces 72, 82, 84
    production instructions 116
    shopping 34, 36, 39, 174, 177, 178–9
    ticket sales 47, 155
    travel booking 2, 42, 132
    training 58, 81, 86, 117, 186–90, 192,
        193
    transactions 26, 84
    see also e-banking, e-billing
Onyx 113, 128
Open 174, 175
operating margin 18
optical networking technology 45
Oracle *ix*, 6, 9, 12, 18–21, 36, 59, 76, 129,
    132, 137, 139, 142, 196
Orban, Ted 46
orders
    automating 19, 23, 23, 24, 26, 67, 69,
        90, 95
    missed/unacknowledged 20, 67, 100
    online 14, 15, 19, 22, 42
    order to delivery web network 85–6
    processing 97–100, 127
    see also STP (straight through
        processing), tracking
organisation models/structures 21, 40, 42,
    208–10
    optimum 17
    and technology 55–6
outsourcing 14, 63, 92, 140, 145, 197, 211
Owens Corning 70
Oyster 77

PA Consulting 76, 77, 105, 119, 156, 208
packet size 124
packet switching 157
paper-based systems 15, 56, 67, 69, 98,
    106, 113
    cost of 97

partnership 13, 14, 28, 87, 93, 102, 104,
    153, 197, 210–11
passport accounts 31
paying for e-service 42, 47–8, 97
PC Magazine 87, 140, 146
PCs 31, 32, 38, 39, 40, 56, 73, 77, 142,
    148, 154, 160, 168, 177, 182, 205
    customised 101
    and iTV 176–8
    laptops *ix*, 111, 130, 149, 161, 164,
        165, 166, 168
    pocket *ix*, 3, 32, 149, 208
PDA (personal digital assistant) 12, 31,
    95, 149, 150, 161, 164, 165, 166,
    168, 177
peer groups 111, 112, 187
performance improvement 2, 6, 18, 48, 50
    see also productivity
personalising *see* customisation
Philips 4, 157
Phoenix Hecht Cash Management
    Monitor 150
pilot and test 50–1, 123, 130, 139, 145,
    185, 197
    pilot projects 20–1, 69, 71, 81, 83
pioneers 40, 50, 64, 66, 76, 87, 122, 126,
    134, 142, 148, 169, 185, 201
    see also companies by name
PKI (public key infrastructure) 79
policing 123–4
portals 4, 87, 159, 193
    employee 110, 111, 113, 119, 187, 214
    learning 188
    online currency exchanges 46
    portal-in-a-box 119–20, 139
    for suppliers 91
    transportation 92, 93
portfolio management 57–8
Postgirot, Sweden 25
Pownall, Stephen 83
price setting 20
Priceline 42
PriceWaterhouse Coopers 133
priorities, setting 28, 60, 61, 114, 120,
    127, 189, 198
privacy 147, 166
Procter & Gamble 4, 80, 179, 200–1, 203,
    210
procurement 4, 13, 14, 15, 19, 48, 51, 54,
    55, 60, 67–83, 87, 90, 97, 119, 184,
    195, 197, 203
    Internet 23–4, 51, 54, 67, 87
    needs analysis 75
    slowness of manual process 23

product codes 19, 82
  coding and hierarchy 76
product demos on Net 21
product design 28, 63, 106
product to market time 28, 63, 85, 98, 115
productivity *x*, 11, 33, 34, 36, 48, 116,
    123, 162, 165, 191
  historical 40
profiling
  collaborative filtering 146
  computer users 120
  customers 21, 37, 52, 86, 91, 102, 109,
    113, 116–17, 128, 130, 132, 136,
    138, 140, 142, 145–6, 147, 168, 183,
    209
  dealers 86
  e-analytics engine 145–6
  location specific information 146
  rules-based personalisation 146
profits *ix*, 12, 13, 15, 17, 18, 24, 63, 100,
    132, 134, 203, 213, 215
  delivered by Internet 42–3
  see also ROI
Progressive Insurance 3, 6, 12, 59, 126
project development 28
project management/disciplined programs
    65–6, 112, 123, 201, 213
  key performance indicators 213
  project management disciplines 66
Provident Central Credit 128
Prudential, UK 25

quadrem.com 159
quotes 67, 71
  RFQ (request for a quote) 71, 72

R&D (research and development) 31, 64,
    98
radio, early development of 39
railways, early development of 40
RCA 39
redundancies 25, 200
  fear of 57, 144
Reed Recruitment 156
regulation 30, 154, 155
Reicheld and Sasser 133, 134
reorganisation 37
report engines 109
resource 19, 65, 144, 200–1
  see also human resources, investment,
    key individuals
restructuring 11, 14, 18, 19, 52, 55–6, 57
  problems of 56–7
  resistance to 19, 56–7

streamlining business processes 11
retailing 12, 35, 62–4, 98, 98, 101, 125,
    149, 166
  impulse buying 167
Reuters 46, 52
RF (radio frequency) identification 96
risk 11, 50, 87, 197, 203
Roddick, Anita 134
ROI (return on investment) 14, 24, 28, 50,
    51, 58, 67, 68, 91, 165, 166, 172,
    175, 186, 214
  see also profits
Royal/Dutch Shell 46, 121
Russell Reynolds 185

Sainsbury 73
sales force 21, 56, 108, 113, 114, 129,
    130, 143, 144
  and wireless applications 164–5
sales teams 16, 17
Salesforce.com 142
Saleslogix 139
SAP 70, 71, 137, 187
satellites 92, 95, 164, 166, 171, 172, 182
scalability 93
Scan 47
scenario simulators 86
Schneiderman, Ron 162
Scotland 130, 183
search 120
  engines 42, 104, 185
  via portals 119
security 21, 31, 45, 72, 74, 79, 93, 148
self-assessment 58, 112, 117
seminars/conferences on Net 21, 118
  see also virtual facilities
set top boxes (STB) 171, 172, 173, 179,
    183
shareholders
  employee 213
  iTV voting 182
shares
  buying online 25
  price 13, 39, 42, 186
Siebel 55, 129, 137, 138, 141, 208
Siemens 12, 13, 52, 157, 185–6, 191, 203
silo mentality 21, 88, 113
simplicity 18, 34, 93
Singapore 39, 49, 91, 126, 155, 156
Singapore Airlines 164
size of organisation 18, 141
Skandia 190
skepticism *ix*, 15, 34, 36, 40, 50, 58, 115,
    123, 197, 204–5, 214

Skryme, David 123
Sky Interactive 172, 173, 174, 175, 181, 182, 183
Slater, Peter 34
SMEs (small and medium enterprises) 26, 31, 43, 73, 142
  number of small businesses 43
Smith, Phil 34
SMS text messages 49, 95, 149, 150, 156, 165
software solutions *ix*, 2, 110, 116, 126, 130, 137, 138, 139, 140, 206, 207
  over-hyped 55
  renting 73, 141, 211
  STB 172
software systems
  incompatible *see* compatibility
  legacy of previous system 19, 37, 50, 52–8, 69, 76, 77–8, 104, 110, 128, 129, 205–7, 209
  national legacies 155
  number of 13
  tailor-made/off the peg 19, 20, 28, 69, 139, 141, 142
Sony 64, 158
sound cards 142
Southwest Airlines 36, 125, 185
Southwestern Bell 116–17
Spain 153, 171
Staff Leasing 144
standardisation 54–5, 92, 93, 138, 207
standards 5, 93, 97, 101, 104, 107, 109, 149, 154, 183, 211
  for digital mobile communications 153
  global 158, 159, 198
STP (straight through processing) 97, 98, 100, 103
Sun Microsystems 30, 31, 150
suppliers 4, 13, 14, 15, 19, 23, 24, 28–31, 38, 51, 60, 67, 69, 71, 72, 74, 75, 77, 79, 81–2, 83, 84, 87, 90, 91, 92, 93, 98, 101, 150, 210
  release of proprietary information to 91
supply chain 1, 4, 13–14, 19, 28, 84–103, 184, 210
  SCM (supply chain management) 84, 90, 96, 97, 103
support services 16, 21, 22, 23, 93, 113, 130, 140, 145
Sweden 25, 39, 47, 49
Swisscom 47
Switzerland 25, 119
Syncrony 140
synergy 11, 17, 52, 91, 195, 196, 210

targets 53, 58, 87, 196, 198, 201, 203, 208, 210, 212
TCP/IP language 124, 159
teams, communication between 11, 209
technology research teams 18
technology/people fit 53, 55–7
  TOPP reviews 57
technophobia 56, 80, 144, 170
telcos 45, 97, 107, 151, 153, 158, 162, 163, 183
telephone 67, 138, 139, 142, 149, 150, 154
  cost of 14, 132, 154, 157
  networks and GPRS 157
  slowness of 46, 124, 165
  see also mobile phones
Telewest 172, 175, 176
terrorism 42, 136
Tesco 12, 126, 134
text messaging *see* SMS
Thus plc 44–5
time scales 13, 58, 75, 81, 114, 123, 189–90, 203
Time Warner 42, 172
TOPP *see* technology/people fit
Torex Meditel 113
Toshiba 115–16, 161
Toyota 212
tracking 2, 166
  advances in 96
  of inventory 96, 140
  of online orders 14, 23, 129, 140
  of sales 86
  of shipments 4, 67, 74, 84, 85, 92–5
trading communities/exchanges 72–3
training 2, 11, 14, 16, 52, 56, 58–9, 72, 74, 81, 104, 114, 117, 124, 130, 143, 7 168, 185–6, 191, 192,207–8, 211
  e-learning 184–93
  returns from 186
  online *see* online facilities
transmission speeds 45, 49, 58, 123, 155, 156, 158
transparency 13, 46, 48, 68, 75, 76–7, 84, 92, 93
transport 84, 90, 92–5, 125, 127, 166
  costs 94
  intelligent transportation systems (ITS) 95
trends 63, 98, 99
T-shaped manager 104–5, 112–13
TXU 12

Ubid.com 73
UBS 46

UMTS (universal mobile telecommunications system) 58, 159
underperformance 3
Unilever 34, 105
Unipart 192, 193
United Kingdom 6, 26, 39, 47, 158, 171,
172, 175, 181, 203
government 4, 49, 64, 170, 173
United States 14, 20, 39, 43, 85, 90, 93,
106, 128, 139, 148, 153, 154, 155,
162, 164, 170, 171, 172, 174–5, 177,
182, 183, 213
manufacturing costs 15
wireless access 150, 153, 154
UPS 95–6, 125, 166
user-friendliness 24, 54, 55, 104, 109,
111, 113, 125, 155, 206

value chain 3, 50, 59–60, 62, 63, 130, 172
values *see* culture
Ventro 72
Verisign 45, 79
Verity 110
Viacom 173
video conferencing 111, 160
video on demand 36, 173, 179, 188, 189
Vignette 110
virtual facilities
virtual learning 105
virtual project management 12
virtual team coordination 112
see also online facilities
virus protection 93, 133
visibility *see* transparency
voice transmission 44, 45, 138, 149, 156
voice over IP 142
voting 182

Wachovia 149–50
Walmart 80, 134, 134
Walton, Sam 134
Wang 130
warehousing 63, 71, 80, 84, 92, 127, 140
Watson Wyatt 193
web browser 2, 13, 31, 55, 62, 69, 87, 91,
110, 130, 142, 156, 205, 206
web sites 36, 112
cost of transactions 132

design changes 155
logging calls for sales leads 21
order to delivery network 85–6
project sites 107
web-hosting services 110
Welch, Jack 6, 81, 184–5, 212
WellsFargo Bank 12, 25, 126, 149
Westco-Bakemart 91
Weyerhaeuser 6, 100, 102
Windows systems *ix*, 30, 32, 140
Wink TV 178–9
wireless applications *ix*, 3, 6, 7, 8, 26, 92,
95, 96, 124, 130, 148–69, 173, 184,
190, 208
access 149–50, 154, 158
for data 150
limitations 148
number of users 150, 154
licensing spectrum 151, 153, 158
PBX (private branch exchange)/in
building networks 162
WAP (wireless applications protocol) 4,
149, 165
WAP 1.0 155, 156, 190
WAP 2.0 159
WLAN (wireless local area networks)
162–3, 167, 168
WLL (wireless local loops) 163
Wireless Rules 164
Wireless Systems 162
workflow management 110

Xcert/RSA 79
Xchange 144
Xerox 123, 165
xHTML 159
XML (extensible markup language) 5, 32,
58, 97, 211

Y2K 37
Yahoo! 119, 185
Yamaha 64
yellow pages, electronic 111
younger generation 39, 42, 148, 150, 181,
186

Zander, Edward 150–1
Zara 62–4, 98, 98, 103